About the Author

Robert Warren Stevens is professor and chairman of the Department of Economics at Roosevelt University, Chicago. He studied at Ohio Wesleyan University and at the University of Michigan, where he earned his Ph.D. He has taught at the City University of New York, the University of Michigan, the New School for Social Research, and Indiana University.

Dr. Stevens also served for five years as economist and financial attaché with the Marshall Plan Mission to the United Kingdom and successor agencies and was senior economist for eleven years with the Standard Oil Company of New Jersey. He is the author of *The Dollar as an International Currency,* published in 1971.

Vain Hopes, Grim Realities

The Economic Consequences of the Vietnam War

ROBERT WARREN STEVENS

New Viewpoints
A Division of Franklin Watts
New York   London   1976

New Viewpoints
A Division of Franklin Watts
730 Fifth Avenue
New York, New York 10019

Library of Congress Cataloging in Publication Data

Stevens, Robert Warren, 1918–
    Vain hopes, grim realities.

    Includes bibliographical references and index.
    1. Vietnamese Conflict, 1961–   —Economic
aspects—United States. 2. United States—Economic
policy—1961–   I. Title.
HC106.6.S785   330.9'73'092   75-8800
ISBN 0-531-05379-2
ISBN 0-531-05586-8 pbk.

Printed in the United States of America

6 5 4 3 2 1

PREFACE

CATCHING UP WITH HISTORY

The government of General Nguyen Van Thieu in Saigon proved to have much less staying power than many observers expected it to have when the United States government withdrew from active fighting in Vietnam and signed a cease-fire agreement with the Democratic Republic of Vietnam ("North Vietnam") on January 27, 1973. In fact, the end of formal resistance in Saigon came only two years later—and quite suddenly—at the end of April 1975.

This book, describing the economic consequences of the Vietnam war, was written mainly in 1972 and 1973. It was completed after the Washington-Hanoi cease-fire of January 1973 but before the April 1975 collapse of the Saigon regime. For most purposes in this book, the cut-off date for estimates of the costs already incurred because of United States involvement in the war was taken to be January 1973, the month when the Washington-Hanoi cease-fire was negotiated. Since in international affairs, however, events sometimes follow upon one another with greater speed than they do in the publishing world, it is now necessary to update those war cost estimates.

Past Budgetary Costs

In 1975 the Department of Defense released estimates of the United States government's direct budgetary cost of the war, which compare as follows with earlier estimates contained in Tables 8-3, 14-1, and 14-13:

	Full Costs	Incremental Costs
Defense Department (January 9, 1975,	*($ in billions)*	
estimates for fiscal years 1965–75)	138.9	110.7
Defense Department estimates shown in		
Tables 8-3, 14-1, and 14-13 for fiscal		
years 1965–74	140.1	112.0
Required Updating Adjustment to Tables		
8-3, 14-1, and 14-13	−1.2	+1.3

Future Budgetary Costs

These adjustments to the budgetary costs of the war that have already been incurred are relatively minor, but more substantial adjustments must be made to the future cost estimates contained in Tables 14-8 and 14-13. In 1973 it seemed probable that the United States administration would continue to be able to persuade Congress to support its policy of using as much military force as necessary to keep anti-Communists in power in Saigon. By 1974–75, however, the balance of forces in Congress had changed, and that body was no longer willing to go along with the administration's Vietnam policy. Consequently, the administration was not able to prevent the collapse in Saigon, and the estimate contained in Tables 14-8 and 14-13 that the United States government would spend $2 billion per year in Vietnam during the twenty years 1975–95 must be dropped. Thus the $40 billion estimate of postwar costs in Southeast Asia (line 2 in Table 14-8) should be eliminated and the estimated total cost of the war ($882–925 billion in Table 14-13) should be reduced by $40 billion.

Indirect Costs and Burdens

By 1975 there was general agreement among economists that the escalation and nonfinancing of the Vietnam war in 1965–66 at a time of full employment was the initiating cause of the "two-digit inflation" of 1974–75. Many economists, although not all, would also agree that the economic mismanagement of the war's deescalation in 1969–71 was the initiating cause of the unacceptably high level of unemployment that plagues us in 1975. However, the relationship of the war to these economic disorders of 1974 and 1975 is more tenuous than is its relationship to the economic disorders of 1969–72, and therefore no increase in the estimated indirect costs and burdens of the war (Tables 14-12 and 14-13) is proposed in order to take account of them.

CONTENTS

INTRODUCTION

CHAPTER 1   *II .*
ECONOMIC CONSEQUENCES OF THE WAR IN VIETNAM:
HOW SIGNIFICANT WERE THEY? 1

CHAPTER 2
THE VIETNAM WAR: LANDMARKS ON THE WAY IN AND ON THE
WAY OUT   27   *A .*

CHAPTER 3
"GETTING THE COUNTRY MOVING": 1961–64   *B .*
40

CHAPTER 4
TAKING THE NEXT STEP: THE ANTIPOVERTY PROGRAM: 1964–65
47

CHAPTER 5
TWO WARS IN CONFRONTATION—ONE AGAINST POVERTY AND
ONE AGAINST NORTH VIETNAM   52

CHAPTER 6
ESCALATING THE WAR IN VIETNAM: HOW NOT TO FINANCE A
WAR   62

CHAPTER 7
THE BREACH OF 1965 BECOMES THE DEADLOCK OF 1966–68
74

CHAPTER 8
THE BUDGETARY COST OF THE WAR 82

CHAPTER 9
THE DOLLAR: A CASUALTY OF THE VIETNAM WAR 103

CHAPTER 10
"MOMENTS OF TRUTH" FOR THE DOLLAR AND FOR U.S. *C*
INTERNATIONAL ECONOMIC POLICY 112

CHAPTER 11
"WINDING DOWN THE WAR": NEW MEN AND NEW IDEAS
TO CENTER STAGE 121

CHAPTER 12
"WINDING DOWN THE WAR": GAME PLAN III—
INFLATION AND RECESSION 132

CHAPTER 13
AFTER THE WAR—THE PEACE DIVIDEND AND NEW WAR COSTS:
WHERE IS THE PEACE DIVIDEND? 144

CHAPTER 14
THE ECONOMIC COST OF THE WAR 163

APPENDIX A
INFLATION AND GOVERNMENT POLICY 191

NOTES 197

INDEX 221

INTRODUCTION

Ｔhe Americans have switched off the war [in Vietnam] as if it were a TV set . . . [and] no longer want any part of it," according to the London *Economist.** The hopes of national grandeur, American style, that once were associated with it have long since foundered on the grim realities of the war and its many painful consequences. Today many Americans would like to pretend that it never happened while others struggle, either consciously or unconsciously, to forget it. But it cannot be fantasized away. It did overwhelm, divide, and confuse the country for several long years and we will have to live with its miserable consequences for many more years to come.

Before the major escalation of the war in mid-1965, the U.S. economy had been performing for several years as well as, if not better than, it had ever done before and the prospect ahead seemed to be for many more years of inflation-free economic growth. In addition, a growing share of the bounteous output of the economy, we were told, would in the future be invested compassionately by the public sector to alleviate the causes of involuntary poverty, both at home and abroad. But both the good intentions and the balanced econo-

*August 11, 1973, p. 12.

my were lost in 1965–66 because Washington had decided to rapidly escalate its involvement on the losing side of an unimportant, but rather ambiguous civil war in Southeast Asia. The careless profligacy with which the Johnson administration bent the U.S. economy to the purpose of fighting that war started up the terrible inflation that has engulfed the economy almost continuously ever since.

The administration of Richard Nixon compounded the economic disorder that Lyndon Johnson left behind him when he retreated from public life. Committed to *laissez-faire* economic doctrines, Nixon announced at his first press conference that his administration would do nothing about the price-wage spiral it had inherited. Then he proceeded to cut back Vietnam war expenditures very sharply, but at the same time he also forced a contraction of demand in the civilian sector. This inappropriate policy combination gave the country, in 1970–71, *both* inflation and recession, or "stag-flation," an affliction of contradictions that, it now appears, may very well plague the economy for most of the 1970s. The second attack of it—a more severe one than in 1970–71—was raging in 1974–75 as these lines were being written.

We can now see that it would probably have been better for the economy if the Republicans had been in power in 1964–68 seeking to balance the budget and reduce federal spending, and if the Democrats had been in power in 1969–73 with their readiness to use fiscal policy and modern techniques of controlling inflation. It was our fate, however, to have Democrats in power in 1965–68 outdoing themselves overspending while ever since 1969 we have had Republicans in power pretending that the economy can take care of itself, by itself.

One of the many tragic consequences of the war was the loss by many economists of confidence in themselves and in the arts of economic policy-making. Instead of protesting against the euphoric "we can do everything at once" attitude of the Johnson administration, the extravagant and ruthless opportunism of U.S. foreign policy, and the careless incompetence that has characterized U.S. economic policy almost continuously since 1965, many economists have turned savagely inward on themselves and on their own profession. "*We* may not know enough to advise governments," many are saying, "although we thought we did."

But, hopefully, this is only a temporary phase. Hopefully with the passage of time more members of the profession will realize that it was the dishonest financing of the Vietnam war that dashed the high hopes we had in the mid-1960s and set the economy off on its present inflationary track; that it was the Vietnam war which enormously sped up the outpouring of money from the vast U.S. economy, exacerbating inflationary problems for other countries; that it was the Vietnam war which disheartened American liberals and paved the way for the Nixon administration—an administration run by men incapable of understanding the problems of cost-push inflation and who, therefore, inaugurated the present era of highly inflationary underemployment. Moreover, we must not forget that the demoralizing political scandals collectively labeled "Watergate" trace straight back to the unconscionable habit Washington acquired in the 1960s of trying to conceal from the country what it was doing in Vietnam.

An Overview of the Book

The story of classic economic blunders perpetrated by two successive administrations during the peak fighting years of the Vietnam war, 1965–72, is the principal focus of this book, and it practically tells itself. The main outlines of the story constitute chapter 1, while the first two-thirds of chapter 2 contain a straight history of the war years to help us recall when things happened. In the core chapters of the book, beginning with chapter 3, we investigate the economic consequences of the war by asking what the economy might have been like after 1964 if there had been no escalation in 1965. Therefore, chapters 3 and 4 describe the Kennedy administration's economic programs and goals which, by a decree of fate, Lyndon Johnson inherited on the early afternoon of November 22, 1963. In chapters 5 and 6 we sort out what happened in the crucial years 1964 and 1965 when the Vietnam war replaced the Great Society as Johnson's top priority. In chapter 7 we recall the political deadlock over fiscal policy that developed between a Democratic administration and a Democratic-controlled Congress as the war was escalating, and observe what effect it had on the economy. In Chapter 8 the story is told for the first time of how Defense Department economists and accountants struggled, with only partial success, to pin down the precise cost of the war in the federal budget. Chapters 9 and 10 describe how the Vietnam war dealt the coup de grace to the dollar's role as the linchpin of the world's monetary system and how the Washington government blamed foreign countries for its own bungling. Chapters 11 and 12 discuss the economic blunders made in de-escalating the war, blunders scarcely less gross than those made while escalating it. Chapter 13 contains one man's attempt to say what happened to the peace dividend and includes a discussion of two of the war's heaviest indirect economic costs and burdens. In chapter 14 we wind up by trying to assign a dollar value to the war's cost to the U.S. economy.

CHAPTER

ECONOMIC CONSEQUENCES OF THE WAR IN VIETNAM:
HOW SIGNIFICANT WERE THEY?

From 1965 to 1972 the involvement of the United States in the war in Vietnam was the most important event in the country's national life. This book assesses the consequences of that involvement for the U.S. economy. Economic consequences have to do with *costs* and much of this book deals with costs. But consequences include more than costs, and in searching for the war's economic consequences we will ask ourselves how the economy might have performed in the Vietnam war years if the government had not escalated the war. That is not an easy question to answer, but that does not mean we should ask a less relevant question.

For U.S. foreign policy, the Vietnam war was an example of bungling on a massive scale, and on the domestic scene this was matched by classic examples of economic policy bungling. Surprisingly, however, many economists seem to be unaware of this, because they wring their hands over what they allege to have been the inadequacies of serious efforts by both "fiscalists" and "monetarists" to stabilize the economy in the years since 1965. But the plain fact is that economic rationalism has not had a chance since 1965. In 1965 the economy had been gently lifted to a level of full employment without serious inflation for the first time in a decade and economists of all persuasions were recommending economic restraint to help ease the growth rate down to a sustainable long-term rate. But just at that moment the country's defense-foreign policy establishment, responding to its own ideological imperative, escalated the war in Vietnam. In the three years 1966, 1967, and 1968, war spending created mounting federal budget deficits that overstimulated the economy, writing finis to economists' efforts to bring about the required delicate adjustments in monetary and fiscal policies. When monetary and fiscal policies were working successfully in 1962–65, responsible economists never went so far as to claim they could "fine-tune" the economy, and neither should they now accept responsibility for the disorderly and inflationary economy we have had almost continuously since 1965. The Vietnam war robbed us of the opportunity to see whether we could sustain a reasonably fully employed economy without inflation.

Casualties

Wars are man-made disasters and, like natural disasters, their primary costs are measured by the number of lives lost and the extent of property damage. While fighting the Vietnam war, 56,245 U.S. servicemen (including eight generals) were killed—45,942 in combat and 10,303 from nonhostile causes. Figure 1-1 shows one way of visualizing the deaths of 56,245 young men. There were 303,640 U.S. servicemen wounded, of whom 153,300 required hospitalization. Casualty figures for the Indochinese people are less precise, partly

FIGURE 1-1

HOW MANY U.S. DEATHS?

U.S. deaths in the war 56,245

> Most of these were young men in the 18-24 age group. In the U.S. population young men of this age group account for 4.9% of the total population.

The American city that would have about 56,000 young men aged 18-24 is Indianapolis.

$$56,245 \div 4.9\% = 1,147,755$$
Population of Indianapolis = 1,110,000

If some modern King Herod had gone through the city of Indianapolis selecting all young men aged 18-24 for premature death, the effect would be about equal to the number of U.S. deaths in the Vietnam war.

---

because most of them were civilians. Official statistics report 183,000 South Vietnamese soldiers and more than 400,000 civilians killed, the two together equaling the entire population of Boston, Massachusetts, in a country with one-tenth the United States population.[1] According to the U.S.-sponsored body count, more than 400,000 Vietcong and North Vietnamese were killed.[2] A rough estimate is that in all of Vietnam 1.3 million civilians were killed and some 3 million wounded (about one in ten of the entire population compared with 1/1,000th of the United States population). It is said that from one-fourth to one-third of all the people in the country became refugees because of the war. The above figures exclude Laos and Cambodia, even less developed countries than Vietnam, where casualty estimates are only fragmentary.

FIGURE 1-2

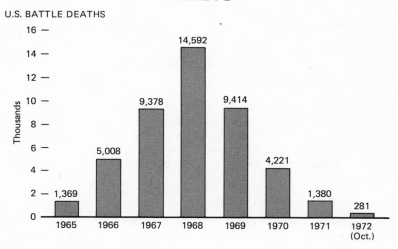

U.S. BATTLE DEATHS

Source: U.S. Department of Defense

The coming and going of the U.S. military establishment in Vietnam appears on graphs as a fairly symmetrical hump, rising steeply from 1965 to 1968-69 and receding in 1970-72.

U.S. battle deaths by year reached a steep peak in 1968 and began to recede in 1969, reflecting Johnson's decision in March, 1968, to commence the de-escalation of U.S. involvement. Thereafter Americans continued to be killed in Vietnam, but in smaller numbers as Nixon gradually withdrew U.S. ground troops, replacing them with sea and air power and grants of military equipment.

Property damage caused by the war is impossible to estimate. The United States routinely bombed Vietnam for eight years, both in the north and in the south, dropping 6.8 million tons of bombs compared with the 1 million tons dropped on Korea and the 2 million tons used in World War II. About one-seventh of the land area of South Vietnam was dosed with poisonous chemical herbicides to reduce vegetation and destroy crops, about six pounds worth for every inhabitant of South Vietnam.[3] Late in the war an American airman, peering out of his plane, ruefully remarked that there were more bombs left than targets, and an economic survey of Vietnam's timber industry found that "fully 50 percent of the trees felled in Tay Ninh Province and taken to sawmills have bomb shrapnel in them. And only the best trees are felled."[4] Under such conditions, how can property damage be estimated?

Even the direct money cost of the war to the U.S. government has not been finally determined, for inside the Pentagon itself two successive comptrollers differed sharply on its costs. The present official estimate is $140 billion from July 1, 1964, to June 30, 1974, but the man who was Defense Department comptroller from 1965 to 1968 insists it was much higher than that.

How Significant Was the Economic Impact?

Some economists believe the impact of the war on the U.S. economy was not very great. Although the Vietnam war was the longest war in the history of the republic, at no time did it seem to make exorbitant demands on the great productive power of the economy.

FIGURE 1-3

HOW MUCH IS ONE BILLION DOLLARS?

If you earned $*10,000* a year, it would take you 100,000 years to earn $1 billion.

If you had begun earning $*200,000* a year at the dawn of recorded history, you would have about $1 billion today.

If you had waited until the year one of our common era to begin earning your $1 billion, you could have earned about $*500,000* a year over the past 1,973 years.

And how much is $140 billion (the approximate budgetary cost of the Vietnam war as estimated by the present administration)? With it you could have paid almost $*2,700* to every family in the United States, which would make a comfortable down payment on a house for most Americans, even at today's inflated prices.

Whereas, at the peak of World War II spending, 41 percent of the nation's total output was absorbed by war expenditures, and 13 percent was taken up at the peak of the Korean War, only 9½ percent was preempted by military spending at the peak of the Vietnam war, and of this only about 3 percent went to the war itself. Moreover, other government expenditures were increasing at the same time— and by considerably more if we include the spending of state and local governments. The war's economic impact looks smaller, too, if we recall that the usual unpleasant accompaniments of a wartime economy—wage and price controls—were notably absent during the Vietnam war, but were used during both World War II and the Korean War. Most Americans were not aware of any serious economic deprivations even during the most active phase of the Vietnam war, 1966–69.[5] In fact, as we shall see, the economic cost of the war in those years was diffused throughout the economy. Finally, while it is clear the United States did not "win" the Vietnam war, it did not fail to do so because of any incapacity of its economy to produce the weapons of war.

The general impression that the impact of the Vietnam war on the vast and powerful United States economy was not very great is held by much of the populace at large, by many businessmen, and by many business-oriented economists.

A directly contrary view may be held by fewer people, but it is probably held more strongly. Most economists who specialize in studying the aggregate behavior of the economy are of this opposite opinion. Also, as one gets closer to those who were directly involved in top-level decision-making in Washington during the peak Vietnam war years, one finds more people who believe the impact of the war on the economy was very great indeed. While agreeing that the war, even at its peak, did not have a very great direct effect on the American standard of living, it is nevertheless held that it had tremendous *indirect* effects on the economy. Consider, for example, the opinion of Arthur M. Okun, a member of the President's Council of Economic Advisers from 1964 to 1968 and council chairman in 1968. Okun is a talented economist who was intimately associated with making economic policy at the highest level during the most decisive phases of the Vietnam war. In his words, "Vietnam plays the Danish prince in the *Hamlet* of recent economic history."[6]

The view that the Vietnam war was much the most important single influence on the economy from 1965 to 1972 has a number of special ramifications. Its central theme is that since the beginning of the Vietnam war—and chiefly because of the Vietnam war—there

FIGURE 1-4

U.S. MILITARY STRENGTH

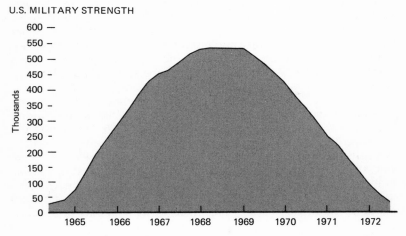

This graph, showing the number of U.S. servicemen in Vietnam, clearly traces a symmetrical pattern starting with 23,000 men at the end of 1964, rising almost 24-fold to 540,000 in 1968-69, and then shrinking back to 27,000 at the end of 1972.

has been almost continuous mismangement of the economy by men whom we would have expected to know better. At the very start, in 1965, the Johnson administration massively escalated the war at the worst possible moment for the economy, just as the country was completing a long, hard climb toward the economists' nirvana—full employment without inflation. Having started off on the wrong economic foot, the administration then compounded the confusion by failing to protect the civilian economy from the intense inflationary pressures generated by the war. In this way, the Johnson administration set in motion the most virulent inflation in the country's history. Lyndon B. Johnson was a man determined to have both guns and butter.[7]

His successor in office, Richard M. Nixon, intensified the damage that had already been done to the civilian economy. In late 1969 and 1970 he rapidly cut back military spending with one hand, while with the other hand, on the basis of a wrong diagnosis of its causes, he attacked the inflation he had inherited. Excess demand associated with the escalation of the war had *set off* the inflation in 1965–68, but by 1969–70 the productive capacity of the country had caught up

FIGURE 1-5

DEMAND-PULL VERSUS COST-PUSH INFLATIONS

Sometimes economic jargon can be very helpful . . .

In a **demand-pull** inflation, sharp increases in demand are *pulling* prices up. In wartime, for example, government spending raises total demand, and the increase in demand *pulls* prices upward.

In a **cost-push** inflation, the pressure comes from the *cost* side, and prices are *pushed* upward by rising costs. Unions may win such large wage increases, for example, that employers could pay them only by accepting lower profits—unless they pass the increase in their wage costs on to the public in the form of higher prices. If they do pass them on, we say that prices were *pushed* upward by rising costs.

Although in practice it is not always easy to distinguish precisely between these two causes of inflation, sometimes it is not at all difficult. In 1966, for example, the U.S. got a dose of demand-pull inflation and in 1969–70 a dose of the cost-push variety.

---

with the higher level of demand, and inflation was being *perpetuated* by rising wages and other costs instead of by excessive demand. However, it pleased Nixon's economic advisers to believe we were still suffering from an old-fashioned *demand-pull* type of inflation and accordingly they chopped away at civilian demand at the same time the Pentagon was sharply cutting back on war spending. This economic overkill produced the unnecessary recession of 1970–71, which failed altogether to quench the inflation but which did, however, increase unemployment by 75 percent. Finally, Americans bought more imports with their inflationary increases in income, and labor leaders, taking their cue from Nixon's version of economic nationalism, blamed imports rather than Nixon's economic policies for the loss of jobs and came out in favor of the most isolationist international trade policy that had been seen in Washington for more than forty years.

At critical moments during the Vietnam war there was a shocking lack of coordination between the military and civilian branches in the higest echelons of the government. The defense foreign-policy establishment knew it had a real war on its hands as early as 1964, but it cooperated with Lyndon Johnson in keeping this knowledge from Congress and from the American people, with the result that the country saw no reason to depart from business-as-usual until long after it was too late. Then, as the war wound down after its climax in March 1968, a new administration took over and intensified the economic disruptions. The Nixon administration, which was under the influence of economic primitivists, adamantly refused to recognize both the realities of a cost-push inflation and the magnitude of the Pentagon's military cutbacks. As a result, the country was forced to pay for the Vietnam war a second time in 1970–71—in the form of an economic recession and a 6 percent unemployment rate.

Some economists have argued that other government spending would have increased more in the absence of the war and would have caused as much economic disorder as the war did. It is almost certainly true that nonwar government spending would have increased more if there had been no war. But it would not have increased nearly so much, nor so suddenly, nor so surreptitiously, and it would not have caused the inflationary bottlenecks in the sensitive capital goods sector that the cascading new orders from the Pentagon caused in 1965 and 1966. Moreover, the nation would have had benefits to show from domestic government spending rather than having its energies wasted on a futile, counterproductive war. Finally, nonmilitary spending would not have been cut back so suddenly and sharply in 1969 and 1970, and the country probably could have avoided the recession of 1970–71.

The nation has been very poorly served by its top economic policymakers since 1965, and it is the thesis of this book that they, like the American people in general, were thrown off balance in the first instance because the defense-foreign policy establishment persistently refused to tell the truth about the Vietnam war.

The Protagonists

At the outset the U.S. military involvement in Vietnam was expected to be short-lived and on a small scale. After all, how could it be otherwise? North Vietnam could not remotely be thought of as a powerful country. On the contrary, it was a small, lightly armed, underdeveloped country, only about one sixtieth of the geographical size and having only one thirty-fourth of the GNP per capita of the United States. By contrast, the United States of America, the giant of the world economy, had a more productive economic system and a higher standard of living than any other country on earth.[8] Moreover, the government of the United States felt itself militarily prepared for any eventuality that might arise. The Johnson administration reflected this confidence in the budget message it sent to Congress on January 25, 1965:

Through determined efforts in the past four years our national defense establishment has been brought to a level of commanding superiority. These efforts have been expensive but they have also been productive. We have largely completed a buildup of the world's most powerful military establishment, and our balanced forces are already superior to those of any potential aggressor. This superiority will be maintained in the future.[9]

In short, on the eve of its escalation of the Vietnam war the United

FIGURE 1-6

According to Many Measures of Economic Strength, the United States Was Hundreds of Times as Strong as the Democratic Republic of Vietnam (North Vietnam)

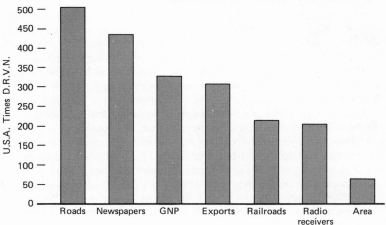

Source: New York Times Encyclopedic Almanac, 1972.

The United States of America and the Democratic Republic of Vietnam (North Vietnam) fought the war to a draw in 1965-72. At first, few people expected such an outcome because the U.S. economy was so much larger and more productive than North Vietnam's. For example, as shown here the United States had 505 times North Vietnam's mileage of surfaced roads, 437 times as many newspapers, 325 times as large a gross national product, and so on and on.

In the end, however, these economic advantages were not decisive. What *was* decisive was that the Vietnamese were fighting for their vital interests, but the United States was not.

States of America was, and knew it was, a big-time, heavily armed superpower. In the Democratic Republic of North Vietnam, the United States faced only a small-time, militarily insignificant non-power. How, the men of Washington asked, could the outcome of a military confrontation between these two be long in doubt? Are not conventional-style wars won ultimately by superior economic power? And the United States, with only 10 times the population of North Vietnam, had 505 times the mileage of surfaced roads, 213 times the railroad mileage, 437 times as many newspapers, 325 times the gross national product, 305 times the value of exports—one could go on and on reciting the statistics of overwhelming preponderance.

"Resources Unlimited:
We Can Have Both Guns and Butter"

At the outset, and for some time thereafter, the Johnson administration had no doubts about the outcome. Certainly no one expected the war to take very much out of the American economy. At first it was believed that the North Vietnamese would simply cave in as soon as they got a taste of the "surge capability" of the U.S. military establishment. And even later, when it became apparent that North Vietnam, instead of caving in, was matching the U.S. escalation, still very few thought the war would seriously affect the U.S. economy. The President, after all, and some of his top advisers had witnessed with their own eyes the miracle of American production in World War II, and they felt confident of its capacity to do whatever they might ask of it.[10] The secretary of defense, himself a conspicuous product of the business sector, was one of the very last to acknowledge the inflationary effects of the war and, as late as January 1967, Secretary of Defense Robert McNamara told Congress, "There are many . . .

FIGURE 1-7

BY GROSS NATIONAL PRODUCT WE MEAN . . .

A country's total output of goods and services, gross national product (GNP) is the most commonly used measure of the size and productivity of a country's economy.

The GNP is measured in dollars (it was $1,290 billion in 1973). Changes in GNP from year to year may be due to inflation (price increases) or to a *real* increase in the country's output. From 1972 to 1973, for example, GNP rose 11.5 percent, of which 5.3 percent was due to higher prices and 5.9 percent consisted of a *real* increase.

---

prices we pay for the war in South Vietnam . . . but in my opinion one of them is not strain on our economy."[11]

Why, then, did the barely 2 to 3 percent of the GNP that was finally required by the Vietnam war prove to be so disruptive? The answer to this question is that, at the margin, it was a very important 2 to 3 percent because it was added just as the country was arriving at full employment. The contrast with World War II could hardly be greater. The massive demands of that war came at a time of severe unemployment, and the government was able to get the real GNP to rise by an *average* of 14 percent a year during the first three years of World War II by drawing upon previously unemployed resources. Later in mid-1950, when the Korean War broke out, the unemployment rate was 5.2 percent compared with 4.2 percent in late 1965. It is the economist's concept of incremental, or marginal, demand that makes the crucial difference here, because a 3 percent increase in total demand, which would have been welcome at any time between 1957 and 1964, was too much for the economy to accommodate without inflation by 1965.

Figure 3-2 summarizes the relationship of the key variables. The actual GNP is shown from 1951 to 1972 by calendar quarters, plotted alongside the hypothetical maximum feasible GNP, referred to in the graph as the *potential* GNP. One can see that the GNP fell short of its potential, beginning in 1956. Beginning in 1961 it began to rise at a rate higher than its long-term potential rate of increase, responding to the Kennedy administration's goal to "get the country moving again." By mid-1965 the GNP had *arrived* at its maximum civilian potential, just on the eve of receiving the impact of the Johnson administration's escalation of the war in Vietnam. Under the lash of production for war, total output actually exceeded its potential during most of 1966–68, as it had in 1952 under the pressure of Korean War spending. Since there were no wage or price controls from 1966 to 1968 (as there were during the Korean War), this extra high pressure of demand pushing against the economy's maximum supply potential brought into being the price inflation from which the economy has suffered ever since.[12]

"You Pump Out Money: It Meets a Bottleneck, and You Get a Price Rise"

In short, the economy in 1965 was highly vulnerable to the inflationary pressures set off by mushrooming war expenditures. The situation was then made worse by the absence of any overall eco-

FIGURE 1-8
U.S. Armed Forces

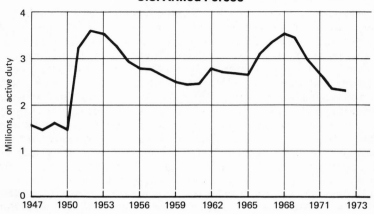

Source: Statistical Abstract

For the first four years after World War II the United States cut the strength of its armed forces to 1.5 million men. This number more than doubled during the Korean war to about 3.5 million and then leveled off at a little over 2.5 million for the decade 1956–65.

With higher draft calls during the Vietnam war, the armed forces went back up to about 3.5 million. By 1973 the number was down to about 2.4 million, lower than at any time since 1947–50.

Military spending was higher relative to GNP in 1973 than in 1947–50, however, in part because the arms race was more advanced, requiring more expensive weapons, and in part because military pay rates had been raised to approximate parity with civilian wages.

---

nomic mobilization machinery to divert resources from civilian to military purposes.[13] The lack of any central political direction of U.S. foreign policy in Southeast Asia, which has been frequently criticized,[14] was fully matched by the lack of domestic economic controls of the sort that would have been appropriate to wartime conditions. Consequently, beginning in 1966 and for the duration of U.S. involvement in the war, the nation's economy was wrenched this way and that almost continuously because of Washington's Janus-faced policies. The bureaucracy was fighting a real war in Southeast Asia for what it regarded as high stakes, but it did not trust the American people, and by its rhetoric and in its economic policies it sought to persuade the public that nothing very important was going on. Anyone who lived through World War II and the Korean War, as well as through the Vietnam war, can testify to the difference in how they were handled by the Washington bureaucracy.

The results for the nation's economy of the Vietnam war duplicity were the most virulent inflation in American history, the highest interest rates in history, a series of balance of payments crises worse than any that had gone before, an unnecessary recession in 1970–71, two serious declines in stock prices (in 1970 and 1972–73), two major liquidity crises at home (in 1966 and 1969–70), a collapse of the housing industry (1966), financial market distortions that bore extremely heavily on small business and that forced state and local governments to retrench on education and other vital services, and the eventual defeat of the most imaginative experimental approach to the problems of impacted poverty that had ever been tried.

This appalling performance by an economy that is capable of performing so magnificently is particularly galling to modern economists because their work over the past twenty years has established that, in principle, such economic malfunctioning is unnecessary if one may assume moderately enlightened and honest policies by the central government. Ever since the federal Employment Act of 1946 it has been the statutory obligation of the President "to promote maximum employment, production, and purchasing power." As the experience of 1961–65 demonstrates, great progress has been made in coordinating the monetary, fiscal, and other policies of government in carrying out this responsibility. In principle, as every elementary economics textbook now points out, the Washington bureaucracy has the knowledge and the power to control without serious inflation any practicable level of spontaneous total demand and any division of resources between the private and public sectors that the American people decide they want to have. What it cannot do, and what no free society anywhere can do for long, is to shield an uninformed, defenseless civilian economy from the disruptive effects of unannounced, undeclared wars that make sudden enormous demands upon it.

The multifarious, indirect impacts of the Vietnam war on the U.S. economy all stemmed from a single direct cause: although adequate resources to fight the war could have been made available by appropriate government policies in 1965–66 and although the war-stimulated economy of 1969 could have been shifted back onto a civilian base without a recession, two successive administrations failed miserably to invoke the right policies at the right times. The Johnson administration seemed to believe that the richly productive U.S. economy was *infinitely* rich and productive, while the Nixon administration seemed to believe that economic prosperity and high levels of employment could withstand the triple blows of military de-escalation, a restrictive fiscal policy for the civilian economy, and an extremely tight monetary policy. Just as the Washington defense-foreign policy establishment blithely set foreign policy goals for the country without stopping to count the cost, Washington's economic policy-makers set tasks for the economy that it could not perform.[15]

Allocating Resources by Catch-as-Catch-Can

Economic decisions involve costs and choices, and at the heart of the economist's concept of cost is the idea that any given use of resources has been achieved *at the cost of* other possible uses to which those resources might have been put. In an economy at full employment there is no way of running a war except by transferring resources away from other forms of employment. Thus, while the budgetary cost of the war may have been in the neighborhood of $140 billion, those billions of dollars really stood for x billion man-years of labor, y million tons of steel poured, z billion barrels of oil pumped, and all the other products of human labor that were yanked out of their existing employments and devoted to the prosecution of the war in Vietnam. A question of great interest in considering the economic impact of the war is how the government—in the absence of overt economic mobilization—accomplished so vast a shift of resources. This question can be considered in two parts, the first having to do with shifts within the sphere of military production and the second with shifts from civilian to military uses.

Within the sphere of military production, the war caused a major shift in the product mix. Outlays for missiles, sophisticated electronics, and strategic aircraft declined sharply in relative importance—and, in some cases, in absolute amount as well. By contrast, outlays were greatly expanded for (1) conventional battlefield ordnance (such as tanks, field and hand weapons, and ammunition), (2) routine supplies needed to support large forces in combat (such as food, medicines, and uniforms), and (3) tactical aircraft (such as fighter planes and helicopters). In these respects, military procurement reverted to the pattern that had prevailed during the Korean War, in contrast to the heavy emphasis on superkill weapons that was characteristic of the intervening cold-war years.

"Once again," Murray L. Weidenbaum wrote during the war, "the traditional industries, such as automotive, mechanical, textile, cloth-

TABLE 1-1

THE CHANGING MIX OF MILITARY PROCUREMENT
(% of Obligations Incurred)

Category	Korean War (Fiscal Year 1952)	Cold War (Fiscal Year 1962)	Vietnam War (Fiscal Year 1967)
Sophisticated equipment	52	70	53
Conventional equipment	48	30	47
Total	100	100	100

Source: Murray L. Weidenbaum, "Economic Environment After Vietnam: An Analysis of Military Expenditure Trends," U.S. Congress Joint Economic Committee, Subcommittee on Economy in Government, Hearings, Part I, June 3, 1970, p. 254.

In the early 1960s expenditures on the cold war went mainly to support an arms race based on highly sophisticated superweapons systems.

In the Vietnam war, however, as in the Korean War, the United States fought a land war. These two wars required, on the ground, more conventional or "old-fashioned" battlefield equipment, such as tanks and hand weapons, while in the air they required tactical aircraft such as helicopters rather than, for example, intercontinental ballistic missiles.

ing, and rubber, have become important military suppliers."[16] The funds going for tanks, artillery, rifles, ammunition, and similar conventional battlefield hardware more than doubled; ". . . the military aircraft budget was reoriented from new long-range bombers to acquiring smaller 'tactical' aircraft, particularly helicopters and supersonic fighters, such as the F-4 Phantom."[17] Also, many ordinarily civilian-type goods became weapons in the war the U.S. government had decided to fight in faraway Asia. Among thirteen industries whose new orders from the Pentagon more than tripled from 1965 to 1967, the three with the largest increases were wooden containers (up more than 1000 percent), paperboard containers, and metal containers (each up more than 500 percent).[18]

The shift toward the more traditional industries favored older, longer-established manufacturing areas of the country rather than mainly the new glamour-weapon producing states such as California, Texas, and Washington. In 1968 military contracts went to eight states at rates at least twice as high as the pre-Vietnam rates. They were Tennessee, Texas, Connecticut, Illinois, Alabama, Mississippi, Minnesota, and Wisconsin. Six states got orders at least 50 percent higher than in 1965. They were Florida, Indiana, Louisiana, New York, Ohio, and Pennsylvania.[19]

It is one thing for Pentagon procurement officers to alter their patterns of shopping when the Pentagon perceives a new kind of threat to the safety of the republic; it is another thing for an already fully employed private economy to be able to produce what the new pattern calls for. At such a time there are several ways open to the government to obtain command over the resources it wants. It can do any of the following, either singly or in combination:

1/ **Promote a larger than normal increase in the GNP and take possession of as much of the increase as possible.**
In both 1966 and 1968 the level of the GNP exceeded its maximum potential, and yet its yearly growth rate was pushed up above its long-term average.

2/ **Cut back other forms of government spending.**
Several times in 1966–68, Lyndon Johnson cut back the federal government's civilian programs, the Pentagon reduced its non-Vietnam activities, and the rate of growth in state and local government spending was curtailed.

3/ **Increase taxes in order to reduce private spending.**
In June 1968, some three years after the war was escalated, Congress passed a 10 percent income-tax surcharge.

4/ **Run larger balance-of-payments deficits.**
This technique of adding to U.S. resources was used steadily during the cold war and was used more intensively for the Vietnam war; net exports fell from $8.5 billion in 1964 to $1.9 billion in 1969.

5/ **Restrict monetary growth and enforce higher interest rates.**
Because fiscal policy had disrupted the economy, the Federal Reserve slammed on the brakes twice in attempts to cut back private spending, once in 1966 and once in 1969–70.

6/ Enact direct controls over wages and prices.

This technique, very unpopular in Washington, was not resorted to until August 1971, ten years after the first U.S. casualty in Vietnam and six years after the main escalation of the war.

7/ Resort to inflation.

Deficit spending at full employment is a method by which the federal government can use inflation to commandeer resources; this method was liberally used in 1966–68.

As can be seen, Washington resorted to all of these methods sooner or later. There was no single coordinated economic plan for fighting the Vietnam war. The Johnson administration, having grossly misjudged the situation in Vietnam, was then for a long time unwilling to be seen passing the real costs of its war on to the American people in the form, for example, of a tax increase or wage and price controls. Thus, it put itself in a position where it had to get the real resources to fight its war by methods that can best be described by the phrase "catch as catch can."

The effects of such haphazardry on the civilian economy both immediately and in subsequent years, on the *élan* of the American people, on the moral climate in Washington, and on the standing of the United States among the nations of the world are by now clear for all to see. Instead of openly resorting to taxation or economic controls when they were most needed, the government passed the cost of its war on to the American people largely through inflation, savagely high interest rates, and the neglect of other government programs. Inflation and extremely tight money are brutal, unjust ways of redistributing income and wealth. The public, never told in so many words what the government was doing, was at first deluded into thinking that its problems were caused by greedy labor unions and businessmen, expensive social programs, and disenchanted college students rather than by the government's scandalous nonfinancing of the war in Vietnam. The resulting confusion, disarray, and obstreperousness of life in the United States in the late 1960s and early 1970s shook the confidence of the American people in their basic institutions—particularly in the honesty of the government in Washington and in the ability of a free society to manage its affairs—even before the nation's attention became riveted on the Watergate crimes. Economists were deceived, no less than other groups. "Demand management won't work," they told the people instead of saying, "The government deceived you by failing to fi-

FIGURE 1-9

Changes in major GNP components (% change from 1963–65)

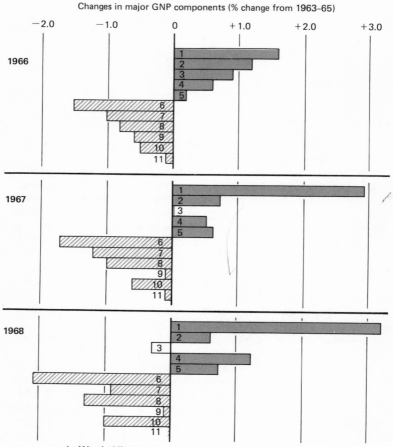

1. War in Vietnam
2. Business Fixed Investment
3. Changes in Business Inventories
4. Consumers' Purchases of Durable Goods
5. State and Local Governments
6. Defense Department, Excluding Vietnam War
7. Residential Investment
8. Consumers' Purchases of Non-Durable Goods
9. Consumer Services
10. Net Exports
11. Federal Government, Excluding Defense Department

FIGURE 1-9 *(Continued)*
Out of Whose Pockets?

The Vietnam war was escalated mainly in 1966–68 and this graph shows all major uses of GNP in those three years as percentage changes from 1963–65. As the graph shows, in 1966–68 the war took steadily larger bites out of the GNP (bar 1 in the graph). But because the war was layered on top of a boom in the civilian economy, both business fixed investment and consumers' purchases of durable goods (sectors in which the boom was concentrated) also took larger shares of GNP in 1966–68 than in 1963–65 (bars 2 and 4).

Who got *less* of the GNP? The Pentagon tells us it was skimping on non-Vietnam projects in 1966–68 (bar 6 in the graph), but larger bites came out of the civilian economy in the form of reduced spending on new housing and on consumers' purchases of nondurable goods and services (bars 7, 8, and 9).* Net exports also fell in 1966–68, which meant that part of the cost of the war was being shifted to other countries (bar 10) because they were accepting ever-larger IOU's from the United States.

Business inventory investment (bar 3) did not change materially; governmental projects other than the Vietnam war (bars 5 and 11) would doubtless have increased more except for the war.

*The graph is drawn to show only percentage changes, not absolute amounts of change.

---

nance its war in Vietnam.'' Clearly, Washington's double-dealing in fighting the Vietnam war laid the foundation for the Watergate scandals that came immediately after it.

1966–68: Who Had to Pay?

We may ask which sectors of the economy had to surrender resources to the government for use in the war in 1966–68, the years of the major war buildup. Such a question cannot be answered with certainty. All we can *know* is what did happen, not what might have happened. However, we can take the years 1963–65 as a benchmark and examine the pattern of the economy's overall use of resources in each of the following three years in order to see which sectors got smaller proportions of the economy's total output in the years when the war's strain on the economy was greatest.

Such a comparison is made in Figure 1-9. It shows percentage changes in the allocation of resources (measured in dollars of constant purchasing power) sector by sector in each of the years 1966, 1967, and 1968, compared with the benchmark period 1963–65. Many other things besides the Vietnam war were going on in those years and the best that Figure 1-9 can do is to show what happened in the years when the main shift in the allocation of resources was toward the war. The absorption of resources for the war went from 0 percent of the total in 1963–65 to about 3 percent in 1967 and 1968. This net absorption of resources by the war determined, year by year, the percentage that had to be surrendered by all other uses combined.[20]

The behavior of the other sectors of the economy in 1966–68 was about what we would expect. The only two sectors of the private economy that took larger shares of total output in 1966–68 than in 1963–65 were business fixed investment and consumers' purchases of durable goods (mainly autos). As we know, the civilian economy was staging a boom while the war was being escalated, and these two sectors nearly always set the pace of expansion during a boom.

Five sectors seem to have felt the pinch of the Vietnam war the most. They were non-Vietnam military spending, housing construction, net exports, and consumers' purchases of nondurable goods and services. The Defense Department's use of resources for the war that would have been used otherwise in the absence of the war was significant, according to the present official definitions of the war's costs. The housing sector of the U.S. economy is known to be very sensitive to high interest rates and to the availability of funds in the capital market, and among the domestic private sectors, it was the hardest hit by the war. Net exports took successively smaller shares of the nation's output in each of the three years, thus accounting for part of the deterioration of the international balance of payments under the pressure of stepped-up military spending. As prices and incomes rise in a country suffering inflation, its exports lose price competitiveness while rising incomes are sucking in more imports.

Personal consumption expenditures show conflicting trends in Figure 1-9. Durable goods purchases remained higher than in the pre-war benchmark period, but there were net declines in consumers' purchases of nondurable goods and services. Since the latter categories are almost five times as large as consumer durable goods purchases, there was a distinct decline in *total* consumption as a percentage of the GNP during the years of the war buildup. This shrinkage in the relative importance of consumption reflected a decline in the real (i.e., inflation-corrected) earnings of American workers during the war. Prices rose faster than money wages. Figure 1-10 tells this story. A hiatus took place during the war in the long-term upward trend of real wages in the United States. Earnings in manufacturing (measured in dollars of constant purchasing power) rose 2.5 percent a year in 1961–65 and 3.6 percent a year in 1971–72, but they actually fell by $1/2$ percent a year in 1966–70.

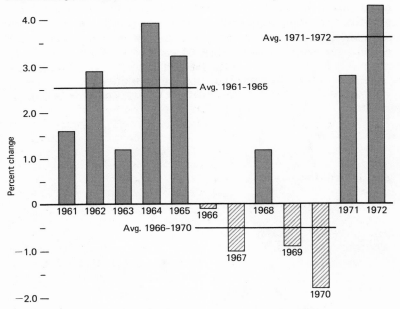

FIGURE 1-10
How Consumers Paid for the War

EARNINGS IN MANUFACTURING
(Percent Change, Constant Dollars)

Note: Data pertain to worker with three dependents

Source: Council of Economic Advisers. Economic
Report of the President, 1972.

Resources to fight the Vietnam war came out of the pockets of consumers to a considerable extent, and changes in "real" wages (which are money wages corrected for price changes) show how this took place.

Wages rose every year from 1961 to 1972, but the buying power of wages did not. In 1966–70 prices rose on the average faster than wages, and in four out of five of those years, workers' *real* earnings actually declined. Over the full five-year period the rate of decline was 0.5 percent a year. This shrinkage in what wages could buy was due to the Vietnam war and its aftermath. In 1966–69 part of what consumers could not buy because of inflation was used by the government to fight the war.

Real wages rose 2.5 percent a year on the average in the five prewar years 1961–65, when price increases were minimal. By 1971–72 wage increases were at the high rate of 7.4 percent; prices rose somewhat less and the government was no longer siphoning off resources for the war, so workers' *real* income started to rise again.

The three sectors of the economy least affected by the war were changes in business inventories, federal nondefense spending, and state and local government spending. Congress had legislated significant increases in federal nondefense outlays in 1964–65, but Lyndon Johnson repeatedly cut these back. State and local government services have long been one of the major growth sectors of the economy, and, like federal nondefense programs, they would almost certainly have grown more in 1966–68 except for the war.

FIGURE 1-11
The War's Effect on Income Distribution
CIVILIAN EMPLOYMENT BY OCCUPATIONAL GROUPS, FISCAL YEAR 1968
(Percentage Distribution)

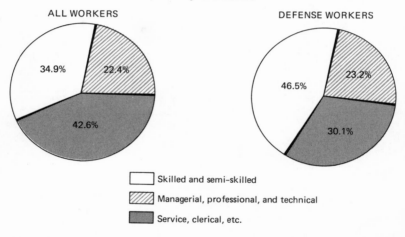

ALL WORKERS   DEFENSE WORKERS

ALL WORKERS: 34.9% 22.4% 42.6%

DEFENSE WORKERS: 46.5% 23.2% 30.1%

☐ Skilled and semi-skilled
▨ Managerial, professional, and technical
■ Service, clerical, etc.

Source: President's Council of Economic Advisers, *Economic Report of the President*, 1971, Pg. 46.

More skilled and semi-skilled workers are employed by defense industries than in the rest of the economy, but these same industries employ relatively fewer people in the less-skilled categories.

Consequently, the sharp increase in defense industry employment in 1965–68—at a time when the civilian economy was also booming—put a squeeze on many categories of skilled workers, with inflationary effects on the wages of those who were already the most highly paid. The newly stimulated defense industries, on the other hand, did not require the service of as many less-skilled and lower paid workers, whose chances to benefit from Great Society programs had also been diminished by Washington's escalation of the war.

In these, as in other ways, the less fortunate bore a disproportionately heavy share of the costs of the Vietnam war.

How Significant the Impact?

The American people as a whole were not involved in either the fighting or the suffering of the Vietnam war. In the main, only those who were drafted or threatened with the draft and the families of those killed, injured, missing in action, or taken prisoner felt themselves deeply involved. For most of the war years (until the recession of 1970–71) most Americans went about their business in a generally prosperous, if inflationary, economy. Within the country the poor and the unskilled felt the impact of the war the most. They contributed proportionally more fighting men than the rich, got fewer jobs in war industries than skilled workers, had the most to lose from the displacement of the war on poverty by the war in Vietnam, were harder hit by inflationary price increases, and were the first to lose their jobs in the recession of 1970–71.

To the general public, the brutalities and horrors of the war were fleeting abstractions on a television screen, which most viewers found they were able to come to terms with. There was no outpouring of war enthusiasm, and perhaps the most representative attitude was that of people who objected mildly to the war but who objected much more strenuously to those who dared to protest against the war. U.S. foreign policy, as someone has said, is often of more vital importance to other countries than it is to the American people—both when it is good (as with the Marshall Plan) and when it is bad (as in Southeast Asia).

The direct budgetary cost of the war amounted to $28.8 billion at its peak (full cost, official definition). In the context of the total GNP of the United States this is not an indigestible sum, being somewhat less than the annual value of consumers' purchases of furniture and household equipment. Costly, yes. Crippling, no—so great was the country's economic muscle. The Defense Department tells us that incremental cost is a better measure of the war's net impact on the economy; the incremental cost never got above 2.5 percent of the GNP. Economic effects are often easier to see at the margins of growth than when they are buried in totals. The war's direct budgetary impact looks even smaller when viewed as a fraction of each year's GNP growth during the years of buildup:

In three of the four major war years the country devoted only a small part of its net growth to the increased cost of the war, and in the total time period only slightly more than 8 percent.

The significant economic impact of the war is not to be found in its direct cost, but in how that cost was extracted from the economy—and in its indirect effects. The Johnson administration unleashed inflation because it was unwilling to level with the country about what

TABLE 1-2

WAR'S BUDGETARY COST

	Increase in Incremental Cost ($ billions)	Increase in GNP ($ billions)	Column I as % of Column II (%)
1966	5.7	65.0	8.8
1967	12.6	44.0	28.6
1968	1.6	70.3	2.3
1969	1.5	66.1	2.3
Total 1966–69	21.4	245.4	8.3

Source: Economic Report, 1973, p. 193.

the war was costing. The Nixon administration allowed the inflation to worsen and subjected the country to an unnecessary recession because it was unwilling to restrain wages and prices and because it failed to ease the economy down from wartime production levels. Because of the escalation of the war, Lyndon Johnson got far more inflation than his Great Society program would ever have generated; because of de-escalating the war without regard to the effect on the civilian economy, Richard Nixon got a larger decline in the GNP and a greater increase in unemployment than his disinflationary policies and his "new federalism" by themselves would have cost. In both cases the American people were the losers and may continue to be the losers for years to come. The economy, once thrown off course by the Vietnam war, has shown few signs of being able to right itself again. When the dollar-quantifiable costs and burdens of the war are roughly calculated—present, past, and future, direct and indirect— the war is estimated to have cost the country about the equivalent of a whole year's gross national product (see Table 14–13).

In 1963 Gen. Earle Wheeler, then chairman of the Joint Chiefs of Staff, called the Vietnam war "that dirty little war." "Dirty" it certainly was, but "little" it was not.

The Costs of Four Major Calls for National Commitment

It is a commonplace that American society is pluralistic. Among other things, this means that it is no easy task to mobilize the vast, often uncoordinated resources of the federal government and to concentrate them on the attainment of definite, clear-cut social goals. At a minimum, the call to do so must go forth from the White House, there must be broad assent in Congress on the desirability of

TABLE 1-3

APPROXIMATE DOLLAR COSTS OF FOUR MAJOR NATIONAL COMMITMENTS (BILLIONS OF DOLLARS)

		$ billions
Federal Interstate Highway Program[1]		53
Man on the Moon Program[2]		25
Great Society Program[3]		199
Aid Directly to People	125	
Grants in Aid, mainly to		
state and local governments	74	
Total, 1964–72	199	
War in Vietnam[4]		260
Costs Already Incurred*	260	
Estimated Future Costs	305	
Estimated Indirect Costs and Burdens	378	
Order-of-Magnitude Aggregate	943	

* Excluding indirect costs and burdens

[1] *America's Lifelines,* U.S. Department of Transportation: Federal Highway Administration. Washington, D.C.: U.S. Government Printing Office, 1972, pp. 11-12. (Expenditures to date, covering 98 percent of the 42,500-mile system.)

[2] U.S. *Statistical Abstract.*

[3] Estimated from U.S. *Statistical Abstract* according to "Major Great Society Programs," analysis by Charles L. Schultze and Associates, *Setting National Priorities; The 1973 Budget.* Washington, D.C.: The Brookings Institution, 1972, p. 11.

[4] See Table 14–12.

The importance of a governmental project is often gauged by how much it costs. Even though the very largest projects make "waves" in the economy that render their cost estimates somewhat imprecise, the record indicates that the costs of the Vietnam war that have already been incurred are about *ten* times the cost of the man-on-the-moon program, almost *five* times as large as the costs incurred thus far for the federal interstate highway program, and about *one-fourth greater* than all of the Great Society programs put together.

Even these comparisons begin to pale when we learn that the costs of the war that have already been incurred constitute only about 40 percent of present estimates of its future costs, burdens, and indirect costs.

accomplishing the goal and articulate sectors of public opinion must at the very least acquiesce in allocating national resources on the scale required.

Since 1955, only four overarching national goals of this sort have been enunciated by U.S. Presidents. In Feburary 1955, President Eisenhower summoned the nation to embark upon the interstate highway building program, acclaimed at the time as the "largest public works project in history"; in May 1961 President Kennedy issued his famous challenge to America's scientific community to "put a man on the moon by the end of the decade"; in January 1964 President Johnson called upon the nation to commit itself to fight an all-out war on poverty as an essential first step toward building the Great Society; the fourth such overriding commitment to which the American people were summoned in this period was to win the Vietnam war, although in this instance it is less easy to pinpoint the specific presidential message that set it in motion.

Of these four national projects, the first two have been or are being carried out successfully. The third, the war on poverty, is less easy to characterize. Almost from the start it was starved for lack of both high-level attention and funds. The parts of it that fit most easily into the familiar pattern of social security are now well established. The most genuinely creative parts of it either were dismantled, failed, or are still operating, but not very effectively. The fourth project, the Vietnam war, ended for the United States—at least for a time—in a draw instead of a win in January 1973.

It is not a simple matter to estimate the dollar costs of national undertakings on the scale of these four because they all had far-reaching implications for the entire economy. Therefore, we must acknowledge that their total dollar costs take on the character of informed approximations. As such, they compare roughly as shown in Table 1-3.

It is apparent that the Vietnam war, besides having brought the country no visible benefits, has been the most costly of the four. The estimates in Table 1-3 of the already incurred war costs and burdens, along with some of the future costs, are by no means inflated estimates; they have been brought together from many sources, all of which are identified in Chapter 14.

CHAPTER 2

THE VIETNAM WAR:
LANDMARKS ON THE WAY IN AND ON THE WAY OUT

The story of how the United States got involved in Vietnam has often been told, and this chapter sketches in only the high points, in order to impart a sense of historical perspective.

In general, indifference characterized the attitude of the United States to Vietnam in the last years of World War II and the early postwar years. Perhaps the main thread of the story begins with the death of President Franklin D. Roosevelt, who had opposed allowing France back into Southeast Asia after World War II. Shortly after Roosevelt's death the U.S. government reversed his judgment and supported France's reestablishing itself in Vietnam as a colonial power following Japan's surrender of its wartime occupation of the country. Early in 1950 Washington agreed to finance the major part of a war France had to fight in Indochina in order to maintain its colonial status there; in return, France agreed at that time to support the U.S. policy of reviving Western Germany as an anchor of anti-Communism in Europe. Later in 1950, with the outbreak of the Korean War in Asia and of McCarthyism in America, France's colonial war in Vietnam came to be perceived differently in Washington:as part of a worldwide grand confrontation between communism and anti-communism. In 1950–54 the United States paid 2.6 billion dollars (80 percent of the total cost) to help finance France's colonial war in Vietnam.

In 1954 the Vietnamese finally defeated the French at the decisive battle of Dien Bien Phu, ending, they thought, an eight-year struggle for independence. At the East-West Geneva Conference that year, which was called to officially end the war, a military demarcation line (not a political boundary) was drawn at the seventeenth parallel to facilitate the military disengagement. Ho Chi Minh's forces controlled territory north of the line, while forces more friendly to the French were in power south of it. Later in 1954 the U.S. government pledged its support to Ngo Dinh Diem, a U.S.-French puppet who had been set up south of the demarcation line to try to form a government. President Eisenhower made the support conditional upon Diem undertaking "needed reforms" in his already corrupt new government. Diem ignored the American call for reform but got the aid, establishing the pattern of the U.S.-Vietnam relations that has now prevailed for more than twenty years.

Diem's rule was ineffective, as well as highly authoritarian. In 1960 a Communist-led National Liberation Front was formed in the south to oppose him and in the same year the U.S. Senate Foreign Relations Committee offered its opinion that "the U.S. Military Advisory Group can be phased out of Vietnam in the foreseeable future." This was only one of many instances of disastrously wishful thinking in Washington about Vietnam. Officials of the U.S. government persisted in their delusion that the Saigon regime enjoyed enough support from the Vietnamese people to be able to govern the southern part of the country on its own authority. By 1961 some 60 percent of the territory south of the seventeenth parallel was under some form of Communist control. The United States responded to these developments by increasing the size of the Military Assistance Advisory Group (MAAG) in Saigon, in part because the Kennedy administration was eager to try out what it thought was an efficient system of counterinsurgency warfare that had just been set up.

The first U.S. combat fatality in Vietnam occurred on December 22, 1961. In the early 1960s Washington received a barrage of poorly informed but highly optimistic reports on the military and political situation in South Vietnam from its official representatives there. The situation steadily deteriorated, however, and early in November 1963, three weeks before the assassination of President Kennedy, the unpopular Diem and close members of his family were deposed and killed as part of a rebellion by his own anti-Communist military commanders. President Kennedy had said two months before he was assassinated, "I don't think that unless a greater effort is made by the Saigon government to win popular support, the war can be won out there." His administration threatened to withdraw U.S. aid and advisers unless Diem made fundamental reforms. Kennedy had personal doubts about the advisability of keeping the U.S. military in Vietnam, but in the time allowed him he did not change the government's official policy.

The year 1964 was critical in determining the course of U.S. intervention in Vietnam. Early in the year both Washington and Moscow announced cuts in their military budgets. In April, after informal negotiations the Soviet Union, the United States, and Britain announced coordinated plans to cut back the production of fissionable materials, thus taking a small but dramatic step toward detente. At the time Khrushchev spoke of "a policy of mutual example" and Washington of "reciprocal unilateral acts." Former Deputy Defense Secretary Roswell L. Gilpatrick wrote in the April issue of *Foreign Affairs* that "if the current detente with the Soviet Union continues the U.S. defense budget could be cut 25 per cent by 1970, from $51 billion to $38 billion." In short, on the eve of the Vietnam war a detente between the United States and the Soviet Union was in the making, and Washington budget makers were looking forward to reductions in military spending so they could finance the Great Society programs Lyndon Johnson was talking about. But Johnson was also wading deeper into the Vietnam morass in 1964. Immediately upon assuming the presidency he had vowed "I am not going to lose Vietnam." He thus closed his mind on the subject of Vietnam at the very outset of his administration. In his opinion the Democrats had lost in Congress after Truman had "lost China" and LBJ did not intend to have his party lose control of Congress.

In Saigon political chaos followed the assassination of Diem, but a military clique gradually established itself in control. In Washington Johnson sought to delay decision-making on Vietnam as much as possible until after the U.S. presidential election. In the election campaign he said, "We don't want to get tied down in a land war in Asia," and, "We are not about to send American boys 9,000 or 10,000 miles away from home to do what Asian boys ought to be doing for themselves." In November he won the election, soundly defeating Sen. Barry Goldwater who had openly proposed escalating the war.

Toward the end of 1964, high U.S. officials spoke of reconsidering U.S. support of unrepresentative "governments" in Saigon, but there was no reconsideration and, instead, as Saigon's authority weakened and hostilities moved from the stage of insurgency to that of a full-scale war, the United States committed itself and its prestige ever more irrevocably to the losing side of the war in Vietnam. Although Johnson, with the backing of a heavy majority in Congress, and the winner of a sweeping election victory, could have escaped from Vietnam in late 1964, he missed the opportunity and did not seriously reconsider why the U.S. military was there until more than three years later, in March 1968.

Early in 1964 Johnson had scorned an offer of French help in trying to bring about the neutralization of Southeast Asia, thus laying the groundwork in Washington for continuing to regard Vietnam as a military, not a political, problem. In August Congress approved the administration-sponsored Gulf of Tonkin resolution by 416-0 in the House and 88-2 in the Senate, unaware that mysterious attacks on two U.S. destroyers in the Gulf of Tonkin had been partly provoked by covert U.S. military operations against the North Vietnamese coast.

In 1965 the U.S. government rapidly escalated the commitment it had made in 1964 to fight in Vietnam, whatever the cost might be. In February, one month after his inauguration, Johnson ordered air attacks on North Vietnam. The North Vietnamese, however, instead of caving in under the air barrage as the Johnson administration had expected, matched the U.S. escalation by sending more men into South Vietnam. In April the President and his top advisers made a crucial decision, secretly deciding to send as many as 300,000 U.S. ground troops into Vietnam.

The major *overt* escalation of the war occurred in July 1965 when the President announced he was raising the troop strength in Vietnam to 125,000 and increasing military draft calls in the United States. At the same time, however, he minimized the significance of the deteriorating situation.

By the end of 1965 the President and his top military advisers were fully aware that they were in for a long and costly war in Vietnam, but in communicating with Congress, with their chief economic advisers, and with the American people generally, they concealed the fact that they had made an open-ended commitment to the Saigon regime, and in general played down the seriousness of the situation. As James Reston of The *New York Times* put it, they had "escalated the war by stealth." There were eight times as many U.S. troops in Vietnam at the end of 1965 as there had been a year earlier, and Johnson was committed to fight a ground war in Asia, reversing a long-standing basic U.S. military policy.

In 1966–67 the United States took over most combat operations in

the war, while South Vietnamese soldiers were assigned to "pac-
ifying" the countryside. In Washington during these years there
was much "looking for the light at the end of the tunnel" but little
real progress to report. Compulsively, Johnson fought on, spurning
peace initiatives in these two years by the British, the Canadians, the
French, the Russians, the Poles, the United Nations, and Pope Paul.
A map of territories controlled by Saigon and by the Communists,
respectively, looked like a leopard skin, and outside of Saigon itself
no one knew who really controlled what in South Vietnam. The crisis
in the war came in early 1968 with the Tet offensive, a simultaneous
attack on nearly all towns and cities in South Vietnam. This shatter-
ing demonstration of the strength and determination of opposition
to the Saigon regime led almost immediately to the first major debate in Washington on the U.S. role in Vietnam. In an atmosphere of
heavy crisis, a top-level study was made in March to decide whether
to send 200,000 more troops to Vietnam. The study concluded that
the troops could be delivered, but to do so would entail calling up
the reserves, increasing the draft, lengthening the period of military
service—and for GIs, second-and-third-trip tours of Vietnam. Treasury Secretary Henry Fowler said that sending that many troops
would require tax increases, price and wage controls, credit restrictions, and perhaps a devaluation of the dollar. These were still un-
thinkable thoughts in the relatively unscarred U.S. economy of 1968.
At about the same time, however, the first of several major international crises of confidence in the dollar broke out. In the face of such
disarray Lyndon Johnson gave up at the end of March. He ordered
an almost complete cessation of bombing (although he continued to
support the Thieu regime in Saigon) and withdrew himself from the
presidential election of 1968.

The Vietnam war was not really at issue in the contest between
Richard Nixon and Hubert Humphrey in the national election of
1968, with both men essentially endorsing Johnson's policies. After
the election the new Nixon administration continued its predecessor's determination to maintain anti-Communist forces in power in
Saigon but, sensing the electorate's opposition to high casualties,
decided to withdraw ground troops and transfer the bulk of the
fighting back to General Thieu's regime in Saigon. Total U.S. troop
strength in Vietnam reached a peak of 543,400 in January 1969,
almost a year after Lyndon Johnson had begun the de-escalation.

In April 1970, after withdrawing 100,000 troops, the Nixon administration launched an invasion of Cambodia, precipitating a crisis of
confidence in the new President's sincerity about withdrawing from

the war. The Senate promptly repealed the Gulf of Tonkin resolution. Withdrawal sped up again, with 150,000 more Americans coming home by May 1971 and another 100,000 by the end of the year. The Paris negotiations for ending the war dragged on through interminable sessions, with each side refusing to compromise its basic position: the United States insisting on keeping Thieu in power in Saigon and North Vietnam insisting that the National Liberation Front should take charge. The negotiations moved off dead center only after Dr. Henry Kissinger, at that time the President's special assistant for foreign affairs, took over. He announced in October 1972 on the eve of another U.S. presidential election that "Peace may be at hand," but after the election the U.S. government sharply re-escalated the air and sea attacks in the final quarter of 1972 before a truce was signed on January 27, 1973.

The above record is sometimes summarized as falling into four main phases of U.S. involvement.

1950–60	Military advisory stage
1961–65	Intensification of military involvement and political commitment
1965–68	Open warfare
1968–73	Gradual disengagement of U.S. ground forces (major troop withdrawals from September 1969 to April 1972)

Whose War?

The Vietnam war was the least popular, least understood war in U.S. history. It had a fuzzy beginning, fuzzy objectives, and a fuzzy ending. At the outset it seemed to be only a small-scale policing incident on the periphery of the vast, far-flung U.S. military establishment.[1] But as it grew into a brushfire type of conflict, the Washington foreign policy establishment doused it with cold-war rhetoric, and in the days when foreign policy was viewed as a moral crusade, the struggle in Vietnam came to be thought of as part of the grand confrontation with communism. Perhaps future historians will regard it as the last chapter of a twenty-five-year period when U.S. foreign policy toward China was blindly fearful and hostile and when the country's foreign policy-makers were seized with the idea of a Sino-Soviet conspiracy. Washington allowed itself to slither deeper and deeper into the conflict until it found it was involved in a full-scale war with an unlovely, incompetent ally that was unable to maintain authority in its own territory. Then a feeling began to spread that something was not working as it should. The Senate

Foreign Relations Committee opened public hearings on the war in February 1966 in a spirit of dissent. Secretary of Defense Robert McNamara expressed disenchantment with the war in August 1967, but by 1966 and 1967 the government's ability to maneuver had been sharply reduced and it could no longer extricate itself as easily as it could have at almost any previous time. In the critical *earlier* years when policy options should have been weighed, Washington had escalated its rhetoric and had verbally linked its own vital interests to the preservation of an anti-Communist regime in Saigon.

By 1966–67 the war had grown out of all proportion. It had moved to center stage in the life of the country and from many points of view it looked grotesque.

For example:

Item: The budgetary cost to the U.S. government of fighting North Vietnam in *each* of the years 1968 and 1969 had risen to at least *nine* times the value of North Vietnam's GNP.

Item: The United States had built its largest overseas airbase at Long Binh, Vietnam, where it occupied seventeen thousand acres, an area larger than the city of Saigon.

Item: In the Vietnam war years, *the cost overruns* on just *two* Pentagon projects—the C-5 cargo plane and the Minuteman II missile (6 billion dollars in total)—exceeded the GNP of *both Vietnams together.*

Item: The U.S. government conservatively estimates the budgetary cost of the war in Vietnam at $140 billion, which is 242 percent of *all* U.S. economic aid to *all* underdeveloped countries in the world from 1945 to 1970.[2]

The U.S. government made a spectacle of itself in Vietnam largely because—almost from the outset—it was preoccupied with military calculations to the almost total neglect of an attempt to understand the historical, political, and cultural realities in that country. Decision-makers, fed on a diet of overoptimistic military reports, kept reassuring one another that just a little more money, just a few more thousand troops, just a few more days of bombing, would surely bring their nightmare to an end, as if the solution to the problem in Vietnam were one vast military engineering project.

To some, it seemed as if by fighting the Vietnam war the U.S. government was performing an unpleasant but necessary duty. Just as the British had employed gunboat diplomacy in the nineteenth century to carry "the white man's burden" to areas of the world that were economically interesting to them, so must the United States in the twentieth century "break a few eggs now and then" as an aspect of carrying out its "unsought burden" of policing the world. But this was a flawed analogy. In the nineteenth century all of the major powers were capitalist countries, among whom the less developed countries had to survive as best they could. In the twentieth century, however, Communist leaders in the less developed countries can rely on two of the world's three superpowers for diplomatic, military, and economic support. In Vietnam, each time the U.S. government "upped the ante" the USSR and/or China would come through with further aid for the beleagured North Vietnamese.[3]

Whose war was it? At the start it was the American people's war, because it sprang directly out of the consensus view of most Americans in the 1950s and 1960s that U.S. foreign policy should concentrate on "winning the cold war." But as more and more people came to feel that the costs of the Vietnam war, in terms of lives, treasure, and political tranquility, were greater than its benefits, that chapter of the cold war lost the support of important sections of public opinion and it became the *government's* war. But the government did not find it easy to explain the war to its critics, especially because the Johnson administration long sought to avoid the appearance of being at war and its announcements of major escalations in the fighting were usually enveloped in clouds of rhetoric about its own peaceful intentions. In attempting to establish the credibility of its armed might abroad, the U.S. government was sacrificing its credibility to the American people. It was during the Vietnam war that Washington developed the habit of governing by dishonesty, a habit that the Nixon White House later transferred from the realm of foreign policy into the domestic political sphere.

Gradually, as the dismal story of the war unfolded, the cold-war political consensus began to fall apart, but the government remained hooked on the war in Vietnam because there had been no preparation of options.[4] Washington had backed a losing cause in Vietnam without first weighing the pros and cons of doing so, and once in, it felt obliged to prolong the agony of its departure. To contemplate the sorry record of successive U.S. presidential administrations in Vietnam is a sobering experience for Americans, brought up, as most have been, to believe in the good sense of the federal government's policy-makers and in the essential justice of the causes that it espouses.

Lest one be carried away by this line of thought, however, it must be recalled that, at the beginning, the government's policies in Vietnam had the solid support of the American people. It is important to stress this because in today's morning-after reappraisals, there is a tendency to lay the blame for the war on one special group or another—on eastern liberals or southern warhawks, on the Pentagon or the intellectuals or the hard hats, or on one or another of the four Presidents whose policies got us involved ever more deeply in the war. But these partial views overlook the fact that at the outset U.S. policy in that most unfortunate country was firmly rooted in the national cold-war consensus view of international relations that was associated with our three most conspicuous recent secretaries of state—Dean Acheson, John Foster Dulles, and Dean Rusk. Only two men in the Congress, one must not forget, voted against the Gulf of Tonkin resolution in 1964—Senators Ernest Gruening of Alaska and Wayne Morse of Oregon—two men who were defeated in the next election.

The President's Two Constituencies
Any government department other than the Defense Department that would maneuver itself onto a runaway spending track would be quickly cut down to size by an aroused Congress, but *defense* spending has first priority on the nation's resources.[5] The American tradition that "politics stops at the water's edge" is often interpreted to mean that the country's foreign policy should be immune from partisan debate, and in the 1950s and early 1960s this stricture also applied to Defense Department appropriation bills. This meant that once the President determined that "national security" was involved in a given line of policy, he received, in effect, a blank check on the U.S. Treasury. Operationally, it is as if the President of the United States has two constituencies: first, the American people who elect him and pay taxes, and second, the defense-foreign-policy establishment which defines the national interest and calls the cold-war moves they say he must make.

During the Vietnam war, successive Presidents did not feel able to resist the demands being made upon them in the interests of "national security," nor were they able to explain adequately to their electoral constituency what their defense-foreign-policy constituency was requiring them to do.

The White House's double constituency places the President in the unenviable position of having to decide between the rival claims of civilian and military priorities as Lyndon Johnson was forced to do in 1964–66. The President must choose his own definition of the national interest—one of the slipperiest, most ambiguous phrases in

Washington. "I will not lose Vietnam," LBJ said late in 1963 as if that country were "his" to possess, and although he tried valiantly thereafter to have both guns and butter, when the pinch came he stinted on the butter, not the guns.[6]

It is almost a foregone conclusion that when the claims of the President's two constituencies come into sharp conflict on his desk, the claims of the defense-foreign-policy establishment will win, as they have done with every President since World War II except, perhaps, Eisenhower. These claims are typically couched in terms of sweeping, simplistic slogans, and they are articulated by men who exude a strong sense of mission ("save the world from communism"). Moreover, they are advanced by men who have been rigorously trained to spare no effort in looking for threats and in devising strategies to preempt them. In such circumstances a President, perhaps without being aware of it, slips into the language of military strategy and into calculations of probability, adopting unconsciously a technology-oriented approach to the subtleties and nuances of international relations.

The claims of the defense-foreign-policy establishment win out over the more diffuse claims of civilian programs because once a man—be he a secretary of defense, a secretary of state, or a President—has partaken of a sufficient number of military briefings he begins to take on, to some extent, the military's premises and thought patterns and thereafter they may unconsciously point him the way to his own conclusions. Psychologists know that, once our basic patterns of thought are established, we tend to ignore information that conflicts with them. We simply don't believe facts that do not conform to ideas we already hold. Each of us prefers to retain his or her private conceptions of the world by tuning out discordant messages.

In the case of the Vietnam war, then, it was no coincidence that after 1966–67 two of the last leaders of the Democratic Party to separate their egos from the idea of "winning" the war were two men who were receiving frequent military briefings—Lyndon Johnson and Hubert Humphrey. These two men, seeing themselves as liberals and humanists in the tradition of Franklin D. Roosevelt, had nevertheless opted to escalate a disastrous war against Asian peasants and in doing so they let slip through their fingers a brief moment of post-assassination political consensus in their country unequaled since the one on which Franklin Roosevelt had built the New Deal. The two led their country into a war in which its vital national interests were not at stake. Lightly taking up war as an instrument of national policy, they thrust themselves into a conflict whose outcome was of more serious moment to Hanoi than to Washington and in which, therefore, Hanoi's staying power outlasted their own. Then, having wanted so desperately to do good, they could not bear to turn and look upon the evil they had done. The American people, sensing all of this and by 1968 believing these two men insincere, turned for relief to the simpler, more comforting nostrums that Richard Nixon was offering.

Economists and Decision-Making

In a deeper sense, it may be that, in the 1960s, the Vietnam war was only that part of the U.S. foreign policy iceberg visible above the waterline. Is it not possible that "a Vietnam war" of one kind or another, in some country or other, had been programmed into U.S. foreign policy in the twenty-odd years following World War II and that it needed only the appropriate circumstances to be triggered into execution? If that is so, then "other Vietnams" are to be expected in the future unless the fundamental premises and/or decision-making procedures of U.S. foreign policy are changed.

In recasting the decision-making machinery of U.S. foreign policy the economist might have something to offer. In recent years economists have developed powerful analytical tools designed to render decision-making more rational. These tools are known to some as cost-benefit analysis and have been used in government under the name Planning Programming Budgeting (PPB). They have the enormous advantage that, as a first step, they require the decision-maker to consider the alternative courses of action open to him and to concentrate on what his precise objectives are. Having done this he must then concentrate on what the costs of attaining his objectives would be in terms of lost opportunities to do other things, and finally he must show, step by step, how the expenditures he proposes to make will help him to reach his most preferred objectives.

Under the label of PPB, public investment projects have been subjected to this rigorous decision-making procedure, and with great advantage. It forces the decision-maker to ask whether society as a whole would be made better off by undertaking a particular project or by undertaking, instead, any of several other carefully defined projects. This approach leads one to reject a project unless he can show that it confers social benefits that exceed its social costs. The procedure can be used with various degrees of sophistication, but the decision-maker who has made use of it at even the lowest level of sophistication is unlikely ever again to fail to examine his premises or to think in terms of all-or-nothing choices.

Ironically, these powerful decision-making tools were introduced into the Defense Department by Robert McNamara in the early 1960s and into other major federal government departments later in the decade—but not even the roughest calculations of this sort seem to have been made by the decision-makers responsible for leading the United States deeper and deeper into the Vietnam war. Instead, the choice of whether or not the government should escalate the fighting in Vietnam seems always to have presented itself as an all-or-nothing choice—win or surrender, fight or retreat—couched in emotion-laden terms that precluded objective analysis. In the main, just one man, the President of the United States, was required to make ultimate decisions about what course history should take without the benefit of any formal decision-making procedures. There were no adversary processes along the way by which alternatives to pressing forward in Vietnam could have been weighed. The saddest irony of all in the Vietnam war may be that, in March 1968, when the U.S. government finally focused serious attention *for the first time* on the costs and benefits of what it was doing in Vietnam, it decided to get out.

The year 1964, perhaps the most decisive single year in terms of U.S. involvement in Vietnam, was a year during which the government was required to make a number of major strategic decisions. Early in the year domestic policy-making was dominant: In January President Johnson declared "war on poverty" and in June he announced his Great Society program; in August he got Congress to pass the Gulf of Tonkin resolution, setting his course in Vietnam.

But the Vietnam war was not the only momentous foreign policy decision that had to be made in 1964. In the spring of that year the United Nations sponsored a conference on international trade and development which held out hope that the rules of international trade and investment, oriented to the world economy as it existed in the nineteenth century, might be brought up to date to the benefit of the less developed countries in particular.[7] But the United States did not respond positively to that initiative and thereby it may have slammed the door on one of the last major opportunities to salvage the United Nations from slow death by neglect and lost the opportunity to work out a cooperative solution to the problem of the developed countries' dependence on the less developed countries for raw material imports, an old problem that has arisen in new and menacing forms to plague international relations in the 1970s.

One strand in the tragedy of our time is that no formal system of decision-making was available to Lyndon Johnson in 1964, and it is doubtful that he was even marginally aware of the historic alternatives that were available to him.

CHAPTER 3

"GETTING THE COUNTRY MOVING": 1961–64

As the American political system operates, it has the opportunity to renew itself once every four years at presidential election time. When a new man enters the White House—especially if he represents a change of political party—those who supported him greet the occasion as symbolizing the arrival of a bright new dawn in the political life of the country. With their man at the helm, they foresee the nation rising above the errors and misguided policies of the past to strike out on a new and more promising course.

In 1961, those who had worked for the election of John F. Kennedy certainly believed that a bright and shining prospect lay ahead for the country. They had sat through an eight-year "reign" by a revered elderly general, waiting to respond to something as stirring as Kennedy's rhetoric on inauguration day, 1961. They believed that Kennedy would, indeed, "get the country moving again" as he had pledged in the election campaign.

Economists in the Kennedy camp were painfully aware that the country's economic growth rate during the Eisenhower years, 1953–60, was one of the lowest of any industrialized country, that unemployment had averaged 6 percent in 1958–60—half again as high as the 4 percent most economists accepted as a reasonable "full employment" goal, and that the economy had had to endure four recessions in the preceding twelve years at a time when, according to the teachings of "the new economics," recessions had become preventable.[1]

The "new economics," as it was still called, was no longer very new in 1961. Its most influential exposition had been at the hands of John Maynard Keynes of Cambridge University, England, in 1935, and it had been included in the staple diet of American college courses in economics for about a quarter century. In the course of those years it had shaped its doctrines to meet the evolving economic situation, but its constant theme over the years had been a central concern with prescribing governmental policies to stabilize the economy.

The early emphasis on economic stability had led to a concentration on devising governmental *fiscal policies*—that is, policies affecting taxation and government spending—that would succeed in damping down the business cycle. The "new economics" had urged governments to compensate for the wavelike oscillations of the economy—shaving off the peaks and filling in the valleys of the business cycle. When private demand fell off, government spending should increase, preventing the economy from sinking into a recession, but in the next phase of the business cycle when the private sector might be stirring up a storm of prosperity, government spending should taper off—and if the private sector should threaten to lapse into overexpansion and its accompanying price inflation, the government should increase taxes in order to siphon off excess demand and thus prevent prices from rising.

By the early 1960s, however, the twenty-five-year-old "new economics" had moved on to a new, more ambitious phase. Fiscal policy was still a principal tool and economic stability the overriding objective, but the intermediate policy goal had changed. As Walter Heller, chairman of the President's Council of Economic Advisers from 1961 to 1964, put it, the focus of economic policy had shifted "from the ups and downs of the cycle to the continuous rise in the economy's potential."[2] What this meant was nothing less than the substitution of the goal of continuous prosperity for the earlier goal of averaging out periods of prosperity and recession. In Figure 3-1 the focus of earlier policy on anticyclical activity is indicated by the shaded areas in the upper panel, while the later focus on "the continuous rise in the economy's potential" is indicated by the heavy black line in the lower panel. As this heavy line is drawn, it represents the economy's maximum potential output as it increases through

FIGURE 3-1

Two different views of economic stability

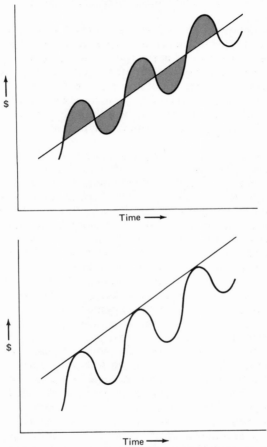

The goal of the new economics in its early years was to conquer the business cycle by shaving off cyclical peaks and filling in cyclical valleys, thus averaging out the good and the bad years. By the early 1960s many economists thought the business cycle could be tamed and the new economics adopted the more ambitious goal of keeping the economy performing continuously at its optimum rate.

The "averaging out" strategy of the early years is portrayed impressionistically in the upper panel of Figure 3-1, while the lower panel illustrates the strategy of attaining continuous full employment.

time. Its appearance on the scene was a natural accompaniment of the shift by economists away from studying the behavior of past business cycles to the study of how the economy could be made to operate continuously at its most satisfactory level.

The translation of this approach to economic analysis into a graphical presentation of how the U.S. economy has actually performed in the last twenty years is shown in Figure 3-2, Actual and Potential GNP. This diagram, originally prepared by the Department of Commerce, represents a way of thinking about the economy that practically requires one to observe whether or not it is living up to its potential. The eye is shifted away from merely contemplating the behavior of cyclical ups and downs and is drawn instead to concentrate on the trend rate of growth, which acts as a pacer for the economy, as it were. The extent of the shortfall of actual GNP below potential GNP came to be called the *performance gap* and by 1961 it had become large. Since early 1957 it had risen from about $10 billion to about $50 billion and the latter figure amounted to about 10 percent of the GNP at the time.

It was this picture of the shortfall in the economy's performance that Walter Heller and his associates on the Council of Economic Advisers laid before the new President in 1961.[3] Their analysis contained a built-in formula for economic activism, because unless the two lines for the actual and the potential GNPs coincide, as they did briefly in the second half of 1955, the graph seems to say "something needs to be done."

President Kennedy despite his forward-looking ideas and his inspiring rhetoric, had come into office holding rather conventional, conservative attitudes toward economic matters. Specifically with regard to government taxation and spending, Herbert Stein reports that "he preferred a balanced budget, being in this respect like most other people but unlike modern economists. But if he brought into the White House no very sophisticated or systematic ideas about compensatory fiscal policy, neither did he bring with him any deep intellectual or emotional commitment to the old ideas. This was partly a matter of his youth. He was the first . . . President . . . who had passed the majority of his life in the post-Keynesian world where the old orthodoxy was giving way to the new."[4]

According to what Stein calls the "new orthodoxy," the all-important economic question for government policy is whether or not *the economy as a whole is in balance* in the sense that it is producing all it is capable of producing. The "old orthodoxy," on the other hand, had placed great stress upon the idea that the *federal government's annual budget ought to be balanced,* just like anyone else's budget.

FIGURE 3-2
Actual and Potential GNP

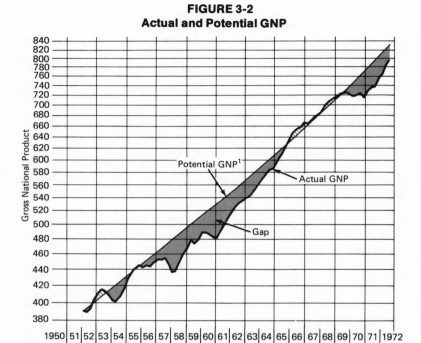

Potentially, the U.S. economy can grow by about 4.5 percent a year (potential GNP line). After the first quarter of 1961, when GNP was below its potential by 9 percent, the Kennedy administration succeeded in "getting the country moving again," and by 1965 the economy had expanded up to its full potential.

At that point, President Johnson decisively escalated the Vietnam war, and for most of the next three years the U.S. economy outdid itself, producing *above* potential. The stresses and strains entailed by that extraordinary exertion, however, set off the inflation that is still with us.

During the Korean war, too, the economy outdid itself (in 1952) but during that period well-timed wage and price controls and higher taxes prevented a serious inflation from getting under way.

The Nixon administration's inept handling of the de-escalation of the war and its ill-advised policies for the civilian economy produced the economic recession of 1970–71 and its accompanying rise in unemployment. In those years the GNP once again fell far short of its potential.

This doctrine had inhibited President Eisenhower's administration from pursuing an activist economic policy in its later years, because such a policy would have called for either more spending or less taxes and would, therefore, have implied unbalancing the federal government's own budget. One simply cannot always have it both ways according to "the new economics," and the attempt to balance the federal budget in 1958–60 had *unbalanced* the economy.[5]

Heller and his associates saw their first task in 1961–62 to be that of finding a way to convince President Kennedy that "getting the country moving again" meant closing the GNP performance gap by a novel, creative use of fiscal policy so that the country could once again make full use of its tremendous productive powers. The young President, whose inquiring intellect was receptive to new ideas, turned out to have a keen interest in the tenets of "the new economics," but he also turned out to be slow to adopt its conclusions as his own.[6] The dialogue that followed—at first between the economists and the President and later between the administration and congressional and business leaders—proved to be one of those rare occasions when economists take giant steps in making themselves intelligible to noneconomists, those who must somehow get the message if economic analysis is to serve the broad public interest.[7]

The President listened long and carefully to his economists. According to Walter Heller, "over 300 economic memoranda went to President Kennedy in the thousand days of his Presidency,"[8] and according to Herbert Stein, "during the period up to the middle of 1962 the President was the chief student in the council's economic seminar."[9]

In the spring of 1962 the economic recovery that had started a year earlier faltered briefly, and in June 1962 Kennedy gave the long-awaited signal that he had accepted his economists' prescription for government action. At the Yale University commencement he delivered one of the most memorable speeches of his brief career, in which he spoke out against the budgetary cliches and mythology of his day and came out in favor of a practical, activist approach to the problem of economic growth.

There was elation at the Council of Economic Advisers at this first public statement in favor of modern economics by an American President, and attention turned immediately to the task of devising a specific economic stimulus that could be passed by a Congress that was generally unreceptive to Kennedy initiatives. The administration would have preferred to attain economic expansion by increasing government expenditures rather than by reducing taxes, but, as usual, there were powerful men in Congress who opposed increases in federal government spending on principle, almost regardless of the object of the expenditure.[10] Upon sounding out congressmen, the President discovered that "much of the opposition to expansive fiscal policy, including budget deficits, would turn into support if the deficits were created by tax reduction rather than by expenditure increases."[11]

Therefore President Kennedy announced in August his intention to ask Congress for a tax cut in the following January. The cut proposed was a large one, intended to lower the full-employment surplus almost to zero from $11 billion at the end of 1963. Individual income taxes were to be cut by almost 20 percent and corporate income taxes by about 20 percent when two Kennedy tax-reduction bills were combined. It was an unprecedented step to ask Congress to cut taxes so much at a time when the federal budget was already in deficit and when the economy was neither in, nor threatened by, a recession. It was possible because an intelligent, open-minded President had been willing to learn modern economics and to accept its activist implications for government policy.

President Kennedy did not live to see his major innovation in fiscal policy become law. Instead, Lyndon Johnson's first major legislative achievement was to get Congress to pass the tax-reform bill in February 1964. Its reductions in taxation amounted to $15 billion and consumers spent most of their increased take-home pay almost immediately. Shortly afterward, business investment also turned upward. Unemployment continued to decline and soon the federal budget deficit was converted into a surplus. In fact, in 1964–65 the Kennedy-Johnson tax cut turned out to be a classic example of modern fiscal policy working effectively in the nation's interest. To recall how it was achieved is a good way to begin a discussion of the economic consequences of the Vietnam war, because today, after we have had to live with the multifarious costs of that war for a decade, it is sometimes forgotten that in the earlier 1960s the atmosphere in Washington was one of confidence and hope.

CHAPTER 4

TAKING THE NEXT STEP:
THE ANTIPOVERTY PROGRAM: 1964–65

President Kennedy's economic advisers had convinced him that after the economy's sluggish economic performance of the late 1950s the promotion of more rapid growth should be the major objective of his economic policy. In their early scenarios they expected an increase in the growth rate to reduce unemployment from 7 percent in early 1961 to their "interim target" rate of 4 percent by sometime in 1963. Unemployment fell steadily throughout 1961, but stalled at about 5 1/2 percent through 1962 and 1963 even though fairly rapid economic growth continued. Apparently something was wrong with the hypothesis that a strong, steady rise in production would always bring with it declining unemployment.

Washington agencies began to study the unemployment problem and gradually came to the conclusion that some Americans were so disadvantaged through no fault of their own that they were not likely to find good steady jobs even when there was prosperity in mainstream America.[1] These were forty million or so people (one fifth of the U.S. population) that Michael Harrington had written about so movingly in 1962: those who, Harrington said, had "dropped out of sight," who dwelt apart in a "culture of poverty."[2] They comprised "a more or less permanent underclass that seemed fated not to share in the nation's growing wealth, even in the best of times."[3] They were the elderly (about half of whom were below the poverty line),[4] the nonwhites in a white man's America (nearly half of whom live in poverty), the poorly educated (more than 60 percent of the poor have only grade-school educations), unproductive small farmers (more than 40 percent of all farm families are poor), they were the forgotten people of Appalachia and of our urban black ghettos—their poverty was the result of social problems that are relatively unaffected by broad economic forces.[5] Impacted poverty of this sort, it was becoming clear, could not be eliminated by the indirect method of stimulating the overall economic growth rate. Instead, society would have to find ways to extend direct help to these poverty victims before they could be expected to help themselves effectively. Studies of impacted poverty at the Council of Economic Advisers, according to Walter Heller, "showed that the tax cut would create two to three million jobs and thus open many new exits from poverty. But those caught in the web of illiteracy, lack of skills, poor health, and squalor would not be able to make use of these exits. . . . By mid-1963 I had sent President Kennedy our economic and statistical analysis of the groups beyond the reach of the tax cut and had offered some groping thoughts on 'an attack on poverty.' "[6] Manpower development and retraining programs that had been started early in 1961 had pointed the way toward the types of direct aid needed.[7] This was the atmosphere of exploratory thinking in the antipoverty field when President Kennedy left Washington for his appointment in Dallas, Texas, on November 22, 1963.

In a sense, the various measures Washington was considering in its attack on poverty in the fall of 1963 hearkened back to the strong social welfare emphasis of Franklin D. Roosevelt's early New Deal in the 1930s. Roosevelt was Lyndon Johnson's greatest hero and the man after whom he had sought to model his political career. It was natural, then, for Johnson, when he succeeded to the presidency, to collect the various embryo antipoverty programs, add to them his own ideas and the stamp of his own personality, and announce to the country as he did in his first State of the Union message in January 1964 that "a war on poverty" would be the main thrust of his administration.

There followed a period of feverish activity in Washington in early 1964 as a team of talented and dedicated administration men, under the general supervision of President Kennedy's brother-in-law Sargent Shriver, put together the details of the antipoverty programs. In May 1964 at the University of Michigan Johnson proclaimed that he would preside over "the Great Society"—great in the sense that it would show compassion by rescuing its less fortunate members from poverty. The new President then succeeded in getting a number of important Great Society measures through Congress even before his landslide victory over Senator Barry Goldwater in the presidential election of 1964. That election victory also brought into Congress the heaviest Democratic Party majorities in a generation. With such large majorities, Congress then proceeded to enact a body of domestic social legislation that had not been equaled since the first New Deal of the early 1930s.

The major thrust of Lyndon Johnson's war on poverty was not to be that of rescuing the American underclass through "handouts," but to enable its members to lift themselves out of poverty through "the opportunity for education and training" and "the opportunity to work," to quote the language of the preamble to the Economic Opportunity Act of 1964. The Office of Economic Opportunity (OEO) set up by that act was created to provide a community-wide focus in each local community for various individual programs offering special education, training, and work experience mainly directed toward young people. The OEO was also to coordinate the activities of local Community Action Programs (CAPs) across the nation through which the poor were to participate directly in planning antipoverty activities in their local communities. The CAPs had considerable local autonomy and sponsored such services as children's preschool activities, vocational and mental health counseling, neighborhood centers, and the like. According to the Johnson administration, these CAPs "are an important new social institution and a major weapon in the war on urban poverty."[8]

A flood of legislation to implement the war on poverty burst from the halls of Congress in 1964–65 (see Table 4-1). It was as if the apparently meaningless assassination of their promising young President at the end of 1963 had released a flood of dammed-up goodwill in the American body politic. Several social reform measures President Kennedy had proposed were taken out of congressional pigeonholes and passed and the country seemed once again to be as eager to promote social justice in the land as it had been under FDR in the 1930s. Not that the war against poverty was costing very much money in 1964–65; those were years when goals were being set, when professional staffs were being assembled, enacting legislation passed, and experimental approaches tried out. The years when large sums of money would be needed to do battle with the forces of fear, ignorance, and prejudice that do so much to perpetuate poverty still lay ahead—in a hoped-for future.

TABLE 4-1

GREAT SOCIETY PROGRAMS OF 1963–66

In a burst of social creativity in the early and mid-1960s, the American people set out for the first time to cope with the problems of hard-core poverty in its contemporary U.S. setting. They sought to help people escape from poverty who, in Michael Harrington's words, had previously been "beyond the welfare state—some . . . simply not covered by social legislation . . . others covered but so poor they do not know how to take advantage of the opportunities, or else their coverage is so inadequate as to not make a difference." In a many-pronged attack on poverty these are some of the legislative acts and government agencies through which the American people sought to express their concern.

Antipoverty Legislation

Appalachian Regional
  Development Act of 1965
Area Redevelopment Act of
  1965
Civil Rights Act of 1964
Demonstration Cities and
  Metropolitan Development
  Act of 1966
Economic Development Act of
  1965
Economic Opportunity Act of
  1964
Elementary and Secondary
  Education Act of 1965
Graduate Public Health
  Training Amendments of
  1964
Health Professions Education
  Assistance Act of 1963
Higher Education Act of 1965
Housing Act of 1964
Housing and Urban
  Development Act of 1965
Library Services and
  Construction Act of 1964
Manpower Development and
  Training Act of 1962 (MDTA)

Antipoverty Agencies & Programs

Adult Basic Education
  Program
Community Action Programs
Community Mental Health
  Centers
Department of Health,
  Education and Welfare
Department of Housing and
  Urban Development
Economic Opportunity Grants
Expanded Work-Study
  Program
Food Stamps Program
Job Corps
Medicaid
Medicare
Model Cities
National Teachers Corps
Neighborhood Youth Corps
Project Head Start
Project Upward Bound
Talent Search
Volunteers in Service to
  America (VISTA, the
  domestic peace corps)
Vocational Rehabilitation
  Service

TABLE 4-1 *(Continued)*

Antipoverty Legislation	Antipoverty Agencies & Programs
MDTA Extended and Amended in 1965	Work Experience Program
Nurse Training Act of 1964	Youth Opportunity Centers
Older Americans Act of 1965	
Urban Mass Transportation Act of 1964	
Vocational Education Act of 1963	
Youth Employment Act of 1963	

CHAPTER 5

TWO WARS IN CONFRONTATION—
ONE AGAINST POVERTY AND ONE AGAINST NORTH VIETNAM

It is very risky to try to generalize about the effect of the war in Vietnam upon the war against poverty. Among the Washington *cognoscenti* you will find two directly contradictory views about the effect of one war upon the other. On the one hand there are those who say President Johnson did *not* cut back on his Great Society programs in order to fight the Vietnam war but, instead, pressed doggedly ahead, fighting *both* the war in Vietnam and the war against poverty. Since the economy could not afford both wars simultaneously, according to this view, it became dangerously overheated and lapsed into the severe price inflation from whose enervating effects we continue to suffer.

Other equally well-informed people argue that the war in Vietnam ultimately won out over the war against poverty—in two stages, as it were. First, top officials in the Johnson administration—and especially the President himself—became so preoccupied with fighting the war in Vietnam that they did not provide the high-level political leadership that would have been essential if as novel a social experiment as the war against poverty was to survive, let alone thrive.[1] Secondly, after 1965 the antipoverty program was rendered ineffective because the funds it needed to grow were spent, instead, to fight the war in Vietnam.[2]

There are, unfortunately, elements of truth in both of these apparently inconsistent interpretations—unfortunately so, because the Vietnam war brought us *both* of the unfavorable consequences that were foreseen—we got a badly inflated economy *and* we lost track of the war on poverty.

LBJ's War on Two Fronts

Let us try to reconcile the two different interpretations of what happened. In January 1966, when it first became apparent to the administration that there would be difficulty about supporting both the war in Vietnam and the antipoverty program, Johnson spoke out "loud and clear" in favor of both. "I am unwilling to declare a moratorium on our progress toward the Great Society [in order to finance the war in Vietnam]," he told Congress. And posing a rhetorical question to himself, he asked, "Can we move ahead with the Great Society programs and at the same time meet our needs for defense? My confident answer is YES."[3] These declarations of his intention to extract both guns and butter from the American economy got wide publicity at the time, and today they are much better remembered than the fact that he subsequently pruned the antipoverty programs because the money they needed had already been spent for the Vietnam war.

It also helps to reconcile the two divergent opinions about the relationship between the war in Vietnam and the antipoverty program to recall that the war in Vietnam turned out to be fabulously more expensive than Johnson thought it would be in January 1966. Because he was grossly underestimating its cost he was able to suppose that he could strike a balance and manage to have both wars. At first he tried to protect the war against poverty (which was closer to his heart than it was to many congressmen's hearts) from being overbalanced by the war in Vietnam. But his failure to accomplish this impossible balancing act brought us the worst of both worlds: inflation for the economy and disappointment for those who had believed him when he promised to fight the war aginst poverty.

The year of the showdown between the two wars was 1966, but the seeds for the confrontation between them were planted and nourished in 1964 and 1965. We have seen that Johnson launched his new administration on the antipoverty theme early in 1964, that his political party obtained a huge congressional majority in November 1964, and that the pace of antipoverty legislation quickened in 1965. At the same time these events were occurring, an ominously parallel momentum was building up in Vietnam. Ngo Dinh Diem had been executed by his own officer corps in November 1963, and in 1964 a series of anti-Communist military regimes in Saigon had run its course. By early 1965 the power of officials in Saigon to influence events in Vietnam had almost reached the vanishing point. Instead of collapsing, however, the regime's slender hold on life was strengthened at this point by powerful evidence of the U.S. government's determination to see it survive. Congress had passed the Gulf of Tonkin resolution in August 1964, and building on this vaguely worded document, President Johnson ordered American planes to bomb North Vietnam for the first time in February 1965, less than a month after his inauguration. Later in the spring, when it became clear that Hanoi could not be bombed into submission, U.S. officials decided to commit U.S. ground forces to the war, and on July 28, 1965, the most notable single overt escalation of the war came when draft calls were raised in order to fight the war.

Clearly, in 1965 the Johnson administration made strong commitments to fight both the war in Vietnam and the war against poverty. It was a heady time in the history of the nation and even critics of the administration found rhetoric for expressing the overconfidence of the day. "If we are going to meet our responsibilities as a society we must do what needs to be done in Vietnam and what needs to be done at home. We shall fail as a society if we do not do both. And the fact is that we can do both." These words were spoken not by President Johnson but by Sen. Robert F. Kennedy of New York.[4]

The year 1965 was also notable for another reason, one not related to the confrontation that was building up for 1966. It was the fifth consecutive year of sustained economic expansion in the United States. The results of the Kennedy-Johnson tax cut—the last installment of which came into effect in 1965—were highly favorable, and for the first time in eight years the economy was back to a full employment level of production.[5] This economic fact of life was an essential ingredient of the confrontation drama that was to be acted out in 1966 between Johnson's two national commitments. The economy, having arrived at full employment, was not able to accommodate any further increases in demand. On the contrary, it was already producing all it could and it was vulnerable to inflationary price and wage increase even without the additional economic stimulus about to be applied to it by the administration.

Hopefulness and Vulnerability
In the fall of 1965 hope and enthusiasm ran high in the Office of Economic Opportunity (OEO), the coordinating agency in Washing-

ton for the war against poverty. There was much intellectual ferment at the OEO because the American people had just made a long overdue policy decision to strike out in new directions in trying to remove some of the deep and intractable causes of poverty. However, as a grim and terrible unfolding of events was about to demonstrate, the antipoverty program was vulnerable to being shot down by its critics, even if the fires had not already been lighted for the war in Vietnam which was soon to overwhelm it.

There were several basic reasons for the antipoverty program's vulnerability. In the first place, it involved a brand-new approach to the problem of poverty by attempting to reach out to the submerged, inarticulate classes in American society whom developments in mainstream America had passed by for one reason or another. The strategy for this approach had been put together hastily by a small group of officials early in 1964 so that Lyndon Johnson could identify his administration with the idea of the Great Society. Some aspects of the program were somewhat experimental in nature since almost no scientific research had been conducted into the behavior patterns of the very poor. Goals for some of the projects were not sharply defined and no one knew what their future costs would be.[6] But to many of the antipoverty workers these were all questions of secondary importance. The main reality was that the program was on its way; once its foot was in the door, many felt, it was bound to grow in effectiveness and in the public's esteem.

To these uncertainties and ambiguities must be added some even more threatening difficulties that loomed in the political arena. The Office of Economic Opportunity had the task of seeing to it that antipoverty activities in each community were appropriately adapted to that community's particular problems since, as someone put it, "the needs of the poor are not the same in East Kentucky and West Harlem." To help in accomplishing this adaptation, Title II of the Economic Opportunity Act had called for the "maximum feasible participation" of the poor themselves in administering and coordinating the various antipoverty projects. As events worked out, this innocuous sounding provision was found to carry within it the seeds of a possible redistribution of power in local communities—toward the poor, away from established local political leaders. Not unnaturally, therefore, it was resented by some local political figures as a direct challenge to their power and prestige, engineered by meddlesome officials of the federal government. Such local-federal tensions provided the OEO's critics in Congress and elsewhere with ready-made clubs that they could use to beat the organization. Congress soon heard these complaints, as well as the sharp differences of opinion over the value and effectiveness of some of the antipoverty projects. In addition, the impression spread that the OEO was having more than its share of administrative difficulties, and some of the organized poor, who were becoming radicalized, turned against the program.

"Teething troubles" such as these are to be expected in any important new venture by government, but in this instance they were made worse by the fact that the antipoverty program did not have powerful friends in Congress with vested interests in preserving it. Both the flowing rhetoric and the overall strategy of the war against poverty had been creatures of the Kennedy and Johnson administrations rather than having been put together in Congress; therefore Congress did not identify with it as it does with most traditional, oldline government agencies.

All of these vulnerabilities of the antipoverty program added up to one essential requirement: if it was to survive and grow it would have to have continuous, active, and imaginative support from the White House. But this it did not get because President Johnson and his staff became more and more preoccupied with plotting the strategy of their other war—the one in Vietnam, which they were also destined not to win.

"Hand Me the Meat Ax"

While escalating the war in Vietnam in 1965, the Johnson administration went to Congress three times to ask for a total of $2.5 billion more to help pay for it, and by the end of the year it was an open secret that much more money would be needed. Therefore, in January 1966 the budget that Johnson presented to Congress was prepared under the shadow of mushrooming war costs. Whereas a year earlier, in January 1965, the administration had urged Congress to double the money appropriated for the war against poverty, *in January 1966, the President's economic message did not even contain a section devoted to the antipoverty program!* The war against North Vietnam had usurped first priority and the Council of Economic Advisers muttered grimly, "National security, of course, has first priority on the budget [sic] and the first claim on production."[7] President Johnson, speaking as if the country were in imminent danger of attack, told Congress, "I have reviewed every program of the government to make room for the necessities of defense. I have sharply reduced or eliminated those civilian programs of lowest priority."[8]

By as early as January 1966, the antipoverty program was no longer a civilian program of high priority. The OEO had received about $1.5 billion in the government's fiscal year 1965–66 (its second year of life), but in 1966–67 it got only $1.6 billion. Since the agency had been expanding its activities during 1965–66, its slim budget allotment in 1966–67 meant that it had to cut back its programs to a level below that already reached at the end of 1965–66.[9] This was a body blow to the agency while it was still in its infancy "and the war on poverty became the first domestic casualty of the war in Vietnam."[10] The war that counted with the administration was against a tiny country in Southeast Asia, not against poverty in America. The latter was to be fought in 1966–67 with a budget *only 8 percent as large as the cost overrun of the Vietnam war in 1965–66.*[11]

But still more cuts were on the way. As the cost of the Vietnam war continued to mushroom in 1966, the pace of price inflation increased and the administration decided to jettison even more of the government's civilian expenditures. On November 29, 1966, Johnson announced at a news conference in Texas a series of "budget cutbacks, postponements, deferments, etc.," intended to reduce expenditures "by more than 3 billion dollars in the next seven months."[12] Of these cuts, 42 percent were in agencies directly concerned with the antipoverty program. Reflecting the garrison-state mentality that was taking over in the administration, Johnson added, "We have put pretty strong ceilings on in regard to the number of employees in all departments already."[13]

"Late in 1966 . . . a malaise of despair and disappointment swept through the Office of Economic Opportunity: as it had to perform the unwelcome task of cutting back on its programs."[14] This, one year after hope and enthusiasm had been so high. James Reston caught the mood early in 1967 when he wrote "The problem [of poverty in the United States] is defined; the programs all have vivid names; the machinery, still new and imperfect, is nevertheless in place; but the funds are lamentably inadequate to the gigantic scope of the problem."[15] As John C. Donovan saw it, "The conclusion is inescapable. Lyndon Baines Johnson became so involved in a war in Vietnam which he did not start and which he did not want that he soon lost sight of the war on poverty which he initiated and which only he could lead if it were to be fought with courage and skill. A controversial social welfare program . . . became particularly vulnerable to Congressional and bureaucratic controls—and to local political resistance—once presidential leadership was deflected."[16]

What Might Have Been

What's done is done. And no one can know what might have been if "it" had not been done. That is the elusive nature of the idea of economic cost (opportunity cost), and all the economist can say for certain is that if "it" had not been done, other things could have been done. Who can say what might have sprung out of the high hopes of 1964–65 for the war on poverty if the war in Vietnam had not bludgeoned it into a foregone opportunity? Lyndon Johnson was a seasoned, resilient politician, and if he had opted to stay with the war he knew more about, quite possibly appropriations for it could have doubled again in 1966–67 and 1967–68, as they had in 1964–65, up to some $6 billion a year.

In addition to simply projecting a trend of doubled expenditures for three years in order to meet a major public need, there are several other ways one can dig up clues to what the war on poverty "might have been" except for the war in Vietnam. One way is to look at the official records of how much money Congress authorized for it that was never spent. In January 1969 the Council of Economic Advisers reported that several antipoverty programs authorized by Congress were underspending in 1969 at rates that added up to $4.8 billion per year.[17] Merely bringing these various projects up to their authorized rates of expenditure for, say, three years would have given the country $14.4 billion of antipoverty efforts.

Another way to peer into the inscrutable world of "might-have-beens" is to build up to a total of projects that competent authorities determined needed to be undertaken to correct some of the injustices that poverty inflicts upon so many Americans. The Council of Economic Advisers also did this, and in its 1969 report it listed desirable new domestic programs in the fields of education, health, job and manpower training, social insurance, welfare, urban development, and others that had been recommended by special task forces or study groups. The council estimated these recommended programs would have cost $30.5 billion per year in 1971–72 if implemented, or $91.2 billion over a period of three years.[18] The total of these "desirable" projects sets an upper limit on what one might have expected in the way of actual expenditures.

A third way to get at an estimate of how much we missed in domestic government spending because of the war in Vietnam is to start with the increase that would have occurred in the federal government's revenues and to suppose that none of the increase had been absorbed by increased Defense Department spending. Arthur Okun, a former chairman of the Council of Economic Advisers, has done this for us. He estimates federal revenues would have risen by "well over 30 billion dollars from mid-1965 to mid-1969 along a non-inflationary, high employment growth track [of the GNP] with no changes in tax rates [excluding social insurance taxes]. . . . During

TABLE 5-1

THE WAR IN VIETNAM CROWDS OUT
THE WAR AGAINST POVERTY
*(Alternative Approximations to Shortfalls of Spending
on Antipoverty Programs)*

Method of Approximation and Year of Projected Spending	Billion Dollars per Year
If OEO Appropriations Had Doubled for Two More Years (value by 1967–68)	6.0
Under-spending on Authorized Programs (1969)	4.8
If All Federal Revenue Increases Had Been Available (1969)	11.0
Upper Limit Set by Total of "Desirable" Projects (estimates for 1971–72)	30.4

The war in Vietnam did not snuff out the Viet Cong or the North Vietnamese but it did snuff out much of the momentum of, and the financial support for, the war against poverty in the United States.

This table suggests that the war against poverty might have received at least 5 billion a year more in federal funds except for the Vietnam war. By 1968 the federal government was paying out some 30 billion a year to fight the Vietnamese war.

that period . . . apart from social security (covered by social insurance taxes) and higher interest costs on the federal debt (not controllable) other nondefense outlays rose by [only] 19 billion dollars."[19] In other words, if the Johnson administration had not lost control of events, it would have been able by 1969 to spend on civilian projects—in a noninflationary environment—something like $11 billion a year more than it did spend.

This figure of approximately $11 billion is of special interest because it would have been more than adequate to have *eliminated* poverty in the United States, defined as closing "the poverty gap" between the actual incomes of the poor and the incomes that would be necessary to place them above the poverty level of income. The cost of this operation in the late 1960s was in the neighborhood of $10 billion.[20] Whether or not "the funds that might have been" would all have been used in an effort to eliminate poverty, it is impossible to say. What we can say with confidence is that they would have been adequate to have had a transforming effect on the quality of life in the United States. An earnest effort to restore dignity and hope to those among us whom Michael Harrington identified as "the other America" might have brought them and their children into the mainstream of American life, might have reduced the use of narcotics and the spread of violence among the poor, and might have made our city streets safe enough for all to walk on once again.

Ten billion dollars amounts to less than 1 percent of the country's GNP, compared with approximately 2 1/2 to 3 percent of the GNP spent on the Vietnam war in each of the years 1967, 1968, 1969, and 1970. As Arthur Okun has said, the cost of eliminating poverty in the United States "is enormous [only] because it strains our will and determination, not because it strains our resources."[21] But in the second half of the 1960s our will and determination were not equal to the task—compared to the zest with which we embarked upon the destruction of the life of peasants in Vietnam.[22]

Often the dollar signs of economic statistics do not convey their real meanings in human terms. When Sen. Robert F. Kennedy asserted that the United States "must" do *both* "what needs to be done in Vietnam and what needs to be done at home" he also spoke directly to the human meaning of the administration's downgrading of its hopeful domestic programs in favor of its hopeless foreign venture. He said, "Cuts [in programs intended to improve the education of disadvantaged children] will be felt most by those least able to afford them . . . particularly the disadvantaged children who live in the vast urban ghettos and the rural hollows of the nation."[23] Who will ever know how many of the young men who might have participated in the Job Corps, the Neighborhood Youth Corps, and other Great Society programs—either as enrollees or as instructors—ended up, instead, as corpses in Southeast Asia, their vigorous, hopeful young lives snuffed out in an unnecessary, ill-conceived war, their names today surviving only as memories cherished by their loved ones?

Martin Luther King, Jr., once referred to the Vietnam war as "America's tragic distraction,"[24] and at greater length he wrote: "There is at the outset a very obvious and almost facile connection between the war in Vietnam and the struggle I and others have been waging in America. A few years ago there was a shining moment in that struggle. It seemed as if there was a real promise of hope for the poor, both black and white, through the poverty program. There were experiments, hopes, new beginnings. Then came the build-up in Vietnam and I watched the program broken and eviscerated as if it were some idle political plaything of a society gone mad on war, and I knew that America would never invest the necessary funds or energies in rehabilitation of its poor so long as adventures like Vietnam continued to draw men and skills and money like some demoniacal destructive suction tube. And so I was increasingly compelled to see the war not only as a moral outrage but also as an enemy of the poor, and to attack it as such."[25]

Today people who should know better lapse into a mood of disillusionment and defeatism when they discuss Johnson's war on poverty, as if the Great Society programs had been so poorly conceived that they were foredoomed to fail. That there were problems with some of the programs, no one can doubt, but let no one forget that the antipoverty program was *mainly* a victim of the Vietnam war. After many years of negativism in American public life, it is important that the story of how Lyndon Johnson scuttled the war on poverty in order to escalate the Vietnam war not be forgotten.

CHAPTER 6

ESCALATING THE WAR IN VIETNAM:
HOW NOT TO FINANCE A WAR*

The American economy was put through a series of violent contortions under the disruptive impact of the Vietnam war. As the war escalated—and later, as it de-escalated—one economic distortion followed hard upon another at a time when the government was guilty of classic mismanagement of the economy. Some observers insisted that "the new economics," so soon after its major success in "getting the economy moving again," in 1961–64, had fallen flat on its face when confronted with the challenge of managing a war economy, despite the fact that in no sense was the economy managed as a war economy should be. Critics from both the right and the left were not slow in coming forward to denounce economists' claim that they knew enough to be able to manage a modern economy successfully. Bitter attacks were made on the new economics that should have been directed instead at the top political echelons of the Johnson administration.

Beginning in 1965–66, the American people have had to learn how

*Readers who would benefit from reading a brief summary of the main outlines of economic stabilization policy and a sketchy account of how they should be carried out by the federal government should read Appendix A before beginning to read this chapter.

to live with economic disorder. The large, rapidly growing demands of the war were superimposed upon a fully employed economy that, already in 1965, was giving signs of being overloaded by the demands of a *civilian-style* economic boom. This set off the inflationary price-wage spiral with which the country is still afflicted. No deliberate decision about how to finance the war was taken until it was much too late, so the Johnson administration carelessly resorted to deficit financing to pay for it. To make matters worse, in the early phase of the escalation, policy-makers added to the war's inflationary effect by seriously underestimating the speed with which the war would affect the economy.

In short, the government's fiscal policy veered off course in 1965–66 and instead of contributing to economic stability, it became a major destabilizing influence. Monetary policy swerved this way and that as the Federal Reserve sought unsuccessfully to stabilize the economy in the face of the government's counterproductive fiscal policy. The relatively new wage-price guideposts that had helped somewhat to reduce inflation in 1962–66 were first undermined and then discredited, and the country's already weakened international balance of payments simply came unstuck.

Later, the Nixon administration tilted unsuccessfully with the inflation. First, in 1970–1971 it subjected the country to its first economic recession in ten years. When that failed to check inflation, it introduced peacetime direct wage and price controls for the first time in U.S. history, and finally, in 1973, it prematurely abandoned the controls that had been introduced too late.

After World War II and the Korean War——A Small War

Some observers thought the country's economy would easily be able to take the Vietnam war in its stride. At no time, they pointed out, did it absorb more than 3.2 percent of the GNP and national defense in total rose only to 9.2 percent of the GNP; by contrast, war expenditures rose to 38 percent of GNP at the peak of World War II and to 13 percent during the Korean War.[1] This rough-and-ready type of economic diagnosis sounded plausible at first, but it did not bear up under closer scrutiny. For one thing, the U.S. economy had a vast reservoir of unemployed resources that it brought into full use in order to fight World War II. Thus, World War II was fought by soldiers who might otherwise have been unemployed, and they used guns, tanks, airplanes, and the other accouterments of war that were produced in factories that might otherwise have been idle. In sharp contrast, at the time of the Vietnam war, a sudden, sharp 3 percent

FIGURE 6-1
Defense Expenditure as a % of GNP

How Do We Use the GNP?

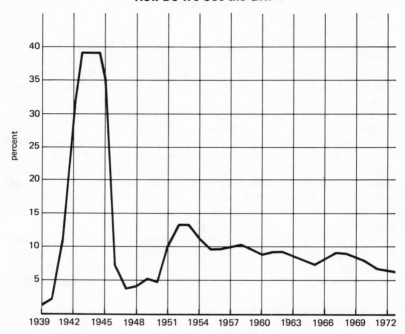

Most of the GNP goes into private civilian uses such as personal consumption and business investment. Some of it goes to meet such public civilian
needs as those for schools, highways, police protection, and the like—and
varying percentages of it are devoted to military purposes. During World War
II the military took almost 40 percent of the GNP. The fraction going into
military uses rose again during the Korean War, but thereafter the proportion
fell because the GNP rose more than military spending, except for a "hump"
during the Vietnam war.

The military has been taking a declining fraction of the GNP since the
Korean War, but the country *could* devote either a higher or a lower proportion of its GNP to the military without serious strain. It is all a matter of the
American people, their political leaders, and their civilian economic policy-
makers knowing what they want and what they are doing. During the Vietnam
war these conditions were not met, and that is why that war so severely
disrupted the economy.

increase in demand proved highly inflationary. Soldiers for the war, guns for them to use, and new factories to make more guns all had to be yanked out of a fully employed civilian economy.

Consider another major flaw in the argument that the Vietnam war should not have proved very difficult for the U.S. economy. The management of a modern democratic country's economy is a difficult task even under the most favorable circumstances. But it cannot be done at all unless the country's economic policy-makers know rather precisely what its problems are, unless they are provided with tools of economic management that are appropriate to deal with those problems, and unless they can count on broad public support for the policies they decide to promulgate. During the highly inflationary early stages of the Vietnam war none of these conditions were met. By contrast, during the Korean War the economy was managed reasonably well. But unlike the Vietnam war, the Korean War broke out suddenly and dramatically on a certain day in June 1950 when, with much fanfare, North Korean troops stomped defiantly across the border into South Korea. World public opinion was shocked. President Truman and Congress were galvanized into action immediately and before long an aroused Congress was even more eager than the administration to resort to increased taxation and direct controls in order to shield the civilian economy from the inflationary impact of the war.

A greater contrast with the Vietnam war could scarcely be imagined. In Vietnam there was no sudden, dramatic defiance of world public opinion. Instead, the United States inched its way in gradually, over a period of many years, always at the initiative of Presidents rather than of Congress or public opinion. Confusing U.S. protestations of peaceful intent accompanied every escalation, clear-cut goals were lacking, and there was very little martial spirit in the country. The Vietnam war was a bureaucratic war rather than a flag-waving war with widespread popular support. Congress and the American people knew only as much about the war and its probable impact on the economy as their Presidents were willing to tell them. And whenever President Johnson described the war he usually employed hopeful, soothing phrases, playing down the war mainly hoping to soften domestic opposition to it. This misleading public relations approach served to deflect Congress and the American people from demanding measures that could have protected the civilian economy. Therefore, measures to shield the civilian economy from the Vietnam war were inadequate and were introduced much too late to be effective. These are some of the reasons why a relatively small-scale war turned out to have such ravaging effects on the U.S. civilian economy.

The overriding fact is that the American economy was never mobilized to fight the Vietnam war. There was no central economic command in Washington as there would need to be in an economy geared up to fight a war. This lack of central economic direction reflected a parallel lack of central political direction in the foreign policy branches of the government. In the State Department, "there was no 'Mr. Vietnam,' " as Chester L. Cooper, a former foreign service officer, colorfully put it.[2] The war's impact on the economy, once it came to be recognized, was treated as just one more variable in a business-as-usual attitude toward economic policy-making in Washington. The government ignored the disruptive implications of the war for the civilian economy as long as it possibly could, pretending they did not exist. The record shows that the 10 percent tax surcharge to finance the war did not take effect until three months after the government began to *de-escalate* the war (which it did in March 1968) and that price and wage controls (which are essential to contain inflation during wartime) were not introduced until August 1971, almost three and a half years *after* the de-escalation had begun.

On the Eve of Inflation, Relaxed Economists

The Vietnam war converted the U.S. economic climate from one of pride and self-confidence into one of frustration, confusion, and demoralization. But on the eve of the war's major escalation in 1965, the nation's economists were in a relaxed, self-satisfied mood.

Business Week reported at this time that a five-year record of "remarkable growth—and remarkable stability—in the U.S. economy . . . has raised the prestige of economists—especially those who espouse the so-called new economics—to an all-time high."[3] The Kennedy-Johnson tax cut had met the high standards of performance expected of it. In 1965, when the second installment of the tax cut had gone into effect, the economy was almost up to its capacity level of operation after a five-year, record-breaking, remarkably well-balanced period of expansion. The price-cost record had been unusually good for such a long period of rising demand, and the economy's unit labor costs were lower in the spring of 1965 than they had been a year earlier.[4] Economists were congratulating themselves on their impressive performance and the economic future looked bright indeed. "The main future task of budgetary policy appeared to be that of distributing the fiscal dividend—providing for expenditure increases and tax reductions that, in combination, approximately matched the economy's normal revenue growth along a rising trend of full-employment GNP."[5]

Some private economic forecasters were predicting an economic *downturn* in the second half of 1965, but the government assured them it stood ready with further tax cuts or increased spending to offset the effects of any tendency for a recession to start.[6] Most professional economists were optimistic about the outlook, although they were also aware of the fact that since the economy was arriving at full employment the task of overall economic management would become more complex than it had been in 1961–64.[7] For example, the GNP growth rate would have to slow down from an average 5 1/2 percent a year to an average 4 percent a year once maximum potential GNP was reached, because 4 percent was about the maximum long-term rate of growth attainable.[8] But these tiny clouds in the generally cheerful economic sky of 1965 were smaller than a man's hand.

Adding to the favorable outlook for the federal government's budget was the prospect of further declines in spending for national defense. After the expensive missile buildup of the early 1960s, national defense spending had leveled off at $50 billion a year in 1963–65. These figures include some price and wage increases; according to Department of Defense records in *real* terms (that is, after deflating current dollar figures for price and wage increases), its military expenditures actually *declined* by 7 percent between the fiscal years 1963–64 and 1964–65, falling from 8.3 percent of the GNP to 7.2 percent—the largest decline since the end of the Korean War.[9] "As late as 1964 the government was considering the abolition of the military draft and the Bureau of the Budget was projecting $50 billion as a long-run ceiling on future defense spending."[10] The federal budget of January 1965, in fact, projected a further decline in defense spending for 1965–66, and the Americans, the British, and the Russians had made a beginning toward military-political detente.

What the Economists Did Not Know in 1965

In 1965 the handful of men who determine U.S. foreign policy made an open-ended commitment to use U.S. military power in Vietnam, but they kept the decision secret among themselves. They began bombing North Vietnam in February, and by April it was clear that Hanoi was matching the U.S. escalation rather than giving in, as Washington had hoped. In June and July the momentous, secret decision to commit ground troops to the war was made. Although the chairman of the Joint Chiefs of Staff, Gen. Earle G. Wheeler, spoke of perhaps needing as many of 750,000 troops and possibly keeping a major force in Vietnam for twenty or thirty years, only a shorter-term interim decision was made to send up to about 300,000 in 1966.[11] In July Lyndon Johnson announced that only 50,000 more troops would go to Vietnam and, except for increasing draft calls, he denied that there had been any basic change in U.S. policy in Vietnam. He spoke of a possible increase of only $2 billion in the cost of the war. The duplicity had begun.

It is well known that each President brings with him to office his own style for the performance of his duties. Lyndon Johnson's biographers all agree that, as a person, he had almost a passion for keeping major policy decisions under wraps until he was ready to announce them himself. They also agree that he was a skilled manipulator of men and that his success as majority leader of the Senate in the 1950s owed much to his use of this skill. In 1965, at the apex of his power, he saw himself as a great benefactor of the poor (in the United States, not in Southeast Asia), and he was determined to get Congress to pass his Great Society legislation. But given the power structure in Congress and the voting records of congressmen, he feared that if he allowed Congress to become aware of how costly the war in Vietnam might become, Congress would appropriate money for the war but would turn down his Great Society legislation. In this situation, he went to work as a manipulator of men, keeping as few people as possible informed about what he was doing in Vietnam.

The Joint Chiefs of Staff were uneasy about the situation in Vietnam in 1964 and 1965, worried lest Vietnam, like Korea, might turn out to be another frustrating war for them in which civilians would unduly circumscribe their military plans. Therefore, they were pressing Johnson to place the country on a frankly wartime footing, which would include, among other things, higher taxes and more money for what they knew might become a very expensive war. Johnson finally overruled them in July by playing down the significance of what he was doing in Vietnam.

True, in his July 29, 1965, news conference he said that "this is a different kind of war . . . but this is really war," just as on August 4, 1964, he had ominously declared that his government was determined "to take all necessary measures . . . in defense of peace in Southeast Asia".[12] These phrases—possibly inserted in the hope of overawing the Hanoi government—were lost on the American people, however, and even as late as the spring of 1966 the country as a whole was not aware that it was at war.

As a result of Johnson's policy of tight secrecy, most high government officials—including his own top economic advisers—knew scarcely more about what was being planned for Vietnam than the mass of the American people knew. "The national security people did not talk to the domestic [policy] people" because Johnson's way was to have "*his own* military planners be less than candid with *his own* economic planners."[13] According to McGeorge Bundy, the President's special assistant for national security affairs from 1961 to 1966, even the political and military leaders did not speak candidly to one another because, at this moment in American history, there was "a premium put on imprecision."[14]

In the fall of 1965 Gardner Ackley, chairman of the Council of Economic Advisers, was projecting $3 to $5 billion as the maximum probable increase in the budgetary cost of the war. At this time he learned that the chairmen of the Senate and House Armed Services committees, John Stennis and Mendel Rivers, were saying that the war's cost could rise by as much as $10 billion. Ackley, after first clearing his facts with Secretary McNamara, then asserted in a speech to the American Statistical Association in Philadelphia in September that such a figure as $10 billion was altogether unrealistic. In 1972, looking back on that occasion, Ackley said that that speech "was a major mistake. Stennis knew more about what the generals were thinking than we knew about what LBJ was thinking."[15]

Enter the War with an Economic Whoosh

Beginning in mid-1965, defense spending took off on an upward course during which it rose 50 percent in only thirty months. This zooming upward of government spending pulled the whole economy up with it—farther up, in fact, than it could go without lapsing into inflation since it was already operating at practically full capacity. In the nine months after mid-1965 the real growth rate of the GNP soared up to 8.5 percent rather than declining to 4 percent as the government's economic planners had wanted. It was during this nine-month period that the economy received the original dose of inflationary adrenalin from which it has still not recovered.

Underestimating the Whoosh

One basic reason the economy veered off course in 1965–66 was because most economists at the time were not aware of what was

FIGURE 6-2
How Contract Awards Precede Production Changes

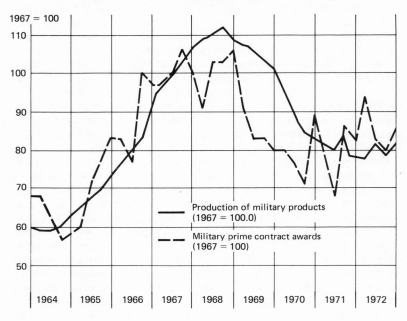

Sources: Production, Board of Governors, Federal Reserve
System; Contracts, DOD *Defense Indicators*.

At times of sharp upward and downward changes in Defense Department procurement, changes in military prime contract awards (that is, in the Pentagon's new orders for military goods) move up or down *before* changes take place in the actual production of military goods.

During the Vietnam war, for example, on the way up contract awards rose most in 1965 and the second half of 1966, while the production of military goods rose more gradually and kept rising until mid-1968. On the way down, contract awards slid off early in 1969, but the sharpest decline in military *production* came in 1970, helping to bring unemployment and recession in that year.

Civilian economic policy makers during the Vietnam war failed to prepare for what the prime contract award series (that is, new orders placed by the Pentagon) was telling them. They failed to do so both during the escalation phase of the war and during its de-escalation phase. As a result of these blunders, both the generation of inflationary pressure in 1966-68 and the recession in 1970-71 were much more severe than they needed to be.

In Figure 6-2 the contract award series is more irregular than the production series because of the "lumpiness" of new orders for entire weapons systems, battleships, and the like.

---

happening until it was too late. Fundamentally, they were not aware because they had not been told about the government's plans for the war, but the situation was also complicated by the fact that most economists were not attuned to the special way in which a rapid military buildup affects the economy.

As Arthur Okun, a member of the Council of Economic Advisers at the time, later expressed it, "Our intelligence system for tracking current movements did not perform well."[16] The reason it did not perform well is because in 1965–66 many economists were looking at the wrong indicators. Usually they concentrate on developments in individual components of the GNP such as consumers' spending for durable goods, business investment, and governmental expenditures. At a time of rapid military buildup, however, such a procedure is misleading because the government's recorded expenditures for military procurement lag behind the Pentagon's real influence on the economy, and therefore understate the extent of its influence. Government expenditures do not get counted until the government receives delivery of what it has bought and writes a check to pay for it. But this check-writing occasion follows with a considerable lag after the Pentagon's *placing of new orders* for defense material has taken place, and it is when the new orders are placed that a rapid defense buildup has its main impact on the economy.[17]

In the second half of 1965, companies that were already almost fully occupied with meeting the booming civilian demand for capital goods and automobiles suddenly received new high priority orders from the Pentagon. These new orders immediately set off inflationary developments in the private sector of the economy as employers began to expand their plants and to raise wages in order to attract more workers into defense production.[18]

At such a time, a rapid increase in military production first shows up in the *private* sector of the economy as an increase in investment, including inventories—several months before it turns up in the *government* sector as an increase in government spending.[19] Consequently, early signs of the inflationary buildup engendered by the Vietnam war were missed by those whose attention was focused on changes in government spending. The largest increases in government spending did not come until after mid-1966. In 1966, as a whole, the increase in business investment—in building and equipping new factories and in stocking up on inventories—was larger than the entire increase in Defense Department spending.

Thus, most economists were underassessing the dangerous implications of the Vietnam war for the economy in late 1965 and in 1966 at the very time when it was already implanting a powerful inflationary seed in the economy.[20]

A Breach Between Policy-Makers; December 1965

It was not until November-December 1965 that a few high economic policy-makers in Washington first recognized the possible danger of incipient inflation. At that time their judgment rested not upon developments in the military sector of the economy—about which they knew little—but upon their interpretation of statistics for the civilian economy. Then, as if to foreshadow the years of bitter controversy to which the Vietnam war would give rise, this first recognition of inflationary danger drove a wedge between the White House and the Federal Reserve System, precipitating one of Washington's most publicized and acrimonious intragovernmental quarrels. Today, several years later and some seventy points higher on the Consumer Price Index, the action the Federal Reserve took on December 6, 1965, of raising its discount rate from 4 percent to 4.5 percent—and the furious, confused controversy that it set off—can be viewed as symbols of how vulnerable and unprepared the economy was for what the Vietnam war had in store for it.

By raising the discount rate, Federal Reserve officials were signaling their belief that the economy needed to be slowed down. This signal shattered the calm sense of economic well-being in which the business and financial communities had been basking for the past five years, dismayed many economists who were still thinking in terms of too much unemployment rather than too much inflation, and foreshadowed many more struggles to come over policy-making in a war-inflated economy.[21] We know now that the Fed's action came several months too late, but at the time it was almost universally thought to be too early—if not altogether inappropriate. Ever since 1961 Federal Reserve authorities had made monetary policy the handmaiden of fiscal policy by seeing to it that adequate credit was available to finance a steadily rising GNP. Thus, December 1965 was the first time in five years that the Fed had openly dissented from Kennedy-Johnson economic policies.

This sudden withdrawal of Federal Reserve support caught the Johnson administration completely by surprise. Johnson had said less than a week earlier that he "didn't consider inflation a major threat at this time," and he reacted to the Fed's action as if it were a serious breach of faith.[22] Tempers flared in the White House and at the Council of Economic Advisers, but "Democrats in Congress were even more critical"[23] and the Congressional Joint Economic Committee opened public hearings at once to try to get to the bottom of this breach between the Federal Reserve and the administration.

In retrospect, two broad judgments on this extraordinary incident seem to be warranted. In the first place, the Federal Reserve "jumped the gun," without adequate advance consultation with the administration's economists, placing them in an awkward position. They were themselves just in the midst of trying to devise an appropriate combination of fiscal and monetary policies to incorporate in the January 1966 budget, and they knew Congress would be less than willing to agree to a restrictive fiscal policy if the Fed was at the same time turning toward a tighter monetary policy. The second judgment can be stated in the words of G.L. Bach, a careful student of economic policy-making in Washington. Bach reminds us that "neither the Federal Reserve, the CEA, nor the Treasury had been able to get Defense Department estimates on defense spending for 1966 . . ." and then concludes that "inadequate information from the Department of Defense on its spending plans underlay the entire situation."[24]

We now know that December 1965 was the last time for many years that U.S. economic policy-makers were to enjoy the luxury of thinking they were prescribing policies for a peacetime economy. One month later, in January 1966, the Pentagon began to disclose the hand it was playing in Vietnam by asking Congress for a $12.8 billion supplemental military appropriation, and the realization began to dawn upon the country that it was at war.

CHAPTER 7

THE BREACH OF 1965
BECOMES THE DEADLOCK OF 1966–68

In the saga of the U.S. government's misadventure in Vietnam, 1964 was the year when the critical political decisions were taken, 1965 the year when the final military decisions were taken, and 1966 the year when the effects of the war on the economy became visible for all to see. In 1966 unemployment fell below the Kennedy-Johnson administration's interim target rate of 4 percent, the GNP exceeded its theoretical potential—both for the first time since the Korean War—and consumer and wholesale prices both rose by 3 percent, beginning a long, uninterrupted climb that is still under way. Within the government's top economic decision-making machinery, the split between the Federal Reserve and the troika of December 1965 was patched over relatively soon, but its place in the parade of disorders caused by the Vietnam war was soon taken by a three-cornered deadlock involving the troika, Congress, and the White House. The new split proved to have far more disastrous consequences than the earlier one, and it lasted much longer—from the beginning of 1966 to mid-1968.

"The Colossal Inflation Goof"

In 1966, as in 1965, the country's economic policy-makers were severely handicapped because the top foreign policy planners kept secret their plans for escalating the war. The President and the Secretary of Defense continued to dissemble rather than leveling with the country, with Congress, and with their own economic advisers about how much the war would probably cost. Their deception stands out as one of the major blunders of the war. Because of it there was no tax increase in 1966, the year when a tax increase to offset the burgeoning cost of the war might have prevented the onset of the most virulent inflation in the nation's history. Edwin L. Dale, economic correspondent for The *New York Times*, has described what happened as "the colossal inflation goof."[1]

A key figure in the story of this "goof" was Secretary of Defense Robert McNamara. At the end of 1965, when he had to submit the Defense Department's budget for the fiscal year 1966–67, he had been informed that Hanoi was reinforcing faster than the United States was and that a long, costly war was probable. Instead of 300,000 troops, military planners were now expecting to need 600,000. And yet, according to McNamara, he wished to avoid the error that had been made during the Korean War of building up large surplus stocks of war material because of overordering while the fighting was going on. For this reason, in making his budget for fiscal 1966–67 he assumed arbitrarily that the war would be over on June 30, 1967, and put its cost into the budget at $10 billion. However, this crucial assumption was not mentioned anywhere in the budget statement presented to Congress, although it had the effect of determining the size of the budget. Meanwhile, he was assuring President Johnson that the Vietnam war would be "the most economically fought war in history," although its cost in fiscal 1966–67 might prove to be as high as $15 to 17 billion.[2]

The administration's economists were not privy to these figures, but during the closing weeks of 1965 they were deciding that the January 1966 budget should be one of economic restraint, at the same time that the Federal Reserve was deciding to raise the discount rate. On December 10 the Council of Economic Advisers sent a report to Johnson advising him that he could not have the Great Society, the war in Vietnam, and no inflation unless he also got a tax increase out of Congress.[3] But Johnson the politician was convinced that he could not get his Great Society programs if he asked for a tax increase at that time, and so he decided to concentrate on getting the rest of his Great Society legislation through Congress in the early part of 1966 before facing up to his financial problem.

Gardner Ackley, at the time chairman of the Council of Economic Advisers, is convinced that Johnson was persuaded of the need for a tax increase in the winter of 1965–66.[4] At any rate, the President met with key businessmen and members of the House Ways and Means Committee to sound out their receptivity to a tax increase. In his discussions with them he told them about the balanced federal budget for the coming fiscal year that he had just presented to Congress, but he did not tell them that the cost of the Vietnam war would probably be much greater than allowed for in the budget. Under these conditions the men he consulted advised him against going for a tax increase, and then, armed with this advice, he went back to inform his economic advisers that the political situation was not favorable to asking for the tax increase they were urging upon him.

Edwin L. Dale, writing before the Watergate scandals, wrote in condemnation of this particular presidential manipulation, that it was "the single most irresponsible act of an American President in the fifteen years that he had covered Washington."[5] Dale believes that by April 1966 President Johnson, Budget Director Charles L. Schultze, and Ackley all "knew . . . that total spending was going to be billions higher than the figure in the budget. . . . By mid-year," he goes on, "McNamara was already arguing privately that it would be politically disastrous to admit the true costs of the war because such an admission would wreck the chances in Congress of the domestic legislation."[6] Dale therefore concludes that the colossal inflation goof of 1966 was "an entirely avoidable error."[7]

As events worked out, "The [Great Society] legislation passed. The cost of the war was finally admitted at the President's ranch in Texas in November, after Congress had gone home, and domestic spending was heading sharply upward as well."[8] And so, for the second time in one year, the defense-foreign-policy establishment substantially raised its estimate of how much the war was costing. In November the figure for the current fiscal year (1966–67) was raised by about $10 billion or by 100 percent over the amount that had been inserted into the government's budget in January. This was highly inflationary in the already overstimulated economy of 1966, because it replaced the administration's approximately balanced budget with a budget deficit of $9 billion. This was deficit financing with a vengeance.[9]

The Terms of the Deadlock
The Department of Defense is the only branch of government that on occasion spends billions of dollars more than Congress votes it, and it went right on spending on the Vietnam war even though the civilian branches of the government had failed to provide for the

war's financing.[10] Responding to the government's nonpolicy for financing the war, the economy moved on from bad to worse in 1966 –68, the remaining years of Johnson's administration. After 1966 the administration urged Congress to pass a general tax increase, but Congress adopted the position that if an unbalanced budget was causing inflation, the remedy lay within the administration's power; it should cut government expenditures (nonmilitary expenditures, that is) by enough to make room for its extra spending on the Vietnam war.[11] Johnson dug in his heels against this, insisting that he wanted the country to have both guns and butter.[12] His unwillingness to deny funds to the Pentagon or to cut back civilian expenditures enough, plus Congress's refusal to vote higher general taxes, made inflation inevitable. Through inflation the government got the resources it wanted for its war, thus denying the use of those resources to other users. In June 1968 when Congress finally passed a 10 percent tax surcharge (two and a half years too late), it revealed its preference for guns over butter by adding a requirement—unprecedented in U.S. history—that the administration must reduce spending by $6 billion on government programs other than the Vietnam war.

Year of Reckoning for the Economy: 1966

The year 1966 was a traumatic one, in part because most people did not realize that the burgeoning economic difficulties of that year were being caused by the Vietnam war. It was a year when the Federal Reserve authorities played the role of Horatio at the bridge—courageously enforcing a tight money policy in an effort to compensate for the highly inflationary consequences of the continuing business investment boom and the administration's deficit financing of the rapidly rising cost of the war. Early in the year the Fed began reducing the supply of reserves available to commercial banks. This monetary stringency in the face of increased government borrowing to finance a growing federal deficit and an "exploding demand for credit from the private sector"[13] drove interest rates up precipitately. The Fed, however, departing sharply from its established policy of increasing the credit supply at times of rising interest rates, held steadfastly to its restrictive policy.[14]

The first casualties of the extreme shortage of credit accompanied by soaring interest rates were the mutual savings banks and savings and loan associations which could no longer bid for funds because they were locked in to lower earning rates on mortgages and other long-term assets. By midyear the liquidity shortage had engulfed the commercial banks. They had been major buyers of state and local government securities ("municipals"), but now they became net sellers in their scramble for funds. For a few days virtually no buyers at all could be found for municipals, and rumors spread that leading bond houses, caught with unsold stocks of them, were about to fall. By late August the intense, unsatisfied demand for liquidity had produced an "atmosphere on Wall Street . . . of controlled panic."[15] By September 1, the Fed had to recognize that it, alone, could not stabilize the economy in face of the government's reckless fiscal policy, and on that day it brought "the credit crunch of 1966" abruptly to an end. Each Federal Reserve Bank president sent letters to all member banks in his district telling them the Fed would resume making loans to banks that could show their own loans to business were for only essential, noninflationary purposes. The Fed also told the banks they could receive Federal Reserve credit on the strength of their municipals, thus immediately making an illiquid asset liquid once again.[16]

As this brief survey of "the credit crunch" brings out, reliance on tight money instead of higher taxes to restrain inflation in 1966 had a very lopsided effect on the economy, severely curtailing the flow of credit to the housing industry and to state and local governments, two classes of borrowers who are unable to maintain their shares of the aggregate credit flow when interest rates rise steeply.[17] On the other hand, the long-lived business investment boom proved remarkably resistant to the effects of tight money because corporations were both better able to pay high interest rates and less dependent on bank credit.[18] Responding to the highest rate of capacity utilization in manufacturing since the Korean War, business investment kept right on surging upward all year and did not recede until 1967.[19]

The inflation of 1966 and the accompanying over-full employment of the country's productive resources also produced a sharp worsening of the U.S. international trade balance as U.S. buyers turned increasingly toward imports for cheaper, prompter deliveries,[20] while U.S. exporters lost relative position in foreign markets. The trade balance fell by 25 percent from $7.1 billion in 1965 to $5.3 billion in 1966. Higher U.S. interest rates drew large sums of capital into the country from abroad, however, offsetting the effect of the deteriorating trade balance on the overall balance of payments. These capital inflows were not reversed until 1970–71, and thus concealed for several years the ominous significance for the dollar of the country's war-induced loss of position in world trade.

The nation's labor markets also became disorganized in 1966–68 under the impact of the sudden, unexpected upsurge of spending on the Vietnam war. During those years more than two million workers were absorbed into the war effort, which was 40 percent of the 5.1 million increase in the total labor force over those years. One aspect of having so many workers siphoned off into participation in and production for the Vietnam war was that unemployment declined from 4.5 percent of the labor force in 1965 to 3.6 percent in 1968. This shrinkage of unemployment below the interim target of 4 percent that the CEA had set in 1962, achieved so rapidly and in response to such extreme pressure of excess demand, set off a sharp increase in wages and prices. In the rush to meet the wartime increase in demand, production ran up against supply bottlenecks. These bottlenecks caused delays and disruptions of production schedules, and in the attempts to overcome or bypass them, prices and wages were bid up, more than physical output. In a variety of ways, such higher prices and wages then fanned out through the rest of the economy.

In 1962 when the Kennedy administration first set out to raise the economy to its capacity level of production, it sought to prevent the expansion from generating inflation by adopting wage-price guideposts to serve as limits for wage and price increases. This decision recognized that as the country moved into a period of continuous prosperity large unions and large corporations could negotiate inflationary wage increases and then pass them along to the rest of the economy in the form of higher prices. The idea behind the guideposts was that if wage increases were limited in amount to the economy's average rate of increase in productivity, then labor costs per unit of output would be unchanged, as would the distribution of income between capital and labor.[21] In 1962–65 the guideposts had helped modestly to keep prices from rising as much as they might otherwise have done,[22] but the Vietnam war inflation beginning in 1966 destroyed their usefulness.

In 1966, 3.2 percent was generally accepted as the rate of national productivity increase and as the maximum amount by which wages should rise. But a necessary condition, if the guideposts were to work, was that prices should remain stable so that when labor limited itself to 3.2 percent wage increases, its real income would also rise by 3.2 percent. By the end of 1966, however, the consumer price index was 3.3 percent higher than it had been a year earlier, and labor was clamoring for an end to the guideposts.

The fatal blow to the wage-price guideposts was struck in August

1966 when the airline mechanics won a boost of between 5 and 6 percent after the longest, costliest strike in the history of the nation's airlines. The White House had intervened directly in the strike and had tacitly accepted the guidepost-defying settlement. This fact was widely interpreted as sealing the fate of the guideposts, and in the flush of a victory for his men, the striking mechanics' leader proclaimed triumphantly that the settlement had "completely shattered (the guideposts) for all unions."[23] The administration clung plaintively to the splinters of its guideposts in the deteriorating economic environment of 1967 and 1968, but as Arthur Okun admits, "the tides of excess demand [attributable to the non-financed Vietnam war] could not be talked down,"[24] and the guideposts were swept away.

A Mistimed Leveling Off: 1966–67

Plain, ordinary bad luck also had a role to play in the deteriorating performance of the U.S. economy in 1965–73 under the stinging impact of the Vietnam war. One instance of bad luck occurred in the latter part of 1966 and early 1967 when a mini-recession broke out unexpectedly, confusing economic forecasters and convincing congressmen that the need for a tax cut had vanished.

After mid-1966 demand eased off greatly, reacting to the Fed's highly restrictive monetary policy. There was a depression in housing, a belated check to the business investment boom, and an unexpected slowdown in consumers' purchasers of durable goods. The dizzying upward sweep of the government's spending on its war in Vietnam continued, however, persuading the administration that the 1966–67 slowdown would be short-lived. In January 1967, therefore, Johnson asked Congress for a 6 percent income tax surcharge to take effect later in the year. "The spurt of demand . . . that followed the step-up of our Vietnam effort in mid-1965 simply exceeded the speed limits on the economy's ability to adjust," he told Congress.[25] The government was getting a second chance to arrange for the financing of its war in Vietnam. The arguments for a tax increase were stronger in January 1967 than they had been in January 1966 because in the interim the country had tasted inflation and experienced the dolorous effects of tight money. The current economic indicators looked weak, however, until late in the year and Congress was not willing to vote an increase in taxes on the basis of a *forecast* of excessive demand.

Thus in the winter of 1966–67 the administration and Congress failed a second time to produce a general tax increase. Reflecting this and the Pentagon's second spectacular revision of its estimate of the Vietnam war's cost, the federal government's budget swung into severe, inflation-making deficits in 1967–68. The full employment budget, which had run an average $3.6 billion surplus in 1962–65, ran deficits of $6.2 billion, $10.7 billion, and $25.3 billion, respectively, in 1966–68. Accordingly, the inflation that began in 1966, instead of receding as expected, took on new life and proceeded to have its way with the economy.[26]

Many debates about government spending, among both the well informed and the poorly informed, ignore the fact that it was mainly the sharp increase in military spending for the Vietnam war in 1965–67 that produced the enormous federal deficits at precisely the wrong time and generated the inflation.

CHAPTER 8

THE BUDGETARY COST OF THE WAR

We live in a time of "information explosion," and today almost any librarian can quickly find the dollar cost to the United States of the Vietnam war. He can find it on page 251 of the 1972 edition of the U.S. government's *Statistical Abstract,* where not one, but *two* war cost figures are shown. "The original war costs" are shown at $110 billion and "the estimated ultimate costs" at $352 billion. But the Vietnam war is not the only one that has been costed out by our contemporary information gatherers. Under the title "Estimates of Total Cost of American Wars, by Rank," the statisticians have obligingly listed, in descending order of costliness, the nine wars in which the U.S. government has been involved since its beginning.

The estimates of the costs of these nine wars in the *Statistical Abstract* provide a convenient way to introduce this chapter and therefore, with slight rearrangements, the table showing their costs is reproduced below.

"The Second Most Expensive U.S. War"

Professor James L. Clayton of the University of Utah, who prepared the figures, told the Joint Economic Committee of Congress when he presented them in 1969 that the Vietnam war has been the most expensive war in U.S. history, excepting only World War II,

TABLE 8-1

ESTIMATES OF TOTAL COST OF AMERICAN WARS, BY RANK

(In millions of dollars, and percents)

War	Original Cost	Total Veterans' Benefits Under Present Laws	Estimated Interest Paid	Estimated Ultimate Cost	Veterans' Benefits to 1971	% of Original War Cost Accounted for by: Veterans' Benefits	Interest	Estimated Ultimate Costs as Multiple of Original Costs
World War II	$288,000	$290,000	$86,000	$664,000	$91,767	100	30	2.31
Vietnam Conflict[1]	110,000	220,000[2]	22,000[3]	352,000	4,700	200[2]	20[3]	3.20
Korean Conflict	54,000	99,000	11,000	164,000	16,055	184	20	3.04
World War I	26,000	75,000	11,000	112,000	50,888	290	42	4.31
Civil War (Union only)	3,200	8,580	1,172	12,952	8,571	260	37	4.05
Spanish-American War	400	6,000	60	6,460	5,481	1,505	15	16.15
American Revolution	100	70	20	190	70	70	20	1.90
War of 1812	93	49	16	158	49	53	17	1.70
Mexican War	73	64	10	147	64	88	14	2.01

[1] Estimates based on assumption that war would end by June 30, 1970.

[2] Medium-level estimate of 200 percent (high, 300; low, 100) based on figures expressing relationship of veterans' benefits payments to original costs of other major U.S. wars.

[3] Medium-level estimate of 20 percent (high, 30; low, 10) based on figures showing interest payments on war loans as percentage of original costs of other major U.S. wars.

Source: U.S. Congress, Joint Economic Committee: *The Military Budget and National Economic Priorities*, 91st Congress, 1st session. (Statement of James L. Clayton, University of Utah). Some figures revised according to *U.S. Statistical Abstract, 1972*, p. 251.

whether it is measured in terms of its initial cost or its estimated ultimate cost (all figures expressed in current dollars). As Table 8-1 shows, in 1970 it had been twice as expensive as the Korean War and its original cost was more than four times that of World War I. But the most striking feature of the table, Professor Clayton suggested, is that the larger costs of wars are incurred after the wars are over. For the twentieth-century wars and for the Civil War (the North only) the estimated ultimate costs are from two and a third to four and a third times the initial costs.[1]

The largest element in postwar expenditures is veterans' benefits. For the earliest five wars shown in the table, those for which veterans' benefit payments are virtually complete, they averaged almost four times the original costs of the wars. Professor Clayton points out that veterans' benefits climb steadily after a war is over and, in the case of the War of 1812, for example, did not peak until 68 years later and did not come to an end until 1946, 131 years after the war was over. He reported that in 1967 dependents of Civil War veterans —1,353 of them—were still drawing benefits of more than $1 million a year, and that in 1969, 52 percent of World War I veterans and 90 percent of Spanish-American War veterans were receiving some kind of compensation. He added that the trend for veterans' benefits is up, with almost half of the U.S. population eligible to receive benefits and with the annual average value of benefits increasing at the rate of 20 percent per decade. This 20 percent rate of increase, moreover, was presumably calculated before the costs of the care and rehabilitation of drug-addicted personnel began to influence the figures significantly. Interest costs on war-incurred debt have ranged from 15 percent to at least 40 percent of the original costs of wars.

Clayton, in his Joint Economic Committee testimony, commented on several omissions from his estimates. He refers to "at least 77,000 Americans stationed in Thailand or serving offshore as support forces for the Vietnamese conflict," who would need to be added to the number serving in Vietnam. He also notes that the government's figures measure the costs of the war only since 1965, whereas "Americans have been stationed in Vietnam since 1954. Between 1954 and 1964 there were a total of 58,885 men stationed in Vietnam, assuming a one-year tour of duty. . . . At $25,000 per man-year . . . this would increase the overall war costs by $1.5 billion.[2] If veterans' benefits and interest costs on the war debt were included, the cost of supporting one GI in Vietnam would be closer to $75,000 per year."[3]

Clayton concluded his congressional testimony by characterizing his $350 billion estimate of the ultimate cost of the Vietnam war as conservative.[4] He went on to say: "The estimate does not include inflationary costs owing to the war, the loss of services and earnings by the 33,000 men killed in the war to date,[5] the cost of resentment abroad, the depletion of our natural resources, the postponement of critical domestic programs, the cost of the arrested training and education of our youth, the cost of the suspended cultural progress of our nation—and nothing of the death and destruction to the South Vietnamese civilians in the war zone itself."[6]

Realizing that $350 billion is a mind-boggling sum, Clayton seeks to place it in meaningful perspective. "Compared with other federal expenditures during the same period of time the war has been on (fiscal years 1960–70), the war in Vietnam has cost ten times more than Medicare and medical assistance . . . 50 times more than was spent for housing and community development. We have spent several times more money on Vietnam in ten years than we have spent in our entire history for public higher education or for police protection. Put another way, the war has cost us more than one-fourth of the value of current personal financial assets of all living Americans, a third again as much as all outstanding home mortgages, and seven times the total U.S. money now in circulation."[7]

Professor Clayton has contributed a novel way of looking at the costs of wars. His concept is that of war-related dollar payments by the government for as long as they last, and by thus extending the time period covered from only a few years to more than a century, his view is far more comprehensive than the views of others. But even so, as he tells us, he has omitted some costs—for example, the foregone earnings of Americans killed in the war that might have been included according to his definition of cost. Also, since his figures are not corrected for the inflation that has taken place over the years, they understate the dollar costs of early wars relative to more recent wars. They do, however, underscore the fact that wars impose real costs not only on the generations that have to fight them, but also on those who come later. They find themselves having to pay taxes to meet interest charges and veterans' benefits with money they might have spent in other ways. Because of the Vietnam war, for example, Clayton tells us that we and our children will have $242 billion more tax receipts and $242 billion less of other things we might have preferred to have.

Nine Estimates of the War's Budgetary Cost in 1968–69

Most people, when they think of a war's dollar cost, have a shorter time perspective than Professor Clayton's. Frequently, the term refers to a government's budgetary expenditures on a war in the years when it is being fought. This meaning is too narrow as a measure of the full *economic* cost of a war, but it does provide a logical starting place for considering a war's full economic cost. Therefore, we take up the budgetary cost of the Vietnam war in this chapter which means looking into the federal government's budget. The government's budget sometimes seems dull and uninteresting, but not when our purpose is to discover what happened in the financial affairs of a great democracy when, for more than a decade, its defense-foreign policy establishment allowed itself to lose control of events.

Today's official estimates show that the budgetary cost of the Vietnam war was shooting upward in 1966 by about a half billion dollars a month and by more than a billion a month in 1967. Such an unexpected skyrocketing of military costs at a time of already full employment in the civilian economy caught the civilian arm of the government off balance. There was great confusion in Congress about what was happening to the cost of the war. Sen. William Proxmire, chairman of the Joint Economic Committee, asked a Defense Department witness with exasperation in April 1967, "Is Congress being adequately informed on the rate of change of defense expenditures right now? That is, are they going up, as some interpret, or are they going down, as other interpret?"[8] And at about the same time, Sen. Stuart Symington, a former secretary of the air force, expressed chagrin over the fact that he had at hand three different estimates of what the war was costing.[9]

In the winter of 1967–68, estimates of what the war would probably cost in the next fiscal year were proliferating. It had cost about $20 billion in fiscal 1966–67 and most estimates were that it would cost about 50 percent more than that in 1968–69. From supposedly official, or at least semiofficial sources, Congress received seven different cost estimates in the course of its hearings on the federal budget for fiscal 1968–69, and later the Department of Defense provided two more.

Senator Symington, using figures he attributed to the staff of the Senate Armed Services Committee, estimated that war costs would run to $32 billion; Congressman Melvin Laird (as he then was) estimated $29 billion; and Secretary of Defense Robert McNamara, when pressed by a congressional committee about these estimates, made a quick mental calculation on the spot and gave his opinion that the *incremental* cost of the war would lie within a range of $17 to $20 billion. The forecast-estimate in the federal budget had been for a cost of $25.8 billion in fiscal 1969, but in February 1968 Assistant Secretary of Defense (Comptroller) Robert N. Anthony brought in different estimates. He set incremental costs at $25.2 billion and "full or prorated" costs at $30.7 billion or $32.2 billion, depending upon how they were calculated. His estimates, along with the others, are shown below in Table 8-2 and compared with Department of Defense after-the-event figures.

TABLE 8-2

ALTERNATIVE ESTIMATES OF THE BUDGETARY COST OF THE WAR IN SOUTHEAST ASIA, FISCAL YEAR 1968-69
(billions of dollars)

Full Cost	
Forecast estimate in the budget*	$25,784
Assistant Secretary Robert Anthony	
"Method A"*	32,200
"Method B"*	30,700
Sen. Stuart Symington (Senate Armed	
Services Committee Staff)*	32,000
Congressman Melvin Laird*	29,000
Department of Defense, after-the-event	28,805
Incremental Cost	
Secretary of Defense	
Robert McNamara*	$17,000-20,000 range
Assistant Secretary Robert Anthony*	25,200
Department of Defense, after the event	21,544

*Estimates brought before Congress

Source: Congressional hearings and Table 8-5.

As the budgetary cost of the war shot upward, far exceeding initial congressional appropriations for it in 1966 and 1967, estimates proliferated of what it would cost in 1968–69. In early 1968 a number of official and semi-official war cost estimates were circulating simultaneously and there was also confusion about how to *define* ts cost.

These various figures, each capable of being called "official," cover a wide range, from McNamara's low figure of $17 billion to Anthony's $32.2 billion (almost 90 percent higher), and in the mood of disputation over the Vietnam war that was beginning to emerge, the public was not disposed to notice what it regarded as fine distinctions, such as the fact, for example, that McNamara and Anthony were discussing quite different concepts of the cost of the war. This proliferation of cost estimates in early 1968 coincided with spreading disillusionment about the reliability of official estimates of the cost of the war, since preliminary forecast-estimates had been only about half as large as later cost estimates in the fiscal years 1966 and 1967. Many people were cynically beginning to take it for granted that Department of Defense cost estimates would always be understated. The conclusion of a Congressional Joint Economic Committee report issued in July 1967 was typical of the credibility gap between the Johnson administration and the rest of the country that had emerged by mid-1967. The committee wrote:

> It is probable that actual expenditures for the Vietnam war exceed the official figures by an appreciable margin. The Department of Defense has conceded that it is somewhat unrealistic to establish a definitive distinction between Vietnam outlays and other defense disbursements. . . . As a consequence, the incremental estimates used for Vietnam expenditures should be considered an understatement. While the absence of any better guidelines makes it necessary to use these figures, it should be realized that the full effect is probably greater than they indicate.[10]

The enormous cost of the Vietnam war had crept up on Congress, as it were. Unbeknownst to the civilian agencies of government, the Washington defense-foreign policy establishment, after its all-out commitment to the Saigon regime in 1964–65, began applying the same philosophy of open-ended government spending to the Vietnam war that previously in American history had been used for genuine all-out-wars—wars that, having been declared by Congress, had broad, enthusiastic public support. But most Americans were slow to abandon the idea that their country was only conducting a small "policing" action in Vietnam. Consequently, during the major escalation of the war when it was getting the same top priority claim on the nation's resources that a major war would get, Congress and the general public were only gradually becoming aware that the country was at war.

How Measure the Cost of a Less Than All-Out War?
Most Americans perceive wars as historical aberrations that come up suddenly, like squalls at sea. Such wars would require for a

short time an all-out effort to survive and then they would die down almost as abruptly as they had started, and the ship of state would sail on in a quieter, more favorable sea. To calculate the budgetary cost of a war like that was easy—its cost would equal the government's total military spending during the war years. Thus, for example, in Table 8-1 Professor Clayton estimates the initial cost of World War II at $290 billion, which is almost exactly equal to the national defense component of the gross national product in the years 1942–45. The national defense component, which had been 1 percent of GNP in 1939, shot up to 42 percent in 1943 and 1944 and was back down to 4 percent in 1947 and 1948.

In Professor Clayton's table the cost of the Korean War is carried at $54 billion, which is not far from the total national defense component of the GNP in the years 1951 and 1952. In the case of the Korean War, however, there is an enormous difference of expert opinion as to its cost. Wilfred McNeil, comptroller in the Defense Department from 1949 to 1959, told Congress in 1955:

> While it is impossible precisely to compute the money cost of a war, particularly a restrictive war in which only a portion of the country's resources are employed, it has been estimated that the United States military expenditures in the Korean area alone were in the neighborhood of $18 billion. This estimate is based on calculations that the Army had expenditures for this effort in the neighborhood of $16 billion.[11]

Later, the Library of Congress staff made an attempt to estimate the cost of the Korean War. The authors of this report took note of McNeil's figure of $18 billion and then concluded at the end of their analysis that "about the best we can do is to say that such a figure (that is, the cost of the Korean war) would lie somewhere between the minimum of $18 billion and the maximum of $79 billion."[12] This enormous range of $18 to $79 billion in estimates of the cost of the Korean War dramatically underscores the difficulty of estimating the costs of wars that—like both the Korean and the Vietnam wars—are less than all-out ones.

The cost of the Vietnam war is conceptually even more difficult to estimate than the cost of the Korean War. The war in Vietnam had a fuzzy beginning and, moreover, while it was getting under way, military spending was already at the very high level of some $50 billion a year. Therefore, the cost estimator must decide, in the first place, when the Vietnam war began and even then he cannot measure its cost by simply adding up the government's military spending for each war year. The reason is that at its peak, Vietnam war spending absorbed only about 35 percent of total military outlays (see Table 8-5); this shows up in Figure 8-1 as only a hump superimposed on top of the country's total military spending. For this reason, the task

FIGURE 8-1
Defense Department Outlays in Total and for
the Vietnam War

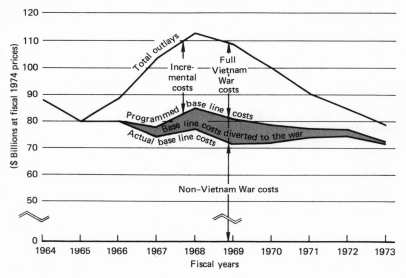

Source: Department of Defense

The budgetary cost of the Vietnam war appears as a lopsided hump atop a curve showing the U.S. government's military outlays over the ten years 1964 –73. Measured in price-corrected dollars, war expenditures surged upward for three years to a peak in 1968 and then commenced a gradual decline.

Incremental costs measure the difference between total outlays and the cost of the base line forces the Pentagon intended to maintain. Demands of the war encroached upon the base line forces, however, and incremental costs plus diversions from planned base line spending measure the full budgetary costs of the war.

Base line military outlays were on a downward trend in 1964–67 as shown in this graph. This trend was overwhelmed and canceled by the escalation of the war, as shown by the upsweep of total outlays beginning in 1966. The reduction of both total outlays and base line outlays in 1969, the first year of the Nixon administration, is apparent in the graph.

of estimating its cost for any one year reduces itself essentially to one of deciding exactly where to draw a line between the identifiable cost of the war and the costs of all other military undertakings. The drawing of such a line proved to be more difficult than it might at first seem to be and required the exercise of judgment at many points. For many types of expenditure, war cost estimators had to decide how much money *would have been spent* if there had been no Vietnam war. Such judgments are not easily made, especially when allocating the costs of supporting services such as training, transportation, communications, medical services, research and development, equipment modernization, and the like. These military support systems are not ordinarily allocated among the various commands, nor even among the individual armed services. The pro rata share of the costs of support systems that should be charged to any one theater of operations must of necessity be determined by methods of statistical approximation since the underlying accounting records provide no basis for doing it. In discussing the Pentagon's estimates of the budgetary cost of the war, Robert C. Moot once told Congress:

> *It is necessary to emphasize whenever Southeast Asia costs are discussed that these figures are estimates. There are no accounting records to identify war costs, nor could there be. Moreover, even granting that war costs must be estimated, there is plenty of room for debate as to how particular items should be reflected. There is no one correct basis for stating the cost of the war.*[13]

My own investigation of how the official estimates of the war's budgetary cost were prepared in the comptroller's office of the Department of Defense led me to conclude that the officials responsible for these estimates made a conscientious effort to draw a clear and consistent line between war costs and nonwar costs, but that they, like the civilian arm of the government, were thrown off balance in 1966–68 by the unexpected speed and cost of the war's escalation. In 1965 the comptroller's office set out to keep one clear set of Vietnam war cost estimates, but serious problems arose as the cost of the war shot upward, and they ended up with *two* sets of estimates rather than one (See Table 8-3).[14]

The comptroller's office defined Vietnam war costs (on both the incremental and full cost bases) to mean all direct expenditures for it (pay, supplies, munitions, equipment attrition, etc.) plus the support costs it could identify as being attributable to the war. The latter

TABLE 8-3

ESTIMATED DEPARTMENT OF DEFENSE EXPENDITURES IN SUPPORT OF U. S. OPERATIONS IN SOUTHEAST ASIA
($ in millions)

Fiscal Year	Full Costs	Incremental Costs	Incremental as % of Full
1965	103	103	100.0
1966	5,812	5,812	100.0
1967	20,133	18,417	91.5
1968	26,547	20,012	75.4
1969	28,805	21,544	74.8
1970	23,052	17,373	75.4
1971	14,719	11,452	77.8
1972	9,353	7,226	77.2
1973	6,987	5,883	84.2
1974	4,618	4,069	88.1
Totals:	140,129	111,891	79.8

Source: U.S. Department of Defense press release, July 18, 1972, for 1965–71; 1972–74 from budget estimates for fiscal year 1974.

Full Costs cover all the forces engaged, plus their support, including the costs of added personnel, aircraft operations, munitions used, equipment lost, and supplies consumed in Southeast Asia or elsewhere in support of those forces deployed.

Incremental Costs cover only the costs for nonbase line forces plus extra costs above the normal peacetime operating level of base line units engaged. For example, full costs include all costs of aircraft operations in the theater, fuel, parts, maintenance, and base operations. In peacetime, the base line units involved would be flying the aircraft in training and other missions and would incur costs. By the same token all ammunition consumed in the theater is reflected under full costs. Since the base line units involved would consume some ammunition in peacetime training, only the difference is included in the incremental cost.

Therefore, the full costs of the war as indicated *do not* represent amounts that could be removed from the budget if there were no war. Incremental costs would.

included additions to the military manpower base (trainees, trainers, transients, patients, etc.); also counted was the cost of civilian manpower added for support activities in both the United States and the Pacific—activities such as supply, transportation, accounting, equipment maintenance and rebuild. Besides these inclusions, there were significant exclusions from the limited concept of cost used to measure the cost of the war. Depreciation of fixed plant and equipment (including ships and aircraft) was excluded since all capital outlays by the government are charged to the budget in the year of acquisition. No general overhead costs were included in the war cost estimate except for the augmentation of specific overhead functions as explained above. Major weapon and equipment items used for the war were costed on the basis of what the Pentagon *bought* for the war, not on the basis of what it *used* to fight the war. Thus war cost estimates include nothing at all for the acquisition cost of *existing*

FIGURE 8-2

WHAT IS FULL COST? WHAT IS INCREMENTAL COST?

Full Cost: Equals all costs incurred to fight the war
Incremental Cost: Equals Full Cost minus what the base line
forces used in the fighting would have
spent anyway, absent the war

TWO EXAMPLES: A MACRO ONE AND A MICRO ONE
Aggregate War Costs, 1965–74

Full cost of the war	$141.1 bil
− Costs base line forces would have incurred anyway	21.2
= Incremental cost of the war	119.9

Cost of Aircraft Fuel Used in Fiscal 1969

Full cost of fuel consumed in Southeast Asia	$231.3 mil
− Amount base line forces would have consumed anyway	
	85.1
= Incremental Cost of Aircraft Fuel Consumed	146.2

Source: Senate Appropriations Committee Hearings, DoD
Appropriations for Fiscal 1971, page 361.

---

aircraft, naval ships, vehicles, communication systems, etc., that were used to fight the war.

The comptroller's department first released its war estimates on the basis of *incremental* cost, which was defined by Secretary of Defense Melvin Laird in 1970 as "the added costs of the war, over and above what would have been spent in peacetime operations." War cost estimates started with the fiscal year 1965, the year in which the first U.S. air strikes against North Vietnam took place but long after U.S. military personnel first entered Vietnam. In the fiscal years 1965 and 1966 the costs that had been *added* because of the Vietnam war would be fairly easily identified, but as the war's costs climbed rapidly it became increasingly difficult to identify the costs that had been added specifically by the war. By late in calendar 1966, according to present Defense Department officials, the special war costs had become difficult to distinguish from the department's regular *base line* (non-Vietnam) costs. The burgeoning cost of the war had overwhelmed the pre-Vietnam budgetary benchmarks, and it had become necessary to *subtract a base line cost estimate* from actual total costs instead of *adding special Vietnam costs* to a base line *benchmark*. But officials were slow to recognize the need for this change.

Consequently, according to present Defense Department officials, by fiscal 1967 the concept of the war's incremental cost had become compromised, and by January 1968 the estimates of the war's costs had shifted away from their original incremental cost basis and full costs were being reported, that is *all* the costs of fighting the war, including some that would have been incurred even if there had been no war.[15] When the Nixon administration took over in January 1969, a review of war cost estimates was undertaken and the decision was made late in the year to release *both* incremental and full cost estimates beginning in fiscal 1970, and to extend the two series backward as far as fiscal 1967. Table 8-4 shows, chronologically by fiscal years, the concepts used when the original cost estimates for each year were released.

The preceding exposition may be summarized by saying that in late 1969 the comptroller's office of the Defense Department made the decision to draw *two* lines to separate the cost of the Vietnam war from the nonwar costs, as in Figure 8-1. The incremental cost of the war consists of the space above the upper line, while the space above the lower line shows its full cost; the space between the two lines measures the difference between its full and incremental costs.

The department paid more attention to estimating incremental cost than full cost because incremental cost was used by decision-

TABLE 8-4
WAR COST CONCEPTS—WHEN THEY CHANGED

Fiscal Years	Concept of War Cost
1965	Incremental
1966	Incremental
1967	Mixture
1968	Mixture
1969	Full
1970	Full
1971	Both separately from this time forward

Source: Department of Defense.
    According to present Defense Department officials, the Vietnam war cost estimates went through a metamorphosis as the war escalated. They started out as incremental costs but they had become full costs by the fiscal years 1969 and 1970. Beginning with the fiscal year 1971 the Department put out estimates on *both* definitions. At the same time they made estimates for the two series back as far as 1967.

makers to estimate the budgetary implications of escalating and de-escalating the war. It was also taken as a measure of the size of the peace dividend the department should return to the civilian economy when the war would be over, and it is presumably a better measure of the *net* impact of the war on the level of the gross national product. Full cost is a better measure of the total impact of the Vietnam war on the U.S. economy, however, because it purports to measure the value of all resources used in the war, including those diverted from their regular employment in the country's base line military establishment. But there are strong reasons to believe that the full cost estimates, even after allowing for the limited scope of the definitions used, are too low. At least three upward adjustments should be made to them, and these are explained in the following paragraphs.

First, the Pentagon estimated the personnel (pay and allowances) cost of the war *only* on an incremental basis, so no official full cost estimates of this important component of the war's cost are in existence. Such a full cost figure would have to include the cost of base line military personnel who were diverted from other duties to fight the war. One way to approximate the size of it is to assume that the only fighting men so diverted were those who were in Southeast Asia at the end of 1964 on the eve of the period covered by the official estimates. There were 23,000 troops on land and 15,000 naval personnel in the area at that time. The ratio of fighting men to their military and civilian backup personnel was about one to one. Therefore, we may take 76,000 men as a conservative estimate of Defense Department personnel who would have been doing other things except for the Vietnam war (23,000 plus 15,000 = 38,000 times 2 = 76,000). The average personnel cost per person at the peak of fighting was $11,000, and 76,000 times $11,000 is $836 million, the amount per year to be added to incremental cost in order to approximate the size of full cost. For the nine years 1965–72, we therefore need to add $7.5 billion ($836 million times 9 = $7.524 billion).

Secondly, the comptroller's office was not making full cost estimates in the fiscal years 1965, 1966, and 1967. In 1970, when it released both full cost and incremental cost figures, it extended the full cost estimates backwards to include these three earlier fiscal years. The three peak fighting years in Vietnam were the fiscal years 1967–69 and in the latter two years full costs were 33 percent greater than incremental costs. In fiscal 1967, however, the year of the most rapid buildup and the year farthest away from the time when the estimates were made, full costs as officially released are shown only 9 percent higher than incremental costs. If, in fact, they should have been 33 percent greater also in fiscal 1967, they would have been $24.5 billion, or $4.4 billion greater than officially estimated.

Thirdly, having adjusted the official full cost estimate for fiscal 1967 so that it conforms more closely to the other two years of peak fighting, we now confront the fact that no full cost estimates at all were made officially for the two fiscal years 1965 and 1966. We can obtain a rough and ready estimate for fiscal 1966 by interpolating between the official estimate for 1965 and the adjusted unofficial estimate for 1967. This gives us $8.8 billion as the approximate full cost estimate for fiscal 1966, which is $3 billion larger than the incremental cost estimate for that year. These three adjustments are summarized in Table 8-5.

Two Comptrollers, Two War Cost Definitions

The London *Economist* once remarked that "the [U.S.] defense economy is a branch of learning of its own."[16] Any analyst of Defense Department economics must perforce live with that disconcerting fact, but in addition an analyst of the budgetary cost of the

TABLE 8-5
PROPOSED ADJUSTMENTS TO DEFENSE DEPARTMENT ESTIMATES OF THE FULL COST OF THE VIETNAM WAR
(billions of dollars)

Nature of Proposed Adjustment	Amount of Adjustment	
	1 Year	1965–73
Military personnel in base line force, omitted from Defense Department estimate of incremental cost*	$0.836	$ 7.5
Full cost in fiscal year 1967 on assumption of average 1968–69 relation to incremental cost	4.400	4.4
Full cost in fiscal year 1966, interpolated between estimate for fiscal years 1965 and 1967	3.000	3.0
Total Adjustments		14.9

*Defense Department did not make a full cost estimate of military personnel.

The author's conclusion after analyzing the Defense Department's official estimate of the full cost of the war is that it should be about $15 billion higher. Of this $15 billion, $7.5 billion comes from adding a full cost estimate of outlays for personnel and $7.5 billion comes from higher full cost estimates for the fiscal years 1966 and 1967.

Vietnam war must also live with the enormously complicating fact that the two inside men who should know the most about it—Robert N. Anthony, the comptroller from 1965 to 1968, and Robert C. Moot, the comptroller since 1968—openly quarrel about what that cost should be.

Anthony flatly rejects the key distinction between incremental and full costs that the Pentagon introduced in 1970 after he had left it. He charges that what his successors defined as full costs are really the incremental costs that were prepared during his tenure as Defense Department comptroller. He insists that it is wrong to subtract from these figures estimates of what the base line forces *would have spent* if the United States had not intervened in the Vietnam war, because as they stand, these figures are *already* incremental costs. According to Anthony, the true full costs of the war should contain a much larger allocation of overhead than Moot and his staff have assigned to them.

Thus, Anthony rejects his successor's estimates of the budgetary cost of the war on the ground that they are too low. The full cost estimates Anthony prepared for fiscal year 1969 when he was comptroller were 9.2 percent higher than those prepared by his successor (compare the Defense Department estimate in Table 8-2 to the average of Anthony's methods A and B). In Anthony's opinion, the Pentagon deliberately understated the cost of the Vietnam war after he left in order to reduce the size of "the peace dividend" that, at one time, it promised to pay to the civilian economy at the end of the war. In this way, he believes, the Pentagon hoped to secure larger post-Vietnam appropriations from Congress.[17]

Long and detailed discussions with present Defense Department officials have persuaded me that they have adequate accounting answers to the objections Anthony has raised against their methods. They can almost completely reconcile their incremental cost figures with his similar series, and they can effectively counter his argument that there should be a larger apportionment of overhead in the full cost series. The Vietnam war was a misbegotten episode in American history and there was much about it that was both sinister and undemocratic. Also, Congress has supinely given the Defense Department incredibly high post-Vietnam appropriations. But it does not follow from either of these statements that the department's estimates of the cost of the war were dishonest. However, the dispute between Anthony and present department officials is by no means resolved. It is beclouded by differences in terminology among other things, and the last word about it has still to be written.

The War, Military Spending, and the GNP

Using the Defense Department's present official definitions of the cost of the war, Table 8-6 shows the relation of its budgetary cost to both total military outlays and the gross national product.

Several features of this table stand out. Concerning the size of the war effort, according to the official *full* cost estimates, it barely exceeded 3 percent of the GNP in the two peak years fiscal 1968 and fiscal 1969. Using the official *incremental* cost definition it reached only about 2 1/2 percent of GNP at the peak. The rapid buildup of the war in the fiscal years 1966 and 1967 stands out. From a negligible cost in fiscal 1965 to a full cost figure of $26.5 billion three years later

TABLE 8–6

BUDGETARY COSTS OF THE VIETNAM WAR

Fiscal Year	Vietnam War Costs		As % of Total Military Outlays		Incremental as % of Full	As % of GNP		Total Military Outlay $M	Gross National Product $B
	Full $M	Incremental $M	Full %	Incremental %		Full %	Incremental %		
1965	.103	.103	0.2	0.2	100.0	—	—	47,098	659
1966	5,812	5,812	10.5	10.5	100.0	0.8	0.8	55,377	717
1967	20,133	18,417	29.5	26.9	91.5	2.6	2.4	68,315	772
1968	26,547	20,012	34.0	26.0	75.4	3.2	2.4	78,027	829
1969	28,805	21,544	36.6	27.4	74.7	3.2	2.4	78,661	897
1970	23,052	17,373	29.6	22.3	75.4	2.4	1.8	77,881	952
1971	14,719	11,452	20.6	16.0	77.8	1.5	1.1	71,545	1012
1972	9,261	7,346	12.2	9.7	79.3	0.8	0.7	75,800	1101
1973 (est.)	7,500	6,200	11.1	8.7	82.4	0.7	0.5	46,500	1213
1974 (est.)	3,800	2,900			75.0				
Total	139,732	111,159							

Source: War costs, U.S. Department of Defense; GNP and total military outlays, U.S. *Statistical Abstract.*

The budgetary cost of the Vietnam war shot upward in the three years after fiscal 1965. In 1968 its full cost was 265 times higher than in 1965.

In 1969, the peak year of spending, it absorbed about one third of total military outlays and about 3 percent of the GNP. The de-escalation of the war was much slower, and in fiscal 1973, four years after the 1969 peak, it was still costing $7.5 billion and absorbing 11 percent of total military outlays.

in fiscal 1968, the war was 265 times as expensive in fiscal 1968 as in fiscal 1965 (273 times on the proposed higher full cost basis). The phasing down of war spending was slower; from $28.8 billion in fiscal 1969 it fell only 68 percent in the next three years to $9.3 billion in fiscal 1972.

The Vietnam war absorbed from 30 to 35 percent of total military outlays in the fiscal years 1967–70 (Table 8-6, column 3). It was the U.S. government's largest single military project in those years but at the same time that the United States was fighting the war it was also pouring out about twice as much money on its other military activities as on the Vietnam war. (Total spending minus 33 percent on Vietnam equals 67 percent on all other ventures.)

According to the official 1970 definitions, incremental cost was from about 75 to 80 percent as large as full cost. This indicates that the military was able to divert a total of some $28 billion of resources from base line forces to the purposes of the war in the fiscal years from 1967 to 1973 ($43 billion on the higher full cost definition.) In the absence of these diversions the war would have overloaded the economy even more than it did. These diversions do not include procurement, construction, and maintenance costs that were postponed during the period of the war.

How Much Did the War Cost?

To date there have been very few independent analyses of the government's estimates of the cost of the war. An analysis of the air war in Vietnam published by the Cornell University Air War Study Group concludes that the official cost estimates are too low, both in the year 1965 and because the estimates do not include the years prior to 1965. The Cornell study found that helicopter combat sorties averaged around 1.7 million a year from 1962 to 1965 compared with 2.3 million in the three subsequent years. It concludes that "helicopter sortie data are too erratic to be precise indicators of activity levels, but they do imply that war costs were incurred."[18]

The Cornell group also estimates that, because of the Vietnam war, a $15 billion backlog of deferred base line investment outlays was built up in the years 1966–71 but was not counted as part of the cost of the war. Such deferred investment should count as a cost of the war, of course, using the economist's concept of cost. As Professor Chandler Morse, a participant in the study, remarked, the group's $15 billion adjustment "is intended to be . . . an addition to the official estimates. Because the deferrals relieved burdens both on the total budget and on the economy, they were a form of current cost avoidance. But because they will be made up in the future . . . they were not permanently avoided."[19]

Deferred expenditures, however, were not counted in the Pentagon's definition of the budgetary cost of the war, which consists basically of a bundle of current purchases made necessary in order to fight the war. To the extent that investment backlogs accumulated during the war had to be made up later, they show up as a rescheduling of base line investment outlays.

Both points raised by the Cornell study team remind us that the Defense Department's concept of budgetary cost is narrowly defined. The team's first objection points to the fact that U.S. military costs in Southeast Asia before 1965 are treated as base line, rather than Vietnam war, costs. Their second point, the "addition" to the department estimates, reminds us that the Pentagon's cost estimates exclude military investment that was deferred because of the war. There were some draw-downs of military supply and equipment inventories too, to fight the war, and these also were not included in the official cost estimates although some of them needed to be replaced later. On this point, former Comptroller Anthony points to an important offset to economic costs of this kind by observing that the Department

". . . consumed inventory of equipment, munitions, and the like, but we have already replaced these with equal quantities of new items, and the new items are more modern. Thus, by and large, the inventory is in better condition now than in 1965. For example, we had huge quantities of bombs left over from World War II. These have now all been consumed, and the inventory consists of much better bombs purchased with funds labeled (quite properly) "Vietnam war costs." The services were asked in 1968 to list deficiencies in their inventories that might have been caused by Vietnam; I do not recollect the details, but the overall list was not large."[20]

The department also came out of the Vietnam war with a larger, newer, and well-tried support establishment and with firsthand knowledge, learned the hard way, about fighting a counterguerrilla war in an unfriendly country.

Some elusive questions still remain unanswered about the best way of estimating the budgetary cost of the war and there will continue to be doubts as long as the dispute between Anthony and his successors at the Pentagon is not finally settled. In addition to Anthony's charge that the Pentagon's cost estimates were crudely self-serving, some Washington observers go further, seeing a relationship between the size of successive war cost estimates and the different situations in which the Pentagon found itself as the war unfolded. According to this view, in 1967–68, as the Johnson administration and congressional committees became increasingly caught up in a determination to press for a military victory in Vietnam, the Pentagon felt a need to prove that its efforts in Vietnam were unstinting and allowed estimates of the war's cost to grow accordingly. Later, when influential people in Washington turned against the war and its enormous cost, the Pentagon's definition of its cost, so it is said, became more restricted. In this chapter the Pentagon's own account of its shift from an initial emphasis on an incremental cost definition to a full cost definition and then back to emphasizing incremental cost is regarded as plausible in its own right, not requiring one to assume that outside pressures were at work. But, one must acknowledge, even in pre-Watergate Washington, before the deceptions associated with the Vietnam war had so badly poisoned the atmosphere, bureaucratic kowtowing to politically motivated pressure was not completely unknown.

CHAPTER 9

THE DOLLAR: A CASUALTY OF THE VIETNAM WAR

The rapid decline in the strength of the dollar as an international currency in the years since World War II can be understood only in light of the politico-military role the U.S. government played on the world stage in the 1950s and the 1960s. Seeing itself as the defender of law and order outside its own territorial borders as well as inside them, it began in the late 1940s to spend huge sums of money abroad on both foreign aid and military projects. As a consequence, for the first time in history, the U.S. balance of international payments was placed under a shadow of massive net foreign spending by the government that vastly exceeded the private sector's capacity to earn foreign exchange. After more than a quarter of a century, this massive foreign spending by the government is still embedded in the structure of the country's international balance of payments.[1]

Trauma for Both the Dollar and the Bretton Woods International Monetary System

For most of the 1950s the international monetary system that had been set up at an international conference in Bretton Woods, New Hampshire, in 1944 worked smoothly. Partly this was because deficits in the U.S. balance of payments caused by the government's

massive foreign spending had the favorable side effect of redistributing international monetary reserves, which had been heavily concentrated in the United States when World War II ended. By the
beginning of the 1960s the rest of the world had more dollars than it
could easily accommodate, but at about that time the net outflow of
dollars from the United States *increased* substantially instead of
subsiding as it would have done if the international economic adjustment process had been working properly. In short, the dollar
shortage of the 1940s had yielded to a plethora of dollars in the
1960s. The overabundance of dollars outside the United States put
increasing strain on the international monetary system of the 1960s
and was a leading cause of the monetary turmoil of that decade.

As one of several measures to reduce the outflow of dollars, foreign economic aid was tied to purchases the aid-receiving countries
were required to make in the United States early in the 1960s. This
meant that economic aid dollars were paid directly to United States
exporters of aid-financed goods and services, thus reducing the flow
of aid dollars to foreigners. No similar tying of expenditures for the
U.S. armed forces abroad was possible, however, so that by 1965
when the Vietnam war was escalated most of the government's foreign spending was already for military purposes.[2] Costly efforts to
"contain communism" on a world wide scale had been planned and
carried forward at the highest level of the government as if there
were no limits to American foreign payments deficits.

There were, in fact, no built-in mechanisms capable of forcing
Washington to reduce or eliminate the country's foreign deficits.
Under an asymmetry incorporated in the Bretton Woods Agreement
of 1944 the dollar became the leading international reserve currency
which countries outside the United States held, alongside gold, as a
monetary reserve. This peculiarity of the international monetary system conferred a privileged position on the Washington government.
Most other countries have to pay out gold when they incur balance
of payments deficits, but the United States was in the enviable position of being able to settle its deficits by simply allowing foreigners
to add more and more to their holdings of dollars. This enabled
Washington to enjoy the illusion of financial omnipotence long after
its reality had passed. Thus, beginning in about 1960, the world's
leading international currency, which should have been as virtuously
above reproach as Caesar's wife, overextended itself instead, and
began its decline.

By the mid-1960s several European creditor countries realized
that this monetary mechanism had lulled them into providing more

credit to the United States than they had intended, and they began to adopt hard-line creditor attitudes toward Washington. After 1964 their holdings of dollars were cut back and the United States had to finance more than 50 percent of its 1965–67 payments deficits in gold, compared to less than 25 percent in 1961–64.

The escalation of the Vietnam war in 1965, despite the fact the dollar had already been weakened by the government's excessive foreign spending on the cold war, was a financially reckless act, but in 1964–65 the defense-foreign policy establishment in Washington was not about to be deterred by "mere" financial or economic limitations from its determination to challenge Communism in a tiny country in Asia. Later, the escalated war was to lead to runs on the dollar in 1968, 1971, and 1973, to the suspension of its gold convertibility in 1971, and to its devaluation in 1971 and 1973. These sharp and unmistakable reductions in the status of the dollar brought home to some of the American people for the first time, a realization that their country's influence in world counsels had shrunk.

Direct and Indirect Effects of the War

How shall we arrive at an estimate in dollar terms of the cost of this shrinkage in the international economic position of the United States? We may begin by noting that the U.S. government's direct foreign outlays for military purposes were increased by almost 70 percent from 1964 to the peak war year 1969 (see Table 9-1). This added burden was heavily concentrated in Southeast Asia, with increases of 700 to 800 percent in Vietnam and Thailand. These direct expenditures for the operation and maintenance of United States military forces abroad have the same effect on the balance of payments that an equal increase in merchandise imports would have, which means that greater foreign military spending worsened the balance of payments directly by about $2 billion between 1964 and 1969, with about $1.7 billion of this deterioration concentrated in Asia. These figures should be viewed in the context of the $2.1 billion size of the country's overall average basic deficit in 1960–70 (see Table 9-1).

Larger purchases of goods and services abroad by the military account for only a part of the total effect on the balance of payments of escalating the war in Vietnam, however. As we know, the escalation was superimposed on the U.S. economy in 1965–66 when it had just arrived at its full capacity level of output and this set off serious inflation. This inflation in turn, was the main cause of the sharp deterioration in the foreign trade balance that began at this time.

TABLE 9-1

U.S. GOVERNMENT'S DEFENSE EXPENDITURES ABROAD FOR GOODS AND SERVICES, BY MAJOR COUNTRY, 1964 AND 1969

(millions of dollars and percents)

Area of Spending	1964	1969	Percent Increase 1964–69	Percent of Total 1969
Western Europe	1,492	1,628	9.1	33.5
Canada	258	296	14.7	6.1
Asia				
Vietnam	64	576	800.0	11.9
Thailand	34	264	676.5	5.4
Japan	321	651	102.8	13.4
Korea	91	364	300.0	7.5
Ryukyu Islands	115	229	99.1	4.7
Philippines	58	189	225.8	3.9
Taiwan	21	80	380.9	1.6
Bahrein and S. Arabia	68	142	108.8	2.9
Subtotal, Asia	772	2,495	223.2	51.4
Other and Unallocated	358	437	22.1	9.0
Grand Total	2,880	4,856	68.6	100.0

Source: U.S. Department of Commerce, *Survey of Current Business,* February 1972, p. 26.

Direct foreign military spending by the U.S. government rose 68.6 percent from 1964 (the year before it began to escalate the Vietnam war) to 1969 (the peak year of war spending). Except for minor increases elsewhere, this rise in direct spending was concentrated in Asia, where a 223 percent increase took place.

The enormous cost of maintaining the U.S. military presence around the world is suggested by the fact that even at the height of this country's spending on the Vietnam war, it accounted for barely more than 50 percent of total direct costs, the balance of which were concentrated in Western Europe and Canada.

From 1969 to 1972 direct military spending declined only 3 percent (not shown in table) and in 1972 more than 40 percent of the total was still in Asia.

This adverse indirect effect on the dollar far outweighed the direct effects of the military's larger purchases abroad. By the time it had run its course, the handsome $5.4 billion trade *surplus* of 1961–65 had been converted into a $6.4 billion trade *deficit* in 1972.

When international trade surpluses turn into deficits, the usual cause is inflation, which has insidious effects on a country's foreign trade. As demand and prices rise, a country's exports lag behind those of other countries, both because they lose price competitiveness in foreign markets and because production bottlenecks develop at home that interfere with the filling of export orders.[3] At the same time, higher money incomes associated with inflation are pull-

FIGURE 9-1
The War and the U.S. Foreign Trade Balance

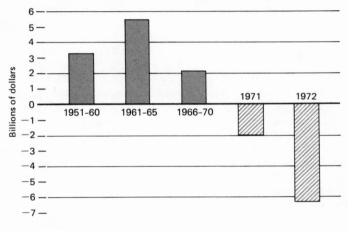

(a) Merchandise only

Source: *Statistical Abstract of the United States 1972*, Table 1281, p. 776.
Economic Report of the President January 1973, Table C–88, p. 295.

The war had a disastrous effect on the U.S. international balance of payments. It converted the country's traditional trade surplus into a trade deficit, setting off a chain reaction that, in the end, dealt the *coup de grace* to the dollar's established role as the key international reserve currency.

The United States earned an average foreign trade surplus of $3.3 billion in 1951–60. This grew to $5.5 billion a year in 1961–65, years of healthy economic growth without inflation. When the U.S. government set off inflation by escalating the Vietnam war in 1965, the foreign trade surplus shrank to $2.1 billion a year in 1966–70.

Because the U.S. government's disagreement from Vietnam was as clumsily managed as the escalation had been, inflation *worsened* during the "winding down" phase, and in 1971–72 the United States encountered its first merchandise trade deficits in eighty-three years.

ing more and more imports into the country from abroad. After 1964, these adverse factors in export and import markets cut into the U.S. foreign trade balance like the two blades of a scissors.

Estimated Dollar Costs to the Balance of Payments

In order to say with certainty what would have happened to the balance of payments if the U.S. government had not involved itself in the affairs of Vietnam, economists would have to have access to occult powers. They have no such access, and all we can know for *certain* is what did happen, not what might have happened. Some economists, however, have conducted econometric studies to *estimate* what might have happened to the balance of payments if there had been no war in Vietnam. In one such study two economists, Leonard Dudley and Peter Passell, estimated the war-induced deterioration in the current account balance was $3.6 billion from 1964 to 1967, of which $1.6 billion was an increase in direct military spending abroad and $2.0 billion was attributable to inflation and other factors.[4] This is approximately the *full amount* of the deterioration of $3.7 billion from 1964 to 1967. In another study, Professor Emile Benoit arrived at an estimate of the effects of the war on the balance of payments that he said could be applied equally well to either the calendar year 1968 or the fiscal year 1969.[5] His figure, $5.7 billion, also accounted for almost all (90 percent) of the actual deterioration between 1964 and 1968.

Table 9-2 summarizes several ways of estimating the war's dollar cost to the balance of payments. Column 1 in the table shows the actual current account worsening from a $5.0 surplus in 1964–65 to an $8.4 billion deficit in the year of U.S. troop disengagement, 1972. As column 2 in Table 9-2 shows, the deterioration was $42.6 billion if all years after 1964–65 are added together to obtain a cumulative figure.[6] This is one way to estimate the war's cost to the balance of payments.

Another way to estimate the cost would be to adjust the Dudley-Passell approximation for 1967 by what happened to the wholesale price index after 1967. As column 3 in Table 9-2 brings out, the cumulative deterioration amounts to $47.8 billion estimated this way. We obtain a larger estimate of the deterioration if we make the plausible assumption that the balance of payments would have continued to *improve* after 1964–65, as it had done at the rate of $1.6 billion a year in 1959–64. If it had improved at a rate of only $1 billion a year absent the war, the cumulative shrinkage attributable to the war would have been $70 billion (column 3 in Table 9-2).

TABLE 9-2

U.S. BALANCE OF PAYMENTS ON CURRENT ACCOUNT AND ALTERNATIVE ESTIMATES OF ITS WAR-INDUCED DETERIORATION

	Current Account Balance	Actual Deterioration from Average 1964–65	Estimated Deterioration Adjusted for Whole-sale Price Index	Current Account Balance, Assuming $1 Billion per Year Improvement	Estimated Improvement Less Actual Deterioration
	1.	*2.*	*3.*	*4.*	*5.*
1965	+5.0	0.0	0.0	5.0	0.0
1966	+2.4	2.6	2.3	6.0	3.6
1967	+2.1	2.9	3.6	7.0	4.9
1968	−0.4	5.4	4.6	8.0	8.4
1969	−0.9	5.9	6.4	9.0	9.9
1970	+0.4	4.6	8.6	10.0	9.6
1971	−2.8	7.8	10.1	11.0	13.8
1972	−8.4	13.4	12.2	12.0	20.0
1966–72	−7.6	42.6	47.8	63.0	70.2

Column 1: President's Council of Economic Advisors, *Economic Report of the President,* 1974, p. 350.
Column 2: $5.0 billion minus column 1.
Column 3: Benchmark estimate by Dudley and Passell for 1967, adjusted to other years by wholesale price index. See Leonard Dudley and Peter Passell, "The War in Vietnam and the U.S. Balance of Payments," *Review of Economics and Statistics,* November 1968, pp. 437–42.

Column 4: Self-explanatory.
Column 5: Column 4 minus column 1.

Cumulative costs of the war in the international balance of payments are reflected in foreigners' increased liquid and official claims against the U.S. economy. The adverse international payments effects of the war on the country's capital accounts were undoubtedly much greater than on the current accounts, but there is no way of estimating these effects.[7]

When we turn to the longer run, we find that the dollar's exchange rate against other currencies proved not to be maintainable in the face of the deteriorating balance of payments. Consequently it had to be devalued—first in December 1971 by 7.89 percent and in February 1973 by a further 10 percent in terms of gold and the Special Drawing Rights of the International Monetary Fund, before the major countries abandoned exchange rate parities and allowed exchange rates to float. After the second devaluation, the dollar had depreciated "against all the world's currencies on a trade weighted average basis" by approximately 12 percent from June 1970 when the Canadian dollar first began to float.[8] A currency devaluation implies worsening international terms of trade for a country, which means that thereafter the country must give up more exports (which are made cheaper for foreigners by the devaluation) to obtain an equal volume of imports (which are made more expensive inside the country).

Currency devaluation thus has an impoverishing effect on the devaluing country which must, in effect, "work harder" and produce more exports after the devaluation to obtain any given volume of imports. There is no way to know in advance, however, by *how much* devaluation will impoverish a country but a reasonable estimate is that the cost to the United States of the 1971 and 1973 devaluations will be equivalent to about a 10 percent increase in the average cost of the country's imports of goods and services. This would amount to a cost of about $8 billion a year, based on the value of goods and service imports in the year 1972.

In Short—

The balance-of-payments cost of the Vietnam war was just too great for the weakened dollar to bear and the war brought it down from its long-established position as the most respected currency. While there is no way a dollar cost can be calculated to measure accurately the decline of a great country in the international pecking order, that does not mean that the decline is any the less real. After the Vietnam war experience it is unlikely that other countries will ever again agree to participate in an international monetary system centered on the dollar, as the Bretton Woods system clearly was.

They now realize that, under such a system the U.S. government felt free, as profligate banker to the world, to pursue for many years an overextended foreign policy that eventually led to the Vietnam war, with its inflationary implications for all countries.

One "lesson" the American people could "learn" from the Vietnam war—a lesson the British had to learn several years ago—is that a country cannot exercise decisive power and influence in the world unless it first takes pains to insure for itself a strong currency. In the vain hope of "winning" by military means in Vietnam, the Washington defense-foreign policy establishment shot down instead the international civilian financial structure, as well as warping, perhaps permanently, the country's domestic civilian economy.

CHAPTER 10

"MOMENTS OF TRUTH" FOR THE DOLLAR
AND FOR U.S. INTERNATIONAL ECONOMIC POLICY

U nder the impact of Vietnam
war spending, we can distinguish two quite separate phases in the
decline of the dollar, each phase—appropriately—punctuated by its
own severe crisis or, if one prefers, by its own "moment of truth" for
the dollar.

In the first phase, 1966–68, the U.S. economy was bursting at the
seams from a severe case of demand-pull inflation because, as we
know, the government escalated the Vietnam war at a time of full
employment without providing for its financing. At such times excess demand at home spills over in the form of an excess demand for
imports.[1] In this phase a crisis of confidence in the dollar broke out
in March 1968. The pound sterling had "fallen" in November 1967
(that is, the British had been forced to devalue it against their will)
and many financial experts believed the "fall" of the dollar could not
be far behind. Between November 1967 and March 1968 the leading
central banks sold $3 billion of gold in a futile effort to stem a world-
wide gold rush. Many individuals and business firms outside the
United States were buying gold in the expectation that Washington
would soon be forced to devalue the dollar which, they thought,
would be done by substantially raising the price of gold.[2]

Inflation was having its way with the economy in early 1968 and the confidence of the financial community in the U.S. government was at a very low ebb. The Viet Cong's Tet offensive had made it clear to almost everyone but the U.S. government that the Vietnam war had become a lost crusade. General Westmoreland was asking for 200,000 more troops, however, and until the end of March 1968 the military had gotten much of what it wanted in Vietnam. Even worse, Lyndon Johnson and the key tax men in Congress had been deadlocked for more than a year over Johnson's belated request for a special surtax to finance the war, and no end of the deadlock was in sight. Against this grim background, confidence in the dollar collapsed. In mid-March 1968 the world's leading finance ministers rushed into emergency conference in Washington, where most observers expected they would raise the price of gold sharply, thus devaluing the dollar. Instead, they decided to abandon attempts to support the price of gold in the free markets without, however, changing its *official* price, a state of affairs they dubbed "a two-tier gold price." The seriousness of the March 1968 dollar crisis, coming so shortly after the Tet offensive, forced the Johnson administration for the very first time to think seriously about where its discredited war policy was taking it. After almost a month of intraadministration debate, Johnson decided to begin the de-escalation of the war and to withdraw himself from the presidency.

In the second phase of balance-of-payments deterioration, 1969–72, the condition of the U.S. economy was different. Richard Nixon had succeeded Johnson as President in 1969, inheriting an inflation that by then had passed into a cost-push phase. By fighting it as if it were still of the demand-pull type, the Nixon administration completely failed to halt the price increases but produced, in 1970, the country's first economic recession in ten years. To cure the recession, the administration and the Federal Reserve lowered interest rates, which set off a massive capital flow out of the United States in the latter part of 1970 to higher interest rate centers in Europe.

The capital efflux continued in 1971, making that year a disastrous one for the balance of payments. The net liquidity deficit, which had averaged $3.2 billion in 1961–70, reached quarterly rates of $10.4 billion, $22.8 billion, and $39.6 billion, building up to the third-quarter crisis. On August 15, 1971, Nixon declared the dollar no longer convertible into gold, thus delivering the *coup de grace* to the Bretton Woods international monetary system and at the same time imposing a wage price freeze on the U.S. economy.

It is generally agreed the administration would not have resorted to the wage-price freeze when it did except for the dollar crisis.

Thus, for the second time in three years, international monetary crises had forced major policy reversals upon the government. In 1968 Washington reversed its escalation of the Vietnam war, and Lyndon Johnson decided to turn his back on the presidency; in 1971 Nixon severed the dollar's link to gold and for the first time in history imposed a wage-price freeze on the country during a nominal period of "peace." To a government that, in its zeal for bombing peasants in Vietnam, was learning to take pride in its capacity for ignoring unfavorable reactions abroad, these forced policy changes were sobering experiences, helping to set the stage for the important reinterpretation of the national economic interest that was about to unfold.

Washington's New Explanation of Our Difficulties
In the long run, probably the most lasting effect of the Vietnam war will be the altered image of themselves that the American people acquired by having experienced it. This self-image was nowhere more subjected to pressure for change than in the field of international economic policy. The story of that pressure begins in early 1971 when President Nixon grew concerned about the enormous capital outflows and created a new, high-level Council on International Economic Policy, the counterpart in economic affairs of the National Security Council, to advise him personally on international economic policy. He brought in as its executive director Peter G. Peterson, until then president of the Bell and Howell Company of Chicago, and asked him to prepare a special report on the changing world economy to be used by the administration as a background paper in formulating its international economic policies. Peterson characterized his report as "a personal overview of the origins and possible policy implications of the new world economy."[3] It was written in the crisp, clear style of a business policy report and it so impressed Nixon that he asked Peterson to repeat it for many officials of the government, congressmen, and selected people outside the government. Because of the widespread exposure given to this report in the spring and summer of 1971, and because Peterson was known to have the ear of the President, it came to have an influence on U.S. international economic policy greater than that of any document since George Marshall's famous address at Harvard in 1947, which launched the Marshall Plan.

In private life Peterson had been an associate of Sen. Charles H. Percy at Bell and Howell, and as a moderate Republican he had espoused liberal views on international trade policy. Reflecting this background in his report, he rejected the idea of imposing new restrictions on imports as "a prescription for defeat and an admission of failure." Instead, he called for improving the productivity and international competitiveness of the American economy and proposed that the United States take leadership in designing new international trade and monetary institutions. This main thrust of his report was consistent with established U.S. policy and was not new except that he placed much greater emphasis upon the need to improve American productivity and competitiveness.

What was distinctly new in the Peterson report was its analysis of the position of the United States in the world economy and certain policy implications that it drew from that analysis. As Peterson phrased it, Americans' "perceptions [of this country's role in the world economy] lagged reality" since "the conviction . . . that the U.S. was dominant, both in size and competitiveness, in the international economy" was no longer true. "Because basic structural and competitive changes had occurred," he said, "much of our thinking and most of our rhetoric about international economic policy have been carried over from another era. As a result, we continuously risk coming up with old answers to new questions." Concerning size, he pointed out that U.S. international trade ranks second to the Common Market's, even before the addition of Britain. Turning to competitiveness, he stressed statistical demonstrations that the U.S. economy was losing ground relative to both Japan and the Common Market.

In listing the main causes of the relative decline of the U.S. in the world economy, Peterson spoke candidly of the situation as he perceived it, and here also he broke new ground. He rejected all single-cause explanations, arguing that "no single error or event explains our present difficulties." He then proceeded to cite four causes originating in the U.S. economy itself, four that stemmed from the actions of other countries and one—"intolerable burdens thrust upon the United States" by the international monetary system for which presumably the international community of nations generally should be held responsible, although the monetary system was designed in 1944 along lines initially laid down by the U.S. government. The causes originating in the United States were an inadequate growth in productivity, increasing energy needs, "excessive domestic inflation over the last half of the sixties," and "a rapid rise in the U.S. labor costs per unit of output." It would serve no useful purpose to dwell on the fact that some of these causes overlap, but it is certainly noteworthy that there is no mention of the escalation of the Vietnam war as a cause of the country's difficulties. As usual, Washington was denying that the war (and the way it was nonfinanced) were the overwhelmingly dominant causes of the dollar's plight.

Something else that was new in an official report of the U.S. government was Peterson's candor in discussing the actions and policies of other governments and his conclusion that, in some sense, other governments' policies toward the United States were unfair. When he referred to "the improved capability of other nations" his point was unexceptionable and it is true that "some of our partners [had introduced] export development programs more aggressive than ours." However, he went on to discuss international trade in agricultural products and "the proliferation of preferential arrangements for industrial products" as "developing inequities" and concluded that the U.S. government must be "more assertive" in demanding "a more . . . fair environment for American exports."

One can easily understand that government officials should have come to feel frustrated over what their economists had told them was the apparently insoluble problem of U.S. balance-of-payments deficits and that they should begin casting around for simple explanations of the problem that could be explained easily to the public. We can sypathize with their frustration over the fact that most conventional explanations of the problem sound either inconclusive or incomprehensible, but we must deplore their seeking refuge in a "blame the foreigner" explanation. This is a disreputable ploy politicians have used down through the ages to deflect public attention from their own shortcomings by inflaming the masses against "the foreigner." Peterson ignored the Vietnam war, which was clearly the dominant cause of the country's foreign payments problem, but instead, told the country that foreigners had been "unfair" to the United States.

The two practices Peterson called unfair—trade in agricultural products and preferential trading arrangements—involve important national interests, and it is simply not true to assert that what the United States believes to be in its interest is "fair" and that what the Europeans believe to be in their interest is "unfair." The fact is that, *at the insistence of the U.S. government,* international trade in agricultural products was exempted from GATT's international trade rules from the beginning and that preferential trading arrangements have gradually come into increasing favor—in Washington as elsewhere—with the rise of preferential regional trade groupings such as the European Common Market, the European Free Trade Area, the Latin American Free Trade Area, and others. The United States itself has a long history of preferential trading arrangements, first with Cuba and now with Puerto Rico and the Philippines.[4]

This is not the place to analyze the pro and con arguments for particular international economic policies. Instead, we must remind ourselves of the real danger, which is that the major governments of the world, following the American lead, will take the easy route of "blaming the foreigner" for their difficulties and that a trade war may ensue that could only be harmful to all. In fact, what was most "unfair" in 1971 was for the U.S. government to blame other countries for the mess into which the Vietnam war and its own neglectful balance of payments policies had delivered it. What was tragic was that the first careful look since 1947–48 at the changing role of the United States in the world economy by a high political personality close to the President should have laid the groundwork for the Nixon administration to assume a self-righteous, injured tone in its dealings with the other economically advanced countries.

Academics, Businessmen, and Labor Leaders Join the Parade

Government officials were not alone in their efforts to explain the dollar's 1970–71 difficulties by ignoring the Vietnam war and concentrating, instead, on the alleged unfairness of foreigners. At about the same time several leading academic economists produced a full-fledged intellectual justification for doing so. Their argument was, in brief, that since most other countries tied the values of their currencies to that of the dollar, the *dollar's* exchange rate was really determined by the sum of all other countries' decisions about the values of *their* currencies. From this they concluded that the size of the U.S. balance of payments deficit was beyond this country's power to affect because it was only the mirror image of surpluses other countries willfully accumulated by keeping their currencies undervalued relative to the dollar. Therefore, these theorists argued, the U.S. government was powerless to affect the dollar's exchange rate and should treat its own balance of payments problems with "benign neglect." The Nixon administration embraced this doctrine in 1970 and in the first seven months of 1971, turned a blind eye toward the difficulties of other industrialized countries—especially West Germany—as an avalanche of unwanted dollars descended upon them, vastly complicating their already serious inflationary problems.

Business spokesmen, too, took up the theme that the cause of the dollar's difficulties was to be found outside the United States, also neglecting the fact that the government itself had long been the principal offender on the international monetary scene. Walter B.

Wriston, chairman of the powerful First National City Bank of New York, thundered that "no one needs to have a balance of payments surplus who doesn't want it" and went on to agree with Peterson that "it is no longer appropriate that the U.S. enter the game [of international trade] with a handicap."[5]

It remained for organized labor to draw the conclusion that if foreigners were responsible for the deteriorating U.S. trade balance, a simple answer would be to shut foreign-made goods out of the U.S. market, and labor was not slow to take up a strongly protectionist stance. While imports were pouring into this country mainly because of the war-induced inflation, the Nixon recession of 1970–71 forced the unemployment rate up from 3.5 percent in 1968 to 6.0 percent in 1971. Responding to the recession, protectionists in the AFL/CIO discovered that the flood of imports was much more visible to most people than the government's deflationary monetary and fiscal policies. Therefore, it was able to convince many union members that it was imports, not the recession, that had robbed them of their jobs.[6]

I.W. Abel of the AFL/CIO was soon echoing Peterson: "We are importing products we should be making. . . . Our governmental policy of allowing other nations to discriminate against American goods, while giving them relatively free access to our domestic markets, tilts the level of international trade against us." Peter Bommarito, president of the United Rubber Workers, put his thoughts into more colorful language: "Plants have been closed and jobs have been wiped out forever. We cannot and will not stand for this. Our people don't want to hear ideological phrases of the learned economists' theories on free trade. What all our members really want is a steady job." In response to these sentiments the Burke-Hartke bill to cut back U.S. imports and private foreign investment was introduced in Congress in late 1971. It was the most restrictive international trade legislation that Congress had been asked to consider in modern times and would apply quotas to almost all imports, forcing a sharp reduction of imports below present levels.

Against this background of grievance, self-righteousness, and protectionism that had been set loose in the country, Richard Nixon went on the nation's television screens on Sunday evening, August 15, 1971, to announce his new economic policy for the United States and a severing of the dollar's convertibility into gold. Although the policies he announced that evening had been forced on him by the Vietnam war and six years' mismanagement of the economy, he did not hesitate to blame foreigners for what he was about to do. In his short text there were no less than five references to "unfair" treatment he claimed the United States had received from other countries and seven references to international currency speculators who, he said, were holding the dollar hostage. He shocked the world that evening by using the only clout Washington had left—access to the large and profitable U.S. market—to bludgeon the country's leading trade partners into complying with Washington's demands. Access to the U.S. market was hobbled by imposing a temporary 10 percent surcharge on all dutiable imports which, the administration announced, would not be removed until the country's major trading partners (1) adopted the exchange rates Washington wanted, (2) modified those of their trade policies that Washington did not like, and (3) increased their military spending.

The Deeper Meaning of It All

How did the Vietnam war affect the dollar and the international monetary system? Because of it, neither will ever be the same again. The dollar, already cut down in stature by prolonged heavy spending on the cold war, finally lost its role as a key currency, becoming just one other world currency. The international monetary system was disrupted and lost its sense of direction when Washington, under heavy pressure from the Vietnam war inflation and its induced dollar crises, abandoned the spirit of reciprocity that had served it well for more than a generation and substituted for it a self-righteous "get tough" attitude toward other leading countries.[7]

This comedown in the position of a great nation is hard enough to bear, but hardest of all was the steadfast refusal of the Johnson and Nixon administrations to admit that it was the consequence mainly of the Vietnam war and of an overmilitarized foreign policy. We were treated to dissemblings, silences, and obfuscations by a bureaucracy that sought to deflect attention away from the Vietnam war. We hear endless discussions of the machinations of currency speculators, of the unfairness of friendly countries toward us, of costs, prices, wages, interest rates, and lagging technology—but we hear almost nothing of the roles of military spending and of the Vietnam war in particular. In its reporting and analysis of economic affairs, the government opened up a yawning credibility gap that may be even more harmful for the long-run health of democracy than its better-known credibility gap in reporting war news.

Candor Seeps Through

Individual government officials tend to be honest men, however, and occasionally they allude—if only obliquely—to the roles of the cold war and the Vietnam war in explaining the country's economic plight. For example, although the five-page summary of the Peterson report almost completely ignores the role of foreign policy in explaining the decline of the dollar, a careful reader of the body of the report could ferret out the following passage:

> *Much of our foreign economic policy has been influenced by, and subordinate to, our Marshall Plan and alliance strategies. These strategies placed security, military-political objectives, and cold war tactics in a dominant position with economic policies largely shaped to serve these ends.* [8]

The meteoric decline of the dollar and the wreckage of the Bretton Woods monetary institutions are fitting testimonials to what happens when a great nation, in Peterson's words, allows "cold war tactics [to play] a dominant position [in shaping] economic policies."

The late Dean Acheson—himself a major architect of the cold war —also once explained the country's balance-of-payments problem to Congress. His explanation made it clear that not only was the Vietnam war carelessly superimposed on an international financial structure that was incapable of supporting it, but that the same charge must also be made against the cold war itself, of which the Vietnam war was only one particularly dismal chapter. Acheson said;

> *The Bretton Woods agreements which were made for commerce were not designed to support military exchange arrangements. They just were not designed for that and we cannot do it. So we have a lot of makeshift agreements by which Germans purchase arms or one thing and another. . . . I am all in favor of foreign trade . . . imports as well as exports. But you cannot take a lot of imports, pay a lot of dollars to support troops, and also make American capital available in the world without going broke. You cannot do it. It just will not work under the rules we have.*
>
> *But it could be made to work . . . a new arrangement . . . by which you had two monetary systems: one for dealing with troops, the other for dealing with commerce.* [9]

The Vietnam war finished off the Bretton Woods monetary institutions, and Acheson's words would make a fitting epitaph for them.

CHAPTER 11

"WINDING DOWN THE WAR":
NEW MEN AND NEW IDEAS TO CENTER STAGE

The Vietnam war was the longest war in American history partly because successive U.S. governments had committed the country to fighting it in the name of such vague, lofty goals that, when these goals proved to be unattainable, it took Washington officials almost five years to find a face-saving way out of the entanglement. The first U.S. serviceman was killed in hostile action in December 1961, and more than six years later Lyndon Johnson abandoned his discredited policy of escalating the war, but, amazing as it seems in retrospect, almost five more years were required before Richard Nixon was prepared to withdraw all U.S. armed forces from Vietnam in January 1973.

Richard Nixon differed from his immediate predecessor in the White House in innumerable ways, great and small. The contrast between the two men is glaring—even stark—whether we consider personal characteristics such as individual mannerisms, rhetorical styles, and relationships with other people, or whether we consider their political views on how the federal government should deal with any number of well-known social and economic problems. But on one point there was scarcely any difference between them—their inflexible determination to maintain the Thieu government in power in Saigon until at least a decent interval after U.S. armed forces could be evacuated. For this reason the Vietnam war, which so rent the American polity and the American economy during Johnson's tenure of the White House, continued to be a major disruptive factor during Nixon's first term.

Under Nixon, as under Johnson toward the end of his administration, the Vietnam war continued to be an unwanted war, an irksome distraction that the administration no longer wanted to have as the centerpiece of its foreign policy. Being still unwanted politically, it remained also underacknowledged economically, with the result that it spread as much, if not more, disorder through the nation's economy in 1969–72 while being phased out as it had done in 1965–68 while being phased in. In 1965–68 an administration bent on enlarging the role of the federal government in the civilian economy ignited the fires of inflation because it underacknowledged the economic impact of the escalating war; in 1969–72 an administration that was determined to reduce the role of the federal government in the civilian economy once again underestimated the war's effect on the economy and landed the country in a recession while at the same time—incredibly—stepping up the rate of inflation.

"Winding Down the War"—but Gradually

The foreign policy framework within which the economic policies of Nixon's administration would have to be worked out were set in the closing months of the Johnson administration and in the first few months under Nixon. U.S. withdrawal from the Vietnam war would be gradual, even more gradual than U.S. intervention had been in 1965–68.

In the most basic sense, the beginning of U.S. withdrawal from Vietnam can be dated from the end of March 1968 when Johnson announced he was ready to accept the necessity of negotiating an end to American involvement in it. Later that year both major political parties endorsed the main outlines of Johnson's decisions. The Republican party nominated Nixon on a platform of de-Americanizing the war plus winning "peace with honor," and just before Nixon was elected in November, Johnson stopped all U.S. bombing in North Vietnam. By mid-1969 the new President had cleared up some of the vagaries in U.S. foreign policy by announcing in June the first U.S. troop withdrawal and by setting forth "the Nixon Doctrine" in July. Later he succinctly summarized "the Nixon Doctrine" as providing that "the U.S. rather than sending men will send arms when we consider it is in our interest to do so."[1] The Nixon Doctrine is a more modest, less costly version of the Truman Doctrine, which it displaced partly because the cost of the Truman Doctrine had become too great for the U.S. economy to bear.

The Economists—Optimistic Once More on the Eve of Economic Disorders

In 1968–69, as in 1964–65, economists were once again in an optimistic, self-congratulatory mood as the country stood on the brink of major economic disorder. In 1965 they were accepting plaudits for having achieved full employment without inflation just as the economy began to inflate under the influence of a rapidly escalating war; in 1968–69 they were feeling sanguine about their ability to guide the country smoothly through a transition from war to peace just on the eve of its first experience with having to endure inflation and recession simultaneously. In 1968–69 they were reassuring the country that the only problem ahead would be to substitute one kind of demand (that for civilian goods and services) for another kind (that for military goods and services). As one official economic report put it, for example, "There is nothing unique about the capacity of military spending to generate jobs. Tax cuts and monetary ease to encourage private spending or government expenditures on civilian programs are also equipped to do the job."[2] In fact, the principal conclusion of this report was that the country faced "a relatively easy transition problem."[3]

An even more self-confidently optimistic tone was set in the last major economic report put out by the Johnson administration, the Economic Report of the President, transmitted to Congress in January 1969 after Johnson's party had suffered defeat in the election of 1968.[4] Appended to this annual Economic Report of the President was a report by the Cabinet Co-ordinating Committee on Economic Planning for the End of Vietnam Hostilities, which Johnson had appointed in March 1967 and which was headed by two successive chairmen of the Council of Economic Advisers, Gardner Ackley and Arthur Okun. The Ackley-Okun committee based its findings on an economic model incorporating a rapid decline in U.S. participation in the war. The committee concluded that "the maintenance of general prosperity is far and away the major part of the economic problem of the transition," and it reported that attaining this would depend upon "the careful and forward-looking management of fiscal and monetary policies."[5] With the ending of the war, according to the committee, a "peace and growth dividend" would emerge that would permit the federal government to spend vast sums of money on other projects. This "peace and growth dividend" would amount to $22 billion according to the committee's projections (later revised to $24.5 billion), and it devoted six pages of its report to describing alternative projects on which this vast sum could be spent.

1969: New Men with Different Priorities Take Over

Not everyone was as optimistic about the economy as the outgoing members of the Johnson Cabinet committee. By early 1969 the country was in the grip of a virulent inflation, the result of bungled fiscal and monetary policies under the Johnson administration. After failing to provide for financing the war in 1965–66, that administration had had a second opportunity to do so in 1967 when in his January 1967 budget message to Congress the President proposed a 6 percent surcharge for the purpose of reducing private demand in the face of burgeoning federal spending. At this point, the Federal Reserve system moved onto center stage. Acting on the assumption that Congress would enact the surcharge, it embarked upon an easy money policy almost at once and hewed firmly to it for the rest of the year. Congress, however, balked and refused to impose the surcharge, insisting instead that the administration should reduce government spending, which the administration, in turn, refused to do.[6] Thus, in 1967 the country was subjected to a highly inflationary fiscal policy and an expansionary monetary policy.

In 1968 Congress finally agreed to pass the income tax surcharge, to take effect June 30. The Federal Reserve System once again reacted by easing credit more than the underlying situation warranted, on the basis of an oversanguine estimate of how effective the surcharge would be in reducing inflation. The unhappy result was that when demand unexpectedly *strengthened* in the latter part of 1968 the economy got what it needed least of all—yet another upward inflationary fillip.

As the year 1969 opened, a new Republican President strode into this scene of escalating inflation, surrounded by new men espousing a new and different philosophy of government and impatient to be back in the seats of power after a long absence.[7] These new men of 1969 had a different set of priorities: They preferred a smaller rather than a larger role for the federal government, they abhorred inflation more than they disliked unemployment, and some of them were disciples of an unconventional monetary theory that they were anxious to try out on the body politic. As they arrived in Washington, the air of expectancy in the Capital in early 1969 was reminiscent of what it had been when John F. Kennedy had arrived eight years before. On both occasions Washington had become bored, if not disenchanted, with things as they were and it was ready for a change: In 1961 to see how young Kennedy and his group would differ from the elderly, slow-moving Eisenhower team, and in 1969 to see how Richard Nixon and company would change the very special style that Lyndon Johnson had imprinted on the Capital.

With Republicans it is almost an article of faith to feel that the country is usually on the verge of succumbing from an overdose of inflation, much as Democrats show a special solicitude for every wiggle in the graph of the unemployment rate. In the Republican year 1969 there was plenty of reason to feel exercised about the inflation that had been brought on by the Democratic administration that preceded them in office.

The Republicans who came to power in 1969 were strongly influenced by the conservative economic views associated with Professor Milton Friedman of the University of Chicago. Professor Friedman is best known as champion of the idea that the money supply is the all-important independent variable determining how large the GNP will be. He believes the growth of the money supply should be set at a rate of 4 to 5 percent a year and then be left alone. He and his followers also believe that government should "interfere" with private economic transactions as little as possible. In particular, they oppose government involvement in wage- and price-setting processes. In their opinion wage-price inflation is simply the result of an oversupply of money and any attempt to influence it directly is worse than useless—worse because it may raise false hopes that they feel are bound to be disappointed.

Professor Friedman provided much of the intellectual backing for the early economic policies of the Nixon administration, *Time* magazine once referring to Nixon as "his most illustrious convert."[8] Friedman himself has declined public office, preferring to maintain his independence as a critic.

Among the Nixon economists most influential in setting policy early in the administration, both Paul McCracken, chairman of the Council of Economic Advisers, and Arthur Burns, economic counselor to the President, acknowledged their debt to Friedman's ideas but they were not true "Friedmanites." In a celebrated remark, McCracken once said that while not a "Friedmanite," he was "Friedmanesque."

It was a Friedmanite article of faith in 1969 that the inflation they had inherited had been caused by the Federal Reserve's overexpansion of the money supply in 1967–68 and that the most urgent order of business was to slow down the rate of growth of the money supply

FIGURE 11-1
How Price Inflation Got Started

CONSUMER PRICE INDEX (% Change)

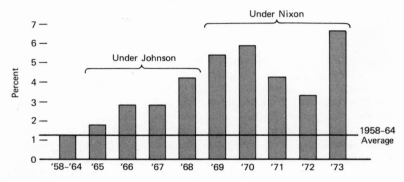

WHOLESALE PRICE INDEX (Industrial Commodities)
(% Changes)

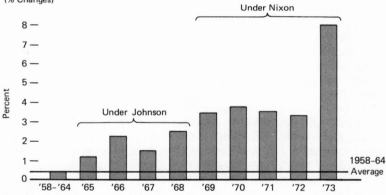

Inflation was not a serious problem in the United States until it was generated by the Vietnam war. In the seven years before 1965 consumer prices rose only a negligible one percent a year and wholesale prices increased less than one-half percent a year. Virile inflation got under way when the Johnson administration escalated the war without making any provisions for financing it.

One of the major blunders of the Nixon administration, upon inheriting an inflationary economy, was to tell businessmen and organized labor that under no circumstances would it interfere with their "freedom" to raise prices and wages. Not surprisingly, the rate of inflation then increased sharply in 1969 and 1970 although total demand in the economy was no longer excessive. This acceleration of inflation confused the administration's economists and in August 1971 they flip-flopped, introducing a "peace time" wage-price *freeze* for the first time in United States history. The wage-price freeze moderated the pace of inflation in 1971 and 1972.

Many economists think the wholesale price of industrial commodities is a better index of inflation than the consumer price index. The Vietnam war brought a proportionally greater increase in wholesale prices than in consumer prices. Wholesale prices also went up more in 1969–73, while the war was being de-escalated, than they had while the war was being paid for by deficit financing in 1966–68.

In 1973 both consumer prices and wholesale prices "took off", foreshadowing the double-digit inflation that was to come. The United States was reaping the consequences of eight years of counter-productive economic policies.

---

while launching a long-range campaign to reduce the federal government's role in the economy. While Friedmanites played down fiscal policy as a matter of distinctly secondary concern, non-Friedmanites in the administration (including the Friedmanesque chairman of the Council of Economic Advisers) were determined to pursue a restrictive fiscal policy as well as a slowing down of the rate of increase in the money supply. Therefore the new men cut back the budget they had inherited from the Johnson administration, and in 1969 the U.S. economy got a double-barreled treatment: simultaneously restrictive monetary and fiscal policies. "The economy was overheated by our predecessors and we must put on the brakes" became the rallying cry of the new policy-makers.

Game Plan I and Game Plan II

The task the Nixon administration set itself—to slow down the very advanced inflation that afflicted the U.S. in 1969 without intervening at all in wage-price bargaining and without precipitating a recession —was an impossible one. A cost-price inflationary spiral such as the United States was enduring in 1969 spins upward with compelling logic: higher prices provide business management with the funds to pay out larger incomes and these incomes become the source of inflationary increases in demand which, in turn, support a further round of price increases. Most countries that have experienced such spirals have introduced "incomes policies" of some sort to moderate them (see Appendix A), but these were not acceptable to the Friedmanesque Nixonians. They were determined to battle inflation on their own terms, by chopping away at total demand in the hope that if sufficient slack would emerge, labor would refrain from demanding higher wages and management would refrain from raising prices. Their policy, called "gradualism," was to stage a very *mild*

FIGURE 11-2
The Real Gross National Product

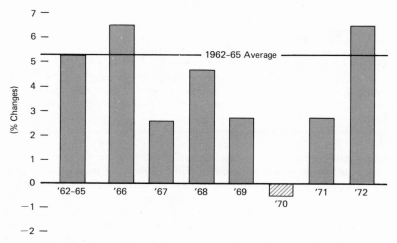

Sources: Economic Report of the President 1973.

The gross national product (GNP), when deflated by an index of price changes to remove the effects of inflation, becomes "real" GNP, a measure of the actual goods and services produced, regardless of their prices. During the main years of heaviest U.S. involvement in Vietnam—1966–71—the real GNP grew by less than it had in the four preceding years, 1962–65.

Total production was pushed against—and slightly beyond—capacity limits by the demands of the war in 1966–68, the years when inflation got its start. In 1969–71 economic mis-management of the war's de-escalation landed the country in recession, with the real GNP actually declining in the year 1970. In 1972 the direct economic effects of de-escalating the war were less than in 1969–71, and real GNP grew by 6.5 percent in that year.

---

recession for one or two quarters only ("so the economy could cool off") and then to return to a path of steady, inflation-free growth. This policy, described on pages 57–62 of the *The Economic Report of the President,* 1970, was doomed to fail.

A *mild* recession was not in the cards because major Vietnam war cutbacks were taking place simultaneously with the imposition of restrictive fiscal and monetary policies. On the wage and price front, moreover, the virulent inflation of 1969 could not have been checked without an explicit government wage-price policy. Before long, in 1970–71, the country lapsed into its first serious recession in twelve years, accompanied by the worst inflation in twenty-five years.

As the grim year 1970 drew to a close a bitter doctrinal strife broke out in the administration, which had more than its share of doctrinaire economists. Both the Friedmanites (monetarists) and non-Friedmanites (fiscalists) pointed with scorn to what they regarded as the failure of the other side's theories "to work out in practice." For Richard M. Nixon, the pragmatist in the White House, the consequences of what had happened became painfully clear when the Republican party suffered widespread losses in the election of November 1970. Nixon was especially disturbed by this election setback because, as Leonard Silk puts it, he "wanted nothing so much as to throw off the Democratic charge that the Republicans are the party that brings depression and unemployment—the charge on which Democrats have been running ever since the Hoover administration."[9]

Demonstrating the light-footedness for which he is famous, in late 1970 Nixon ordered a shift to economic "Game Plan II," which meant that his economists' fight against inflation was to yield pride of place to the need to reduce unemployment. The administration prevailed upon the Federal Reserve to step up the rate of monetary expansion and then, having given up its original plan of trying to choke off inflation by increasing unemployment, clung to a hope that inflation would somehow proceed to exorcise itself. Under Game Plan II, major reliance for combating unemployment was placed on expanding the money supply. In the first seven months of 1971, it proceeded to grow at an explosive annual rate of 11.6 percent, a rate far higher than the much-criticized inflationary rate of 7.6 percent by which it grew during the last two Johnson years, 1967 and 1968.[10]

"The Four-Point Do-Nothing Plan"

Nixon's Game Plan II, or "operation end the recession," was destined to have an even shorter life than Game Plan I, or "operation fight inflation," had had. The first sign that all was not well with Game Plan II came in the form of dissonance among the members of the quadriad, the four highest-level economic policy-makers.[11] Arthur Burns was the highly respected, nondoctrinaire economist in charge of the Federal Reserve, the organization with the leading role to play in Game Plan II, and he became the first member of the quadriad to lose confidence in Game Plan II. He said he doubted that the traditional indirect methods of exercising economic controls only through fiscal and monetary policies would be adequate to cope with the economic problems the nation faced while "winding down" the Vietnam war.[12] He therefore reversed his earlier opposition to an explicit wage-price policy and urged the President to create a voluntary wage and price review board capable of asserting the public's interest in more moderate wage and price increases. This form of direct intervention by the government, he thought, might succeed in curbing inflation.

Burns continued to argue his case in the spring and summer of 1971. In July 1971 he told Congress that, as he saw it, there had not been "any substantial progress" against inflation and he argued more strongly than before for the creation of a wage-price review board. The President himself had delivered a strong *indictment* of wage and price controls in a speech at Kansas City on July 6, and Burns's public reaffirmation of his dissenting opinion later in the same month touched an exposed nerve at the White House. In a move reminiscent of Franklin D. Roosevelt's proposal to "pack" the Supreme Court in 1937, a presidential aide confided to reporters that his chief was considering asking Congress to terminate the independence of the Federal Reserve and bring it under direct presidential control. To say the least, this open quarreling over economic policy at the top level of the government confirmed the worst fears of many observers: Hopeful gradualism was a failure, both in the "operation fight inflation" version and in the "operation end the recession" version.

Under modern conditions, when confidence falters in a government's economic policies, investors transfer capital out of the country, and by the summer of 1971 the flow of capital out of the United States had soared to the highest level ever. The realization that neither the international exchange rate of the dollar established in 1946–47 nor its convertibility into gold could be maintained any longer after twenty-five years of overspending on the cold war came very slowly in Washington. In the summer of 1971 such ideas were not acceptable at all. Consequently, the massive outflow of dollars that summer caused great consternation and confusion.

Even without an unsustainable dollar outflow, however, the administration had pressing problems enough. The stark essentials of its politico-economic dilemma had finally become agonizingly clear.

1 Nixon wanted a more expansionary economic policy in order to reduce unemployment before the presidential election, which was little more than a year away;

2 But faster economic expansion without controls over wages and prices had to be ruled out because it would speed up inflation;

3 And all of the administration's economists except Arthur Burns, the rebellious chairman of the quasi-independent Federal Reserve, had set their hearts and minds against government "interference" in the setting of wages and prices.

At the end of June the President summoned his closest economic advisers to a weekend meeting at Camp David where they decided not to budge one iota from their outworn policy of hopeful gradualism. They did decide, however, to substitute a politician for a professional economist as the policy's main public defender. John Connally, the newest member of the team, "the conservative Democrat from Texas," and the only member of the troika who was not a professional economist, emerged at the beginning of July as "the President's chief economic spokesman," and promptly spoke his piece. The existing economic policies were working well, he told the country, and people should be more patient with them because the administration saw no reason to change them. According to the pundits, Connally's first assignment had been to expound "Nixon's Four-Point Do-Nothing Plan":

1/   Not going to institute a wage-price review board
2/   Not going to impose mandatory wage-price controls
3/   Not going to ask Congress for tax relief
4/   Not going to increase federal spending

CHAPTER 12

"WINDING DOWN THE WAR":
GAME PLAN III—INFLATION AND RECESSION

In the summer of 1971 the unfolding drama of the impact of the Vietnam war on the economy arrived at another of its sudden climaxes—one that shocked and surprised both the Nixon administration and the country at large, because it struck at the hallowed myth of the omnipotence of the American economy. At home, the economy had reached a pathological state. It was by then clear to all that the administrations's first two game plans had produced more inflation and more unemployment rather than, as intended, less inflation and less unemployment. As if this were not trouble enough, shortly after the administration reaffirmed its standpattism in early July, the flight of capital out of the country became a rout and it was soon apparent that the United States would have to begin paying out its remaining $10 billion worth of monetary gold to redeem dollars held by certain foreign central banks. It was this atmosphere of a pressing dollar crisis more than the languishing domestic economy that spurred the administration to action. To prepare for it, a second weekend meeting of economic advisers was summoned to Camp David on August 14–15.

Game Plan III, Ironies, and the Vietnam War
This was the more memorable of the two summer 1971 Camp

David conferences, because at this one standpattism was thrown to the winds and nothing was quite the same afterward. It introduced Game Plan III, which gave the country a wage-price freeze, a dollar no longer convertible into gold, certain tax cuts roughly matched by spending cuts, a 10 percent temporary surcharge on imports, and the most take-it-or-leave-it attitude toward other countries that had been seen in Washington in more than forty years.

Like some of Nixon's other celebrated *volte-faces* in policy, the switch to Game Plan III was rich in ironies. In speech after speech he and his advisers had strongly denounced wage and price controls, promising that never—but never—would they stoop to impose them. But the logic of events had taken over from rhetoric and dogma, and here they were imposing them. John Connally, as the man who six weeks before had promulgated the "do-nothing plan," found himself on August 14–15 presiding over a meeting that had been called to adopt the "interventionist" policies of that heretic Arthur Burns. Meanwhile, "The Great Arthur," as his detractors called him, now found himself vindicated, of course, although later than he would have wished. But surely the crowning ironies of August 15, 1971, were tied up in its associations with the Vietnam war.

From one point of view, Washington was finally equipping the United States to deal with the exigencies of a wartime economy—but doing so seven years after Congress had passed the Gulf of Tonkin resolution, which "authorized" the escalation of the war. Why had it taken so long? Why seven years? Why did consumer prices have to rise more than 30 percent before steps were taken to protect the civilian economy? Such questions are easier to ask than to answer. The broad answer seems to be similar to answers to other questions that have been asked about Vietnam. It is that while Washington fought the Vietnam war like a real war on the battlefields of Southeast Asia, it was never prepared to go one step farther than absolutely necessary in asking the American people to treat it like a real war by making sacrifices at home.

Protecting the civilian economy was a distinctly secondary objective in Washington during most of the years we are analyzing. The primary goals, especially in the White House, were loftier, more "glorious" ones associated with foreign policy. In this scheme of values, if the civilian economy got battered, that was only a necessary cost of establishing the credibility of American arms against the peasants of Asia. When wartime types of economic controls were imposed in August 1971 it was because of international developments, not mainly in order to protect the country's civilian economy.

The dollar, as the world's main key currency, was in a state of collapse and in Washington it seemed necessary to convince foreign investors that the administration could shore up the civilian economy when necessary to defend the prestige of the dollar abroad. Of course, the prestige of the dollar abroad could not be defended by such a last-ditch gesture, but in the years since 1964 Washington has not been deterred from its grandiose plans by considerations of a more practical sort.

There is another, different vantage point from which we may view the imposition of economic controls in August 1971—we may ask why wartime type controls were necessary at all. They were only imposed, after all, three and a half years after Johnson decided not to press the war any further and two and a half years after Nixon came into office pledged to get the United States out of the war. Why should wartime-type controls be necessary—at all—so long after the peak of fighting and so long after the beginning of the end?

The political answer to this question is that U.S. involvement in the Vietnam war itself dragged on interminably—long after it could have been terminated—because the United States was searching for a way to save face while disentangling itself. The economic answer to this second question is not so simple, but it can be summarized in the form of seven major points:

1 The Johnson administration, by failing to finance the war adequately or in time, allowed excess demand to set off a virulent inflation that, once launched, developed a life and a momentum of its own.

2 When the Nixon administration came into office it gave top priority in its domestic policies to fighting the inflation it had inherited, relegating all other economic goals to subordinate positions.

3 Nixon and his economic advisers had a doctrinal bias that led them to view the inflation as mainly of a "demand-pull" type, even though excess demand had in fact been eliminated and the inflation had passed into a predominantly "cost-push" phase.

4 Perceiving the problem as it did, the Nixon administration limited itself too long to fighting the inflation indirectly by cutting back total demand, a remedy that would have been appropriate in 1965–68 but which it was too late to rely upon exclusively in 1969–71.

5 Because its method of attack was inappropriate, the Nixon administration failed in its effort to check inflation, which actually accelerated in 1969–71.

6 The sharp production cutbacks associated with the rapid de-escalation of the war in 1970, when added to the effects of the administration's restrictive policies, landed the country in a recession that saw production decline and unemployment rise from 3 1/2 percent in 1969 to 6 percent in 1971.

7 The acute dollar crisis of 1971 required decisive action and with the presidential election of 1972 only fifteen months away, the administration was eager to restore its fortunes with the voters; accordingly, it seized the opportunity to make the dramatic gesture of imposing a wage-price freeze in the hope it would break the inflationary psychology.

How to Have Both Inflation and Recession

In part, we have dealt with these seven points earlier and it remains now to concentrate upon two underlying aspects of the matter. First, why did the inflation get worse instead of better after 1968, and secondly, why did the country also have to have a recession with a $185 billion loss of production and 5 million people unemployed?

First, why the inflation? The Nixon administration came into office determined to fight a demand-pull inflation that had been caused by an oversupply of money and—regardless of what the country's problem was—that is the kind of inflation it fought. The fact that already by 1969 the inflation had become predominantly a cost-push inflation was not acceptable to the administration because cost-push inflations require some kind of government intervention in the wage-price setting process (that is, they require an incomes policy of some kind) and such intervention the new administration would not countenance.

At his very first press conference, Richard Nixon said:

> *I do not go along with the suggestion that inflation can be effectively controlled by exhorting labor and management and industry to follow certain guidelines. . . . The leaders of labor and the leaders of management, much as they might personally want to do what is in the best interests of the nation, have to be guided by the interests of the organizations that they represent.*[1]

With these words the new President said to labor and management, in effect, "Fighting inflation is our business, not yours, and we will fight it indirectly on the lofty plane of fiscal and monetary policy. You and your organizations may do as you like in the marketplace, but leave the fighting of inflation to us. We do not intend to try directly to help you 'do what is in the best interests of the nation,' however much 'personally you might want to.' "

Given that the nation was caught in an inflationary spiral, the government, by withdrawing altogether from the marketplace, was giving labor and management a green light to charge what they thought the market would bear. The impression was not even created that the government *might* step in here and there to say "enough is enough." In the inflationary environment of the day, this meant that labor unions could push on an open door as long as management thought it could pass price increases on to the public. And how should management interpret the President's statement? "One business advisory service promptly translated the Presidential message into simpler language for its clients: 'The President has just said you can raise prices.' "[2]

A key aspect of an inflationary *environment* is an inflationary *mentality,* which, in turn, amounts to the public's holding inflationary *expectations.* The way several years of rising wages and prices engender inflationary expectations and alter marketplace behavior was described by Robert Roosa, a distinguished former Undersecretary of the Treasury for Monetary Affairs. "Once an inflation becomes as rapid and pervasive as that in the U.S.," he said, "it takes on a character of its own. Everyone now has a share in the perpetuation of inflation, and not merely as victims. We all—as consumers, savers, investors, businessmen, workmen, or government officials—have come to inject a new dimension into our decisions or demands: We assume that prices or wages or interest rates will be so much higher next year that every claim or every purchase we can make must be crowded into today or tomorrow."[3]

The simplistic notion that all wages and prices would gently cease rising if only monetary demand could be held back overlooked too many strongholds of market power from which inflationary wage and price policies can be imposed upon the rest of the country. Professor J.K. Galbraith called attention to these in congressional testimony. He described "a diminishing conflict between management and labor, an increasing tendency to resolve difficulties not by the traditional conflict but, after some ceremonial insult, for the corporation to concede the more urgent demands of the unions and pass the cost along, in higher prices, to the public. This the modern corporation has the market power to do. . . . The occasional strike, conducted as it is now is with considerable decorum, does not alter this pattern of accommodation."[4] But Nixon administration economists were in no mood to discuss wage-price controls. Even as late as July 28, 1971, Paul McCracken published a letter in the *Washington Post* soundly denouncing Professor Galbraith for proposing them.[5]

One reason modern economies have an inflationary bias is that demand-pull inflation, once under way, kindles cost-push inflation. Such practices as negotiated wage agreements covering several years and the insertion of escalation clauses into wage agreements and price contracts add to the wage-price spiral as each center of market power moves to defend its own economic interest, once prices start to rise. If total demand is cut back by the government at such a time, employers may reduce production and their demand for labor at the same time they are raising prices on a lower volume of sales in order to protect their profit margins. The more primitive economic theorists in the Nixon administration refused to recognize these effects of market imperfections, so great was their zeal to "cool off the economy" by reducing total demand.

Some of the evidence supporting the conclusion that the nation was suffering from mainly a cost-push inflation rather than a demand-pull inflation is provided by the behavior of wage increases negotiated by major unions in 1969–71. Table 12-1 shows a steady increase in the size of negotiated wage increases beginning in 1966. These increases accelerated after 1968 when the Nixon administration began its abortive attempt to curb inflation, an acceleration that persisted in 1970–71 even though unemployment was sharply rising.

The second fundamental economic question about the 1969–72 experience concerns why the country, having had to endure inflation, also had to undergo recession. A large part of the answer is that the Nixon administration in 1969–70, like the Johnson administration in 1965–66, was determined to stamp its own image on the economy and, in its rush to do so, underacknowledged the effect the Vietnam war was having at the same time and in the same direction. Johnson forced a rapid increase in war spending upon a fully employed economy; Nixon pushed disinflationary policies upon an economy that was already disinflating under the impact of Vietnam war cutbacks.

When Richard Nixon was inaugurated in January 1969 the federal government's budget was already exerting powerful restraint. In the fiscal year ending June 30, 1968, there was a $25.3 billion deficit in the full employment budget that was being almost entirely eliminated in the fiscal year ending June 30, 1969.[6] Figure 12-1, showing full employment budget surpluses and deficits for the ten years 1962–72, makes startlingly clear what a great stimulus was injected into the economy by rising war spending in 1966–68, as well as the abrupt

TABLE 12-1

NEGOTIATED WAGE RATE INCREASES AND THE RATE
OF UNEMPLOYMENT, 1965–71
(in percentages)

	Negotiated Wage Rate Increases *(medians)*	Rate of Unemployment *(all workers)*
1965	3.9	4.5
1966	4.8	3.8
1967	5.7	3.8
1968	7.2	3.6
1969	8.0	3.5
1970	10.0	4.9
1971	12.5	5.9

Source: President's Council of Economic Advisers, *Economic Report of the President,* February 1971, p. 58, and January 1973, p. 62.

Wage increases negotiated by major unions are an important link in the inflationary process. The size of these increases kept rising during the 1965–69 period of full and over-full employment, but when *unemployment* increased sharply in 1970–71, negotiated wage increases shot up to more than double the 1965 rate instead of declining as the Nixon administration had hoped.

This inflationary behavior of the wages paid to unionized labor is a strong indication that the Nixon administration was facing a cost-push inflation, although it refused to admit this because it preferred to pursue policies that would have been appropriate for fighting a demand-pull type of inflation.

cessation of this stimulus in the fiscal year extending from July 1, 1968, to June 30, 1969. The effect of disinflationary fiscal policy had already become evident in the fourth quarter of 1968 when excess demand was finally eliminated from the economy. The real increase in demand that quarter fell to an annual rate of only 2 percent, roughly half of the potential growth rate. Demand increases were even less in the first three quarters of 1969 before the actual decline in demand in the final quarter signaled the beginning of the recession. As Figure 12–1 shows, the full employment budget ran considerable *surpluses* in 1970 and 1971, registering the Nixon

FIGURE 12-1
When Fiscal Policy Was Counter-Productive

FULL EMPLOYMENT BUDGET SURPLUS OR DEFICIT

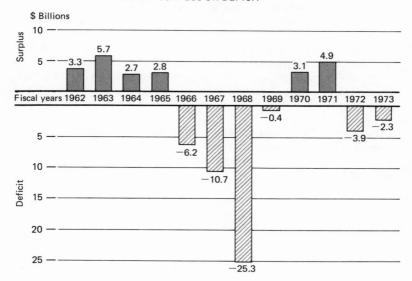

Source: The Budget of the United States, fiscal year 1974 and earlier issues. U.S. Government Printing Office, Washington, D.C.

The full employment budget concept clarifies the role of fiscal policy in stabilizing or de-stabilizing the economy. It was first introduced as a tool of economic planning by the Kennedy administration in 1962. The Nixon administration spurned it in 1969 and 1970, but embraced it as "central to [its] budget policy" in 1971, and it now seems to be here to stay.

The balance shown by the full employment budget is a *hypothetical* balance, telling us what the net surplus or deficit *would* be in the federal government's budget *if* the economy were operating at full employment. The economy seldom operates precisely at full employment, but the full employment budget is a useful tool because it tells the analyst what effect the government's budget policy is exerting on the economy.

There was too large a full employment budget surplus in 1962–63 and it put a ceiling on possible GNP increases. The Kennedy-Johnson tax cut of 1964 reduced the full employment surplus and nudged the economy toward full employment in 1965. Enormous *deficits* in the full employment budget emerged in 1966–68 because of deficit financing of the Vietnam war. They were highly inflationary because super-imposed upon a booming civilian economy. Fiscal policy became *deflationary* in 1969 as shown by the $25

FIGURE 12-1 *(Continued)*

billion reduction in the full employment deficit. The Nixon administration budgeted for full employment surpluses in 1970 and 1971 despite the rapid decline in war spending and landed the country in recession. In an effort to restore prosperity, Nixon turned to a full employment budget deficit in 1972.

administration's Game Plans I and II. These game plans were also responsible for the sharp decline in the rate of increase in the money stock, which rose only 2.9 percent in the year ending January 1970 compared to a rate of increase more than twice as high in the two preceding years.[7]

Once Again, the Underacknowledged War

Against this brief review of the Nixon administration's disinflationary fiscal and monetary policies, what is to be said about the Vietnam war cutbacks?

FIGURE 12-2
How Much Money For National Defense?

NATIONAL DEFENSE AS A PERCENT OF FEDERAL FUNDS OUTLAYS

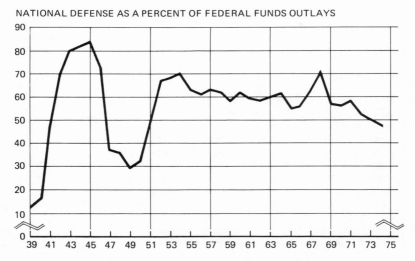

At the time of the Korean War (1950–53) national defense costs shot up to 70 per cent of federal outlays. Their share then drifted down to about 55 percent on the eve of the escalation of the Vietnam war. At the peak of United States intervention in Vietnam, defense spending again reached 70 percent of federal outlays.

Like other government spending, national defense spending should not be judged as a fraction of total government spending, but in terms of its effectiveness in accomplishing its purpose compared with alternative ways of pursuing the same objectives. For example, was it wise for the American people to spend 675 times as much on military programs in 1968 and 1969 as they invested in the United Nations?

The war did not end the way the Ackley-Okun Committee thought it might—first with a truce, followed by a decline in military spending. Instead, such a truce as there was came 3 1/4 years after a frustrated U.S. government began a rapid withdrawal in mid-1969. There was no sharp "peak" in expenditures on the war; instead, they leveled off on a high plateau in 1968–69 and, measured in current prices, definitely started down in the second quarter of 1970.[8] Thus if one draws a parallel between actual disengagement in 1969–72 and the hypothetical disengagement pattern envisaged by the Ackley-Okun Committee, as in Table 12–2, it is only approximate. The parallel fits best if we assume a "truce" to have been signed in the third quarter of 1969, followed by the first significant spending cutbacks in the second quarter of 1970, which is the time sequence built into Table 12-2.

Table 12-2 makes it clear that the actual decline in spending was considerably faster than the Ackley-Okun Committee had expected, especially in late 1969–early 1970 and again late in 1971. The rapidity of decline is noteworthy because in 1969 the committee had written about its own projection, "This is a rapid demobilization—*probably the most rapid that could realistically be assumed.*"[9] Other measures of the war effort also reflected a very rapid decline in spending, concentrated in 1970–71. The Defense Department's prime contract awards turned down in the first quarter of 1969 and were off 25 percent a year later, foreshadowing further cutbacks in war-related production and employment. The manufacture of military products peaked in mid-1968 and was down 27 percent by the end of 1970 (see Figure 6-2 and Table 12-3).

It is not surprising that the combined effect of disinflationary monetary and fiscal policies and the very rapid, uncoordinated cutback of war spending reduced real demand too much, causing in 1970 a decrease in total production for only the third time in twenty-three years. The Nixon administration, in its single-minded determination to reduce federal government spending whatever the cost, completely ignored the Ackley-Okun Committee's conclusion that general prosperity could be maintained despite Vietnam war cutbacks if the government would adopt appropriate fiscal and monetary poli-

VAIN HOPES, GRIM REALITIES

TABLE 12-2

COMPARISON BETWEEN ECONOMIC IMPACTS OF U.S. WITHDRAWAL PATTERN PROJECTED IN 1969 AND ACTUAL WITHDRAWAL PATTERN FOLLOWED IN 1969-72

Decreases in Real Defense Spending

	Ackley-Okun Committee Projection	Actual Pattern, 3rd Qtr. 1969 to 4th Qtr. 1971
	(percent)	(percent)
After four quarters	− 5	−14
After six quarters	−13	−18
After ten quarters	−10	−23

Decreases in Employment

Defense Department Military and Civilian, After six quarters −970,000	Defense Department Military and Civilian, After eight quarters −902,000
Private Employment, After six quarters −750,000	Private Employment, FY 1969 to FY 1971 −871,000
Total Employment 1,720,000	1,773,000

Source: Projections: President's Economic Report 1969, p. 192; Actuals: U.S. Department of Labor.

In its final economic report the Johnson administration released the Ackley-Okun Committee's projection of the probable economic effects of a rapid U.S. withdrawal from the Vietnam war.

In the Nixon administration's withdrawal, the decline in defense spending (corrected for inflation) was faster than the Ackley-Okun Committee had projected, but a slightly longer period of time than they had expected was required for roughly the same decrease in war-related employment.

---

cies. Once again, as in 1965–66, the government's civilian arm seemed oblivious to what was taking place in the military sector. So far from trying to maintain the economy on an even keel while the military authorities reduced their demands, it joined the military in chopping away at the total. As an indication of the effect on unemployment of the Vietnam war cutbacks, it is significant that there was an increase of 2.0 million in total unemployment from 1968 to 1972, while the decline in defense-generated jobs alone over the same period was 2.3 million.

As a dismal sequel to this sorry record, the administration boldly blamed the "winding down" of the Vietnam war for unemployment, lamely trying to deflect attention away from the role its own inept fiscal, monetary, and inflation control policies had played in failing to coordinate the military and civilian economies. In thus trying to cover its own tracks, the administration confirmed the idea held by millions of Americans, and Marxists around the world, that war spending is a necessary prop if the U.S. economy is to function well.[10]

TABLE 12–3

NATIONAL DEFENSE OUTLAYS
(Fiscal 1973 Prices)*

Fiscal Year	$ Billions	% Change
1968	107.8	
1969	103.7	−3.8
1970	94.5	−8.9
1971	85.2	−9.8
1972	78.8	−7.5
1973	73.5	−6.7

*(Excluding Retired Pay)

Source: U.S. Department of Defense (Comptroller), *The Economics of Defense Spending,* July 1972.

Simultaneous Military and Civilian Retrenchments

In the de-escalation of the Vietnam war, national defense outlays in real terms (that is, corrected for inflation) were cut back most severely in fiscal 1970 and 1971, at the same time that other restrictive fiscal and monetary policies were being applied to the economy. This combination proved to be a formula for recession.

CHAPTER 13

AFTER THE WAR—THE PEACE DIVIDEND AND NEW WAR COSTS: WHERE IS THE PEACE DIVIDEND?

The final economic report issued by the Johnson administration, that of the Cabinet Committee on Economic Planning for the End of Vietnam Hostilities (the Ackley-Okun Committee), singled out a "peace and growth dividend" of $24.5 billion[1] which, the committee foresaw, would become available to the federal government after the Vietnam war. Now that the U.S. government is no longer actively fighting in Vietnam, it is a fair question to ask: What became of the dividend?

The commonsense idea of the peace dividend (or the peace and growth dividend, as the Ackley-Okun Committee called it) is that when a war ends its cost to the government should end and the funds formerly used to pay for the war should therefore be available for other purposes. Most discussions centered on three possible postwar uses of the Vietnam war's peace dividend. First, the government could use for other, that is, nondefense, purposes the income no longer needed for the war; it could, for example, get on with funding some of the Great Society projects that were crowded out by the war. Second, it could cut taxes, thus returning the cost of the war to the taxpayers. Third, the funds that formerly paid for the war could continue to go to the Defense Department, which could divert them to other defense uses. These choices seem clear-cut and it ought to be a simple matter, once the cost of the war has fallen off sharply, to find out what happened to the peace dividend. But there are complications.

Peace Dividend Complications

There is no one "correct" method of finding out what happened to the peace dividend. On the contrary, we shall find that the quest for the peace dividend is like trying to keep track of cloud formations as they form and reform while scuttling across the summer sky. The very size of the peace dividend depends, in the first place, upon how it is *defined.* Once it is defined, if we are serious about finding out what happened to it, we must trace out the influences upon it of tax cuts and inflation, of the phasing out of some Great Society programs and of the sharp rise in the cost of others such as Medicare and Medicaid, of built-in growth factors in the U.S. economy, of the fact that the Pentagon is still spending money in Southeast Asia, and of changes in overall military policy such as the shift to a smaller base line force and to a volunteer army. None of these developments took place with the peace dividend in mind, and yet its size and disposition were intertwined with all of them.

At the outset we must decide upon the size and composition of the peace dividend. Even within the Defense Department it was no simple matter to arrive at a clear-cut figure for the cost of the war that could be expected to disappear when the war was over. But because it is the only figure we have, the Defense Department's revised estimate of the war's incremental cost is often taken as the approximate size of the peace dividend. It was at its peak in fiscal 1969 at $21.5 billion (see Table 8-3). The Ackley-Okun Committee, however, worked with a peace *and growth* dividend rather than with only a *peace* dividend. It added $3 billion to its estimate of the size of the peace dividend to allow for the natural growth of federal revenue from fiscal 1968 to fiscal 1972—the year in which the committee assumed the war would be over.[2] Thus, if we adhere to the simple peace dividend concept, it would be about $21.5 billion, but the peace and growth dividend would be about $24.5 billion.

Department of Defense:
"The Peace Dividend Has Been Paid in Full"

A good place to begin tracing the peace dividend is with the Defense Department's claim that it has been "paid in full."[3] Defense officials are sensitive on the subject because they have been accused by some of their critics of making off with the peace dividend

TABLE 13-1

DEFENSE DEPARTMENT'S TOTAL MILITARY OUTLAYS
($ billion current prices and index numbers)

Fiscal year	$B	1964=100
1964	50.8	100
1968	78.0	154
1973	74.8	147

Source: Department of Defense Budget Statement for fiscal 1974.

by burying some of the costs of the Vietnam war in the costs of other (non-Vietnam) defense projects and thereby getting larger post-Vietnam appropriations than they would be getting if they had returned the peace dividend to the civilian economy. But the department insists this is not so.

A cursory look, however, at Department of Defense military outlays in the three fiscal years 1964 (before the war affected the figures significantly), 1968 (with 1969, a year of peak-rate spending), and 1973 (a year when the incremental cost had fallen by about 70 percent) lends credence to the charge that the Pentagon kept the peace dividend for its own uses.

Total spending rose more than $27 billion to the peak war years and fell only $3.2 billion as the war de-escalated, suggesting that the Pentagon simply transferred most of the money it had formerly spent on the war to other, or non-Vietnam, purposes. Or, to put the matter of the apparent disappearance of the "peace dividend" differently, since $50.8 billion was adequate in 1964 before the Vietnam escalation, why should the Pentagon spend 47 percent more in 1973 when most U.S. forces were out of Vietnam?

This second way of phrasing the question points the way to its answer. The Pentagon claims it cost more in 1973 to maintain its military forces because of inflation and pay increases. When the Pentagon deflates the figures in Table 13-1, converting them into 1973 price equivalents, as in Table 13-2, they look very different.

The year 1968 still stands at the top, but now a large difference opens up between 1968 and 1973, disclosing that military outlays were *smaller* in real terms in 1973 than in either 1968 or 1964. The Pentagon supports its claim that "The peace dividend has been paid

TABLE 13-2

DEFENSE DEPARTMENT'S TOTAL MILITARY OUTLAYS
($ billion 1973 prices and index numbers)

Fiscal year	$B	1964=100
1964	78.2	100
1968	104.4	134
1973	71.6	92

Source: Department of Defense (Comptroller), *The Economics of Defense Spending,* July 1972, p. 3. (Figures exclude retired pay.)

in full" by pointing to the figures in Table 13-2. In addition, it has prepared the following analysis of changes in its military budget between 1968 and 1973 to show that, in its own words, "reductions in defense programs since the fiscal year 1968 would have produced a $24 billion expenditure reduction, [but] pay and price increases have absorbed $22.5 billion, so that spending has dropped just $1.5 billion."[4]

In Table 13-3 the Pentagon shows that while its total military and civilian manpower was *reduced* by 1.4 million persons from 1968 to 1973, its payroll and other personnel costs *increased* by $16.3 billion. According to an analysis by the Brookings Institution, four major factors account for this arresting paradox that personnel costs have risen so steeply while the number of people employed has fallen off.[5]

1/ "Catch-up" pay increases in 1969 and 1970 intended to bring federal salaries up to levels prevailing in the private sector and annual increases in subsequent years equivalent to those in the private sector.

2/ The Selective Service Act of 1971, "the all-volunteer bill," increased the pay of enlisted men just entering military service and others in the lowest grades by roughly 60 percent.

3/ In the sharp personnel cuts after 1968, personnel with the fewest years of service tended to be separated, resulting in a grade structure disproportionately heavy in higher paid ranks.

4/ The number of military retirees has more than doubled since 1964 and their pay (that is pensions) has been increased to take account of inflation and higher regular pay levels.

TABLE 13-3

ANALYSIS OF CHANGES IN DEFENSE OUTLAYS, 1968-73

	$ billions
The military budget in the fiscal year 1968 was	$78.0
By 1973 military and civilian service manpower had been cut 1,440,000 (30 percent) and purchases from industry had been cut (in real terms) by 40 percent. These cuts should have reduced spending by	−24.0
So fiscal year 1973 spending at 1968 pay rates and price levels would be	54.0
But we must add: Pay raises for the personnel remaining, plus increased costs of military retirement	16.3
And purchase inflation (22 percent)	6.2
So fiscal year 1973 spending is	76.5

Source: Department of Defense (Comptroller), *The Economics of Defense Spending,* p. 150.

This table, prepared by the Defense Department comptroller, represents an effort to simplify the department's account of the effect pay increases and inflation had on its budget between the fiscal years 1968 and 1973.

First, real cuts in department manpower and purchases from industry since 1968 are subtracted from the 1968 budget to derive a hypothetical estimate of what 1973 spending would have cost at 1968 prices and pay levels. This hypothetical figure must then be raised to take account of the higher pay levels and prices that actually prevailed in 1973. The result of this procedure is that we arrive at the department budget for 1973. The budget forecast for 1973 was $76.5 billion; the $74.8 billion in Table 13-1 is for actual outlays.

There has been a considerable contraction in the size of the armed forces since 1964. "There have been reductions of one-fifth in the number of army divisions, close to one-half in the number of aircraft

FIGURE 13-1

THE DEFENSE DEPARTMENT'S CLAIM THAT "THE PEACE DIVIDEND HAS BEEN PAID IN FULL"

The Defense Department's total expenditures were more than 50% greater in fiscal 1968 than they had been four years earlier, before the Vietnam war was escalated. After the war's de-escalation, the Department was still spending almost as much in 1973 as it had in 1968. These developments are shown in Table 13–1.

However, this increased spending owed much to pay increases and higher prices. When defense outlays are corrected for pay increases and inflation as in Table 13–2, real spending is seen to have followed a different pattern. In 1968 it was only 34% higher than in 1964 and by 1973 the extra dollars spent by the Department bought *less* in terms of materials and man-hours than *fewer* dollars had purchased in 1964.

This decline in total *real* outlays is the basis for the Department's claim that "the peace dividend has been paid in full." In other words the Department, is saying, Table 13–2 shows that *real* military spending after experiencing a "hump" during the war, has returned to a lower level than before. The military, therefore, was pre-empting *fewer* goods and services from the civilian economy in 1973 than it had in 1964.

---

carriers and other naval vessels, and 17 percent—about 450,000 men —in military manpower on active duty."[6] The Pentagon's calculations, based on these reductions, show that as the war ended the military reduced its absorption of real resources (including manpower) from the civilian economy to a lower level than it used in 1964 (Table 13-2). In this sense it is "returning" to the civilian economy all and more of what it withdrew during the Vietnam period. Thus, it has "paid the peace dividend in full" and the fact that its *money* costs are now higher than in 1964 (Table 13-1) is because it has to pay *more* to buy *less* from the civilian economy today than it bought in 1964 as a result of inflation and higher pay levels.

Second Thoughts About the Peace Dividend

The Pentagon's case that, in real terms, it took less from the civilian economy in fiscal 1973 than it did in fiscal 1964 is a persuasive one. But before we agree that this means it has paid the peace dividend in full, we must recall that what the Defense Department has "paid in full" was its own definition of the peace dividend. Among the eight factors listed above that jointly determined what happened to the peace dividend, the Pentagon considered only two —inflation and its own shift to a smaller base line force.

There are also problems about *defining* the peace dividend that are overlooked in the Pentagon's definition of it. One problem is that its definition makes no allowance for the growth of the economy and of the federal government's tax revenues as the Ackley-Okun Committee's formula did. Moreover, neither of these two government-inspired definitions of the peace dividend takes account of productivity growth within the Defense establishment itself—a subject with a controversial history dating back at least as far as Secretary McNamara's insistence, over the opposition of the services, that it be given weight in budget analyses. The potential effect on the Department of Defense budget of introducing an allowance for increases in productivity is very great; the introduction of computers, for example, increases work output while simultaneously reducing manpower requirements. However, expert opinion is divided on how and whether increases in Defense Department productivity (or increases in the productivity of other government agencies, for that matter) should be explicitly introduced in estimating its contribution to gross national product. The two following citations show how great the effect of introducing productivity calculations into the computation of the peace dividend could be. By implication, they also give order of magnitude appraisals of how much of its own increasing efficiency the Defense Department is "hoarding" rather than returning to the civilian economy.

A defense study sponsored by the Urban Coalition concluded that "defense managers . . . [would] be able to offset approximately $600 million of annual price increases through a yearly productivity gain of slightly more than one percent, made possible by . . . operating improvements."[7] A $600 million annual productivity increase for 1969–73 would amount to $3 billion, which should be added to the size of the peace and growth dividend. A second illustration is taken from legislation of the late 1960s providing pay increases for Defense Department personnel. This legislation was designed to make their pay scales competitive with those in the civilian sector and it "includes an allowance for imputed growth in productivity equal to the gain experienced in the private sector . . ."[8] This provision by law to recognize productivity growth in the Defense establishment was introduced in order to increase the financial rewards of defense personnel, but clearly it also imputes to the work they do a growth in real productivity equal to that "experienced in the private sector." Average productivity gains in the private sector are estimated at some 3 percent a year. If we apply a 3 percent rate to the same base used in the Urban Coalition study it would add $7 billion to the size of the peace dividend the civilian economy could have expected to receive from the military establishment between 1968 and 1972. This would have increased the size of the $21.5 billion peace dividend by one-third and of the $25 billion peace and growth dividend by 28 percent.

Another problem, besides the important one of definition, with the Defense Department's claim to have returned the peace dividend to the civilian economy is that it rests upon its own analysis of its own aggregate spending. The department is saying, in effect, "If our aggregate real spending is now less than it was in fiscal 1964, we must have returned all and more of the resources that we were using for the war." Economists at the Brookings Institution have taken a different approach to the question of the peace dividend. They examined, year by year, the Defense Department's Vietnam war and non-Vietnam spending, respectively, and their findings for the period 1969–72 were as follows.

TABLE 13–4

YEAR-TO-YEAR CHANGES IN VIETNAM AND NON-VIETNAM COSTS
(1973 $ billions, total obligational authority)

	Vietnam War Costs	Non-Vietnam Costs	Total
1969	+0.1	+0.6	+0.7
1970	−7.5	−2.0	−9.5
1971	−5.7	−0.6	−6.3
1972	−4.2	+2.3	−1.9
Totals	−17.3	+0.3	−17.0

Source: Charles L. Schultze and Associates, *Setting National Priorities, The 1973 Budget* (Washington, D.C.: The Brookings Institution, 1972), p. 75.

This method of approach, working with year-to-year changes rather than budget aggregates, has the merit of showing that by fiscal 1972 Vietnam war spending had been cut back by only $17.3 billion, or by less than its 1968–69 peak rate of $26.6 billion, measured in 1973 dollars. In this sense, of course, the peace dividend had *not* been repaid in fiscal 1972. Instead, defense spending was less than in 1964 because decisions had been made to cut back the *base line* (non-Vietnam) forces, but Vietnam spending had been cut by only about two-thirds. A year-by-year analysis of changes in Defense Department spending reminds us that the peace dividend cannot be said to have been paid in full as long as military funds are being spent in Vietnam. What the Brookings approach does show in the Pentagon's favor for fiscal 1972 is that total Defense Department spending in real terms had fallen by practically the full amount of the cutback in spending on the war or, in other words, that practically all of the $17.3 billion reduction in real war costs had been returned to the civilian sector.

Thus far we have considered how the Defense Department and economists at the Brookings Institution have analyzed what happened to the peace dividend. There is one more approach to the subject that should be examined. We can compare the Ackley-Okun Committee's 1969 economic forecasts in which the peace dividend was officially defined for the first time with what actually happened in the forecast year, fiscal 1972. This comparison is shown in Table 13–5.

TABLE 13–5

FEDERAL EXPENDITURES AND RECEIPTS, FISCAL YEAR 1972: ACTUAL AND AS FORECAST BY THE ACKLEY-OKUN COMMITTEE IN 1968–69

(billions of dollars)

	Ackley-Okun Committee Forecast	Actual Out-turn(actual	Difference − forecast)
Federal Government Spending			
Defense Department	73	74	+ 1
Other	127*	159	+32
Total	200*	233	+33
Federal Government Receipts	226	213	−13

* Excluding peace dividend

Source: Forecast: President's Council of Economic Advisers, *Report of the President,* January 1969, p. 199; Actual: U.S. Department of Commerce, *Survey of Current Business,* July 1973, Table 32, p. 31.

As this comparison shows, in fiscal 1972 federal nondefense spending was $32 billion dollars larger (excluding the peace dividend) than the Ackley-Okun Committee had expected it to be, and federal receipts were $13 billion less because of unforeseen tax cuts. Of the greater-than-forecast increase in outlays, 40 percent were from trust funds and would not represent a distribution of the peace dividend. The remaining 60 percent of above-forecast outlays, or $20 billion, could, along with the $13 billion tax cut, be regarded as a legitimate use of the peace dividend. Therefore, we may suppose that a $25 billion peace dividend was divided proportionately between increased federal fund outlays and tax cuts in the ratios that each bear to the $33 billion sum of the two. In that case, as shown in Table 13–6, $11 billion, or 60 percent, of the $18 billion of the peace and growth dividend that was available for distribution was being received in fiscal 1972 as increased non-defense federal spending and $7 billion, or 40 percent, as a tax cut.

Further Thoughts About the Peace Dividend
Another difficulty with the concept of the peace dividend is that it might be interpreted to mean that, at the end of the Vietnam war, the level of defense spending *should* revert to what it was in fiscal 1964. Such an expectation that, after many years of costly fighting in Southeast Asia, the level of Defense Department spending should return to the *status quo ante* would imply that U.S. foreign policy is

TABLE 13–6

APPROXIMATE DISTRIBUTION OF THE $25 BILLION VIETNAM WAR'S PEACE AND GROWTH DIVIDEND IN THE FISCAL YEAR 1972

	$ billions
Still being spent to fight in Vietnam	7
Diffused through the economy by tax cuts	7
Being spent on nondefense federal programs	11
Peace and Growth Dividend	25

Source: Table 13–5 and accompanying text.

even more inflexible and ossified than it really is. On the contrary, the size of a national defense budget should be decided on the basis of current need, not on the basis of a past benchmark. The Department of Defense calculates, in fact, that both its manpower and its real outlays in fiscal 1972 were 3 percent less than they were in fiscal 1964.[9] This respite in the burden of defense may be short-lived, however, because the funds the Defense Department is authorized to spend on its non-Vietnam forces are rising from $70.7 billion in fiscal 1972 to $82.1 billion in fiscal 1974, and the authorization is projected to rise to $114 billion by 1980.[10]

In contrast to these hefty escalations of defense spending, some independent studies of the subject have concluded that, for a variety of reasons, the United States could make substantial *reductions* in defense spending. Without going more deeply into this involved question, it is significant that responsible unofficial groups are proposing alternative defense budgets markedly lower than Washington is prepared to consider. A 1973 Brookings Institution study projects the Nixon defense posture five years into the future and compares it with projections of three alternative defense budgets of its own making and finds that by fiscal 1978 the country could save from 10 to 35 percent in defense costs by shifting to one or another of the Brookings defense postures.[11] A 1971 study sponsored by the Urban Coalition gave a detailed analysis of a four-year projection of an alternative defense budget that was 30 percent lower than that proposed by the Nixon administration for 1972.[12]

Finally, a former Secretary of Defense, Clark Clifford, recently recommended an alternative to present Defense Department planning that, he estimates, would save $80 billion over the next five fiscal years.[13] The fact is that the budget request for fiscal 1974–75 contains 566 times as much money for national defense as for supporting the U.S. share of all activities of the United Nations.

On a more fundamental level, if the idea of a peace dividend is to have meaning that the ordinary man can understand, it should be capable of bringing to the country more of a sense of security and serenity. However, given the present regime of international relations under which we live—which is essentially a military threat system—real security and an atmosphere of national serenity are probably unattainable. Despite our knowledge that we do not obtain more security by spending more for defense, the arms race continues to spiral upward, blithely indifferent thus far to whether political tensions among the major powers worsen or improve.[14] If the nation is ever to earn a *genuine* peace dividend that could bring a surcease from militarism, it will have to reconsider its foreign policy goals, its foreign policy decision-making machinery, and probably also it will have to take the lead in sponsoring a revision of the United Nations charter that would give more power and influence to that neglected institution.

In considering what happened to the peace dividend we must recall that it was officially defined by one administration, while a different administration was in power when decisions about it had to be made. Clearly, a political leader interested in trying to heal some of the nation's wounds could have made use of the peace dividend concept to sequester funds for the more imaginative parts of the aborted antipoverty program and to try to recapture some of the enthusiasm that animated that program in 1964, before it was crowded out by the Vietnam war. But the Nixon administration had quite different objectives, and, as we have seen, in 1972 some 28 percent of the peace and growth dividend was still being spent to fight a lost cause in Southeast Asia and another 28 percent had been dissipated through the economy in the form of tax cuts.

Other and Greater Costs of the War

At the same time that the peace dividend was getting lost as a tool of social policy, the economy became stricken, for the first time in history, with a simultaneous attack of inflation and recession because the government's handling of the economics of war de-escalation in 1969–71 was as inept as its handling of the economics of escalation had been in 1965–68. In the following paragraphs we try to arrive at estimates in dollar terms of the social burdens of the war-induced inflation and of the postwar recession.

As a point of departure, we adopt the widely accepted view that the economy would be operating in a broadly satisfactory manner if unemployment could be held down to 4 percent of the civilian labor force and if increases in consumer prices could be held down to 2 percent a year. Actually, the achievement of this satisfactory combination of minimal unemployment and minimal inflation has eluded U.S. economic policy-makers in most of the past twenty years as shown in Figure 13-2. Prior to the Vietnam war years the combination was more often missed because unemployment was too high than because price increases were too high. It was almost attained in the two years 1955 and 1965. Prior to the latter year, as Figure 13-2 shows, economic performance had steadily improved in 1961–65 as unemployment was reduced without any significant increase in inflation.

FIGURE 13-2
Inflation and Unemployment, 1960-72

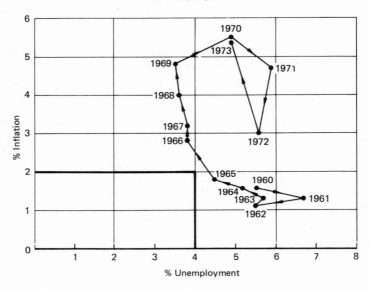

DATA SOURCE: Council of Economic Advisers
The Economic Report of the President 1973 and 1974.

The boxed-in area in the lower left corner of Figure 13–2 shows how the U.S. economy *would* look if it were functioning properly: unemployment would be at or below 4 percent and inflation would be at or below a rate of 2 percent a year. The large black dots, beginning with 1960 and ending with 1973, show how it actually *has* behaved.

In the early 1960s there was very little inflation, but unemployment hovered between 5 and 7 percent until, by 1965, it had been reduced to 4.5 percent. Thereafter, during the most active years of the Vietnam war, 1966–69, unemployment fell below 4 percent, but inflation took over and got as high as 4.8 per cent in 1969.

While Washington was "winding down" the war in 1970–72, the economy became afflicted with *both* 5–6 percent unemployment and 3–5.5 per cent inflation, to the great consternation of many economists.

Since the economy's performance is more unsatisfactory the farther away from the boxed-in area the black dots lie, Figure 12–1 contains a graphic indictment of economic policy in the years after 1965, the years of the Vietnam war and the early years of its economic aftermath. Economic pathology became so severe after 1973 that it would not fit on this graph. In early 1975 unemployment had risen to 8.5 percent and price inflation to an annual rate of 12 percent.

In 1965 before the stunning size of the cost of the Vietnam war became known, there was a soundly based hope that the ideal 4 percent / 2 percent combination could be maintained for the latter part of the 1960s. Unemployment had been cut from 6.7 percent in 1961 to 4.5 percent in 1965 and prices had not risen by more than 1.8 percent a year. Administration economists in 1964–65, blissfully ignorant of the war inflation that lay ahead, were making plans to shift away from the combination of fiscal and monetary policies that had been so successfully used for expansion in 1961–65 and to substitute for them a combination of policies that would have been appropriate for maintaining the economy on an even keel at about 4 percent unemployment and about 2 percent inflation. We shall never know whether the high hopes of those days could have been realized, since after 1965 they were snuffed out by Washington's determination to have a showdown with communism.

In seeking some quantitative measure of the cost of the economy's malfunctioning during the war, we can use this combination of the two leading measures of a satisfactory aggregate performance—a 4 percent unemployment rate and a 2 percent inflation rate—as a standard of measurement and then see how far short of it the economy's actual performance fell. In an impressionistic way Figure 13–1 shows us how poor the performance was. The higher rates of inflation in all years after 1965 stand out clearly, but after 1969 when the rate of unemployment rose to levels about the same as in the early 1960s, *inflation did not decline* to the rates of less than 2 percent that had characterized the early 1960s but instead remained up in the range of 3 to 5 1/2 percent a year.

In recent years we have had comparative rates of inflation and of unemployment dinned into our ears so often that, grim as the record they describe is, it tends to lose its impact. A more effective way to tell the story may be to convert the percentages into rough dollar value equivalents. The government already uses one aggregate economic variable in just this way to assess the overall performance of the economy. The Department of Commerce, Bureau of Economic Analysis, calculates the capacity, or potential level of total output (GNP), and then compares it with the actual, or realized, level of the GNP. The difference between the two is called the GNP gap and it is intended to measure the amount by which actual GNP fell short of (or exceeded), its theoretical potential. In making this calculation of the theoretical potential GNP, the statisticians assume unemployment to be 4 percent.

These official Commerce Department estimates of actual GNP, potential GNP, and the GNP gap for the years 1966–73 are reproduced in Table 13–7.[15] As shown in this table, the country actually exceeded its potential GNP by some 1 or 2 percent in both 1966 and 1968 under the lash of producing for war in an already fully employed civilian economy, while it lost very much more in potential output during the years of the Vietnam war recession, 1970–73.[16]

TABLE 13–7

**THE COST OF THE RECESSION OF 1970-73
IN TERMS OF LOST GNP**
(minus sign indicates GNP greater than potential)

Year	Actual GNP ($ billion)	Potential GNP ($ billion)	GNP Gap ($ billion)
1966	749.1	737.7	−11.4
1967	791.6	791.3	− 0.3
1968	865.4	856.0	− 9.4
1969	930.2	933.2	3.0
1970	976.3	1025.2	48.9
1971	1049.8	1119.9	70.1
1972	1152.2	1203.5	51.3
1973*	616.7	631.6	14.9

Cumulative GNP Gap (Current $)		
	1969–73	188.2
	1966–68	− 21.1
	1966–73	167.1

* First and second quarters only

Source: U.S. Department of Commerce, Bureau of Economic Analysis, *Business Conditions Digest,* various issues; U.S. Council of Economic Advisers, *Economic Report of the President, 1973.* (U.S. Government Printing Office, Washington, D.C., 1973), p. 196. (Official GNP data in 1958 dollars multiplied by the official GNP implicit deflator to convert them into current dollars.)

It has been said that the U.S. economy paid for the Vietnam war twice—once by diverting real resources away from the rest of the economy in order to fight it and later in the form of an unnecessary recession while the war was being de-escalated.

The first cost is estimated to have been about $140 billion and was incurred mainly in 1966–69; the second cost, shown in this table as the cumulative shortfall of total output below its potential level, was about $185 billion and was incurred mainly in 1970–72.

According to the Commerce Department's estimates, about $185 billion of the GNP was lost in this latter period, a sum that compares with $140 billion as the government's estimate of the budgetary cost of the war. Thus, when the American people were required to pay for the Vietnam war a second time in the form of a recession, the cost in terms of goods and services foregone was even greater than the cost of goods and services diverted from the civilian economy to fight the war.

When we turn to consider the question of the aggregate cost to the American economy of the *inflation* caused by the Vietnam war we confront a more complex situation, one in which the usual concept of economic cost does not apply. The point has been made that the concept of economic cost requires that something be foregone or not produced. In applying this cost concept to the war we have shown that some $140 billion of civilian type goods and services were foregone because the government diverted resources away from the civilian economy to the purposes of the war and that some $185 billion of potential goods and services were not produced in 1970–73 because productive resources were made idle by the Vietnam war recession. But we cannot calculate the aggregate cost of the Vietnam inflation as easily as the cost of the recession because, while inflation has many deleterious effects, when experienced as the United States experienced it in 1966–73, it probably does not reduce total output appreciably, if at all. In short, from the standpoint of the country as a whole, inflation enriches some and impoverishes others, but nothing seems to be foregone.

Inflation significantly reduces total GNP only when it becomes so extreme that people work less because their incentives are undermined by a loss of confidence in the money they would earn by working. But, as the country is learning the hard way in 1974–75, inflations create widespread dissatisfaction and social tensions by arbitrarily redistributing income and wealth, processes which involve social costs that may be at least as distasteful—if not quantitatively measurable—as the economic cost of nonproduced goods and services would be.

The inflation engendered originally by the Vietnam war has transferred vast sums of wealth and income to the highly organized, well-placed sectors of the economy. Unionized labor in favored industries, landowners, and the managers and owners of many oligopolistic industries benefited at the expense of unorganized workers, minority groups, many small businesses, state and local governments, and the poor and the elderly whose incomes did not rise in step with the cost of living. The mainstream public, receiving most of its information from the mass media, is only dimly aware of these transfers and of their incidental human costs because the costs are borne most heavily by the least well-organized, the least articulate sectors of society. But the redistributive effects of the inflation do surface in some areas of national life. During the war, while military budgets and price levels soared, the quality of civilian life in America deteriorated. There was a broad-scale reduction in the level and quality of services provided by state and local governments despite their efforts to keep up with inflation by raising property, income, and excise taxes. The deterioration ranged across the board, from more crumbling sidewalks and potholed streets to the longer delays in court calendars, overcrowding of antiquated prisons, and cur-tailed educational services. The condition of many nursing homes for the elderly deteriorated further; crime rates went up; teachers went on strike for higher salaries, smaller classes, and better schools; college professors and many state and local employees became unionized; many small private colleges were forced to close; and early in 1973 the United States experienced its first large-scale consumers' boycott of meat. All of this, of course, in addition to the aborted war on poverty.

But this catalog of costs is only anecdotal. Economists have no objective way of estimating in dollar terms the social burden of transferring X amount of real purchasing power or income from the unorganized and the poor to the highly organized and well-placed.[17] Instead, modern economics asserts that the satisfactions enjoyed by different individuals from consumption, and deprivations suffered by different individuals from nonconsumption, are not to be compared. Therefore, the burden of inflation can only be "sensed," not mea-sured. One way to try to comprehend the order of magnitude of the inflationary burden would be to multiply the value of each year's GNP by the "excess" inflation of that year (defined as inflation in excess of 2 percent). This would provide a quantitative notion of how much the monetary value of the GNP, but not its real value, was directly affected by "excess" inflation as defined. The result of com-paring hypothetical inflation rates of 2 percent a year with the infla-tion rates actually endured during the war years is shown in Table 13–8.

It is immediately apparent from the table that, while inflation ex-tracted some toll in every year from 1966 to 1972, the main increases in the burden during these years were in 1969 and 1970—incident-ally, long after March 1968, the decisive moment in the war, had passed

TABLE 13-8

ESTIMATED AGGREGATE BURDEN
OF EXCESS INFLATION, 1966-72

	Actual Inflation	Target Rate of Inflation	Excess Inflation	GNP	Net Effect of Excessive Inflation on Value of GNP
1965	1.7%	2.0%	0.0%	$685 bil.	— —
1966	2.9	2.0	0.9	750	$ 7 bil.
1967	2.9	2.0	0.9	794	7
1968	4.2	2.0	2.2	864	19
1969	5.4	2.0	3.4	930	32
1970	5.9	2.0	3.9	976	38
1971	4.2	2.0	2.2	1,050	23
1972	3.3	2.0	1.3	1,152	15

Seven-year Cumulative Inflation Bill: $141 billion

Source: President's Council of Economic Advisers, *Economic Report of President,* January 1973. (There was a close correlation between consumer prices and overall inflation in 1968-72.)

This table represents an attempt to quantify the burden of excess inflation on the economy as a whole during the most active years of the Vietnam war. In 1966-72 the Consumer Price Index increased by an average of 4.1 percent a year; excess inflation is defined as any increase in it greater than 2 percent a year. Keeping inflation down to a rate of 2 percent a year should not be thought of as an unattainable goal; in the seven years (1958-64) before the war was escalated, the Consumer Price Index increased only 1.2 percent a year.

For each year excess inflation measures the amount greater than 2 percent by which the merely monetary value of the GNP increased, unaccompanied by any increase in real output. An individual receiving a fixed dollar income would lose real income by the full amount of inflation, but this table measures only the loss caused by inflation in excess of 2 percent a year.

The Indirect Costs and Burdens of the War

The Vietnam recession also imposed its cost on the country during the "winding down" phase of the war, mainly in 1970-72. Clearly the

American people were forced to endure both inflation and recession simultaneously, even though these burdens may not be additive, as economists perceive them. The recession and inflation both struck hardest at the same groups in society, those least able to defend themselves because they are the ones to lose their jobs first and the ones whose incomes are least likely to keep pace with rising prices. The estimated cost of the recession in 1970–72, $185 billion, was considerably greater than the $142 billion budgetary cost of the war, and the estimated effects of "excess" inflation from 1969 through 1972, shown in Table 13–6, were some $140 billion. Placing these magnitudes in juxtaposition may seem surprising at first, suggesting as it does that the costs of the war to the American people were greater during its winding-down than during its earlier, more active phase. But on second thought this conclusion accords with the observation that, except for Americans who might have benefited from the antipoverty program and except for those who lost a loved one in the war, *most* Americans felt the direct impact of the war more painfully through the inflation and unemployment that came in its winding-down phase than they did in any other way. And even greater social costs were to surface later, of course, in the form of the post-Vietnam war inflation of 1973, 1974, 1975. . . .

CHAPTER 14

THE ECONOMIC COST OF THE WAR

In this chapter we attempt to bring together in one place various estimates that have been made of component parts of the economic cost of the Vietnam war. That is by no means simply a task of adding up estimates that have been made by different economists and research agencies. On the contrary, it turns out to mean that we must first evaluate and then try to fit together the work of different estimators who relied on a variety of sources and used a number of different assumptions and estimating procedures. All this in order to obtain results that will still be necessarily untidy. Some of the calculated dollar figures, for example, cover a span of more than one hundred years, which means employing dollars of widely differing purchasing power and present values.

It may be helpful to specify at the outset what must be done. Essentially the task is to *separate out* the costs of the Vietnam war from the vast sums of money that the defense-foreign policy establishment regularly spends on the cold war. That is, we are really grappling with a problem of *cost allocation* and, as any accountant can testify, it is impossible to allocate costs in a purely objective way. But, on the other hand, most of us would be unwilling to admit that the cost of the Vietnam war was literally incalculable. A good way to open up the subject is to review briefly some of the estimates that others have made.

Some of the Estimates

Inside the Defense Department a struggle occurred over what fraction of its total spending should be allocated as the *specific budgetary cost* of the war—a struggle that is not over yet to judge by the dispute that still rages between the two men who should know the most about it—the present comptroller and his immediate predecessor. Professor James L. Clayton made a valiant attempt to estimate the *ultimate budgetary cost* of all wars in which the United States has been involved, including the Vietnam war, and his estimates have received official sanction by being incorporated in the U.S. government's Statistical Abstract. Professor Robert Lekachman estimated that the costs of the Vietnam war added up to $400 billion plus;[1] in a doctoral dissertation Tom Riddell concluded that the war had cost $676 billion;[2] and Professor Murray Weidenbaum has worked extensively on the role of military spending in the economy. Professor Robert Eisner made a comprehensive market-oriented estimate of the added cost of the war attributable to the drafting of servicemen to fight at rates of pay far below what they would have been willing to accept voluntarily, while a group of Cornell University faculty members, writing as the Cornell Air War Study Group, made some war cost estimates as an aspect of its work. More estimates, of course, may come to light before this book is published.

We can take a major step toward bringing order out of this seeming cacophony by distinguishing four broad cost categories that should be considered in estimating the war's full economic cost:

1/ The budgetary cost to the U.S. government incurred at the time of fighting the war

2/ Budgetary costs that the government will have to meet in the future because the war was fought

3/ The various extra-budgetary economic costs that the war imposed upon the American people and the American economy

4/ Some indirect social costs and burdens that are properly attributable to the war

The Budgetary Cost at the Time of the War

The Defense Department Estimates of Direct Cost / To isolate the effect of the war on the economy, logic suggests the use of the official estimates of its incremental direct cost rather than of its full direct cost as these terms are explained above, because full cost includes some base line force costs that, presumably, would have been incurred even if there had been no Vietnam war. In this instance, however, logic alone cannot be decisive because there are doubts about the inclusiveness of the war cost estimates as made in the Defense Department. Many subjective judgments had to be made in preparing them. In the words of Defense Department Comptroller Robert C. Moot, "It is necessary to emphasize . . . that these figures are estimates. . . . There is no one correct basis for stating the cost of the war."

On several counts the judgments made by Defense Department estimators in preparing both the full cost and incremental cost estimates were conservative in the sense that they produced smaller cost estimates than other methods would have done. For example, procurement costs were defined as equipment *purchases to replace war losses* rather than as equipment *used;* deferred construction and maintenance costs were not included; and no estimates of the full personnel costs of the war were made at all. These procedures are understandable since the estimates were prepared for internal govermental purposes—as guides to the war's effects on the budget and on the GNP—but by the same token, they were not intended as measures of the war's economic cost. Moreover, the estimates have not been subjected to the analysis and criticism of outside experts— as, e.g., the GNP accounts and many other official statistical series have been. Therefore, doubts about their inclusiveness cannot be allayed, especially as long as Moot's predecessor as Defense Department comptroller, Robert N. Anthony, continues to attack them as being too low.

For these reasons, some will feel that the official incremental cost estimates understate the "true" incremental cost of the war to the economy and that the full cost figures (which Anthony insists really are incremental costs) should be used instead. Logically, however, full costs are *too* inclusive because they are intended to include elements that were not added to the budget only because of the war. For these reasons, Table 14–1 includes both the incremental and the full Defense Department estimates of the cost of the war.

Other Past Budgetary Costs

In estimating the cost of the war the Defense Department begins with fiscal 1965, the year in which the United States launched its first air attacks against North Vietnam. But the summary of the history of U.S. intervention in Vietnam in chapter 2 shows that the U.S. government's military activity there antedated 1965 by fifteen years. Professor Murray Weidenbaum puts the military costs incurred by U.S. armed forces in Vietnam prior to 1965 at about $700 million.[3] Tom Riddell has brought together from a number of sources estimates of the U.S. government's spending in Southeast Asia over and above the Defense Department's estimates of its direct outlays for the war, including aid that was nominally labeled "economic" because it did not consist of military hardware. After personal conversations with him, some of his data which do not overlap other categories in the table are included in Table 14-1.

TABLE 14-1

PAST BUDGETARY COSTS INCURRED TO FIGHT THE WAR
($ billions)

---

1. Direct Defense Department Outlays, 1965–74
   Full Cost Estimates
   a. Official Estimate (Table 8–3) $140.1
   b. Plus Unofficial Adjustment (Table 8–5)   15.0
                                                                         155.1

   Incremental Cost Estimate
   c. Official Estimate   112.0
   d. Direct Defense Department Outlays
      (Range of estimates) $112.0–155.1

**2. U.S. Military Spending in South Vietnam,
   Prior to 1965[1]**   0.7

3. U.S. Military Aid to:
   France and Emperor Bao Dai, 1950–54 ....   2.7
   South Vietnam, 1954–66[2]....................................   2.4
   Laos and Thailand, 1950–66[2]..............................   1.1
   Cambodia, 1950–74[2] 1.0

**4. U.S. "Economic" Aid to Southeast Asia,
   1946–74[3]**..   7.5

**5. Cost of Supporting "Third Country" Troops
   from South Korea, Philippines, Thailand,
   New Zealand, and Australia[2]**...............................   1.0

6.   Total Past Budgetary Costs 128.4–171.5

---

[1] Murray L. Weidenbaum, *Economic Impact of the Vietnam War,* Center for Strategic Studies, Georgetown University, Washington, D.C. 1967, p. 21.

[2] Tom Riddell, unpublished doctoral dissertation at the American University. After 1966 military aid to South Vietnam, Laos, and Thailand was included in the official war cost estimates.

[3] The U.S. *Statistical Abstract* shows $6.5 billion for 1948–71; Riddell shows $7.5 billion for 1946–74.

Future Budgetary Costs of the War

Anyone who looks into the future is making a forecast, whether or not he is aware of it. And when one looks into the *economic* future, one is willy-nilly joining company with that band of iconoclastic practicing economists who spend most of their working hours preparing economic and business forecasts. These people will forecast any variable you can mention, ranging from the size of the aggregate gross national product in the year 2001 to the number of pink, scented bars of soap housewives will pick off grocers' shelves in the year 1984. Although they use hunch and conjecture as well as the more showy economic, econometric, and mathematical forecasting tools, even the most sophisticated of their forecasts may turn out to be wrong. They were notoriously wrong in the 1940s when they warned of another great depression that was to have followed hard on the heels of World War II. Again in the late 1950s most forecasters thought the major economic problem of the 1960s would be unemployment, slow growth, and economic slack rather than excess demand and inflation. More recently they have had to be reminded that they were leaving environmental considerations out of account and that the environment may soon no longer be able to support some of the profligacy to which American consumers have become accustomed. But, imperfect as economic forecasts are, we must now make use of some as we turn to consider the probable *future* budgetary costs of the war; as we do so, we should remember that some forecasts have been egregiously wrong in the past.

Postponed Military Investments

Official war cost estimates make no allowance for the postponement of substantial Defense Department investments in military facilities such as naval ships, troop barracks, medical facilities, dependents' housing, and the like which occurred because of the war. However, to the extent such investment must be made up later it should be counted as part of the cost of the war. The Cornell University Air War Study Group estimated that a $15 billion backlog of such investments accumulated during the years 1966–71.

When the subject came up at congressional hearings in June 1969, Defense Department representatives placed the cost of such postponements at $13.5 billion. Subsequently, however, defense officials have argued that the cost of these postponements turned out to be much lower—if it exists at all. "The backlog and deferrals were real, but they disappeared," according to one official.[4] Part of the explanation for the disappearance is that equipment lost in the war was replaced by more modern versions, so that the military is now equipped with better weapons than they had on the eve of the war. Weapons were acquired in 1967 or 1968 that, except for the war, might not have been bought until the early 1970s. In addition, the Defense Department reports that the reduction in the size of its post-Vietnam base line force compared to its size on the eve of escalation in 1964 has reduced the need for much of the postponed investment. If the base line armed forces should be raised again toward their 1964 size, the need for facilities not built during the war would presumably emerge again. Their economic cost cannot be precisely estimated, but it must lie somewhere between zero and $13.5 billion and in Table 14–8 it is carried at 6.7 billion.

Cost of Continuing a U.S. Military Presence in Indochina

In the afterglow of World War II the U.S. government initiated international aid programs to assist the economic reconstruction of formerly "friendly" and "enemy" countries. At one stage in the Paris negotiations with the government of North Vietnam, President Nixon sought to build upon this precedent by offering to provide $7.5 billion of postwar economic aid to be divided among the countries of Southeast Asia.[5] The negotiations took a different turn, however, and the aid proposal never entered the realm of practical politics. Moreover, the conditions under which the U.S. government extracted itself from Vietnam were not conducive to a national mood of reconciliation and it now seems unlikely the government will accept financial responsibility for helping to rebuild the economy of any Communist-controlled country in the area. Instead, the defense-foreign policy establishment is more likely to try to use military aid funds to maintain non-Communist governments in power where it can. Therefore, "postwar" costs in Southeast Asia are likely to be mainly military instead of economic in character.

Economists at the Brookings Institution speak of "residual expenditures for Vietnam" in fiscal year 1974, and they believe the Defense Department's $2.9 billion request for new obligational authority is a better guide to cost levels than its $4.1 billion estimate of fiscal 1974 *outlays* (both figures measure incremental cost).[6] The budget was prepared before the cease-fire was signed in January 1973 and it was based upon the assumption that a small number of U.S. troops would remain in Vietnam and that U.S. Air Force operations there would be "moderate." As a result of the cease-fire, incremental cost was expected to fall about $1.2 billion unless heavy fighting continued. The full cost can be calculated roughly as follows: There are approximately 65,000 base line U.S. air force and naval personnel in the Southeast Asia combat area and they are not engaged in active combat. According to the Defense Department budget for fiscal 1974, an average soldier in that year cost about $32,500. This sum times the number of base line personnel in the area would yield $2.1 billion as the cost of the base line force in Southeast Asia. The *total full* cost, then, of maintaining a U.S. military presence in the area would be about $3.3 billion ($1.2 billion + $2.1 billion) in the absence of heavy fighting. The fiscal 1974 budget also asked $0.5 billion economic aid for South Vietnam, raising the total cost estimate to $3.8 billion as a minimum estimate of the "residual cost" of maintaining non-Communist governments in power in Southeast Asia by the force of American arms. The cost estimate, in detail, is as follows:

TABLE 14-2

ILLUSTRATIVE COSTS OF MAINTAINING U.S. MILITARY FORCE IN SOUTHEAST ASIA
($ billions, full cost)

U.S. forces, base line costs	$2.1
U.S. forces, incremental costs	0.5
Military aid to South Vietnam and Laos	0.7
"Economic" aid to South Vietnam	0.5
Total Cost	3.8

Source: Accompanying text and Edward R. Fried and Associates, *Setting National Priorities, The 1974 Budget* (Washington, D.C.: The Brookings Institution, 1973) pp. 331–333.

Would "residual costs" remain at about this level year after year? Looking farther into the future, the Brookings economists remark that "the present administration posture would permit further sizable reductions in military assistance to South Vietnam and the removal of part or all of the U.S. forces now in Thailand . . . if the cease-fire proves to be a transition to political stability and economic reconstruction in Southeast Asia".[7] In this event, they suggest that "American programs in Korea following the 1953 cease-fire there provide at least an indication of possible trends after fiscal 1974 in the level of U.S. assistance to Vietnam. During the period of 1953–61 U.S. military and economic assistance to Korea averaged $450 million a year, which in 1974 dollars would come to an average annual program of about $700 million, higher at the beginning of the period and declining thereafter."[8]

However, analogies are always dangerous and in Southeast Asia where the political situation appears to be more complex than in Korea, a more intensive use of military force might be necessary to keep anti-Communist regimes in power. Therefore, $700 million a year should be regarded as a minimal estimate of "economic" and military *aid* required. *Actual* "residual costs" in Southeast Asia—including the cost of keeping U.S. forces there and adding some costs for Cambodia (which is not included in Table 14–2)—are likely to be nearer $3.8 billion, especially in the early years. The most critical variable in this estimate, of course, is what the balance of forces will be in the U.S. Congress. If it continues to support Washington's defense-foreign policy establishment, costs in Southeast Asia could continue to run at a high level for many years. In 1965, General Earle Wheeler thought the United States might need to keep a major force in Vietnam for perhaps as long as twenty or thirty years.[9] Tom Riddell foresees a period of twenty years, based on the Korean analogy.[10]

Recalling the *caveat* that all politico-economic forecasts are certain to err, we conservatively project the "residual cost" to the United States of maintaining anti-Communist regimes in power in Southeast Asia for twenty years at $2 billion a year ($0.7 billion "aid" and $1.3 billion for U.S. forces) which is only half the cost of U.S. forces there in fiscal 1974, as shown in Table 14–2, and only two-thirds of the Pentagon's request for fiscal 1975.

Vietnam War Veterans' Benefits

Among the various estimates of war costs, the largest by a considerable margin is the $233 billion in benefits that Vietnam war veterans may collect from the government.[11] An estimate of this variable was originally presented to the Joint Economic Committee of Congress in June 1969 by Professor James L. Clayton of the University of Utah and has subsequently been published in the U.S. government's *Statistical Abstract*. It is necessarily an "iffy" forecast because it allows for the fact that Vietnam war veterans may still be collecting these benefits one hundred years from now. Few indeed are the economic forecasters who would be willing to stake their reputations on the accuracy of quantitative forecasts running that far into the future.

In making his projection, Professor Clayton had data at hand showing the size of veterans' benefits compared to the original costs of wars in which the United States has been involved, a record summarized in Table 14–3. His estimate of the cost of Vietnam war veterans' benefits is based upon his interpretation of that record.

TABLE 14-3

VETERANS' BENEFITS AS A PERCENTAGE OF WARS' ORIGINAL COSTS

	Percent
American War for Independence	70
War of 1812	53
War with Mexico	88
Civil War	268
Spanish-American War	1,500
World War I	288
World War II	100
Korean War	183
Unweighted Average	319

Source: Table 8-1.

Table 14-3 is no ordinary table. It covers eight very different war and postwar experiences and a sweep of almost two hundred years, showing that veterans' benefits have ranged from barely 53 percent of the original cost of a war (War of 1812) to as high as 1,500 percent (Spanish-American War).

The situation is not quite as baffling as it looks, however, because in attempting to forecast Vietnam war veterans' benefits we need not assign equal weight to the veterans' experiences after all of the wars shown. We can discount the significance of the first of the three wars shown because they reflect the social value judgments and political realities of a society very different from the one we have today. Likewise, the experience following the Spanish-American war is not a helpful guide because it was an extremely short and inexpensive war. This leaves four wars—the Civil War, World War I, World War II, and the Korean War—to consider. The unweighted average percentage of veterans' benefits to original cost for these four wars is 210 percent, very close to the 200 percent ratio that Professor Clayton used in arriving at his estimate.[12]

In the nature of the case, we know more about veterans' benefits from the first two of these four wars than from the last two, which are of quite recent occurrence. In fact, the largest parts of veterans' benefits from World War II and the Korean War are still to be paid, whereas almost all payments have been made to veterans of the Civil War and 63 percent of Professor Clayton's estimate of World War I veterans' benefits have already been paid.[13] If we should rely mainly upon the experience of two of the last four applicable wars for which we have the most complete pay-out data, the average ratio of veterans' benefits to original cost would be 278 percent rather than 210

TABLE 14–4

VIETNAM WAR VETERANS' BENEFITS, ESTIMATED BY ALTERNATIVE INTERPRETATIONS OF PAST WAR EXPERIENCES

Example Number	Selected Past U.S. Wars	Average Veterans' Benefits as % of War's Original Cost (%)	Vietnam War Cost Estimate to which % Applies[1] ($ bn)	Corresponding Estimate of Vietnam Veterans' Benefits ($ bn)[2]
1	2	3	4	5
I	Four wars most relevant in estimating Vietnam veterans' benefits (Civil War, World War I, World War II, Korean War).	210	112 140 155	235 294 325
II	Two relevant wars for which veterans' benefit information is most complete (Civil War, World War I).	278	112 140 155	311 389 431
III	Two wars immediately preceding Vietnam war (World War II, Korean War).	141	112 140 155	158 197 219
	Unweighted Average of Above			284
	Mid-point of Range			295

All averages are unweighted; all cost figures in current dollars.

[1] $110 billion was the full cost estimate through June 30, 1970, used by Professor Clayton and almost equal to Defense Department incremental cost estimate through June 30, 1974 ($112 B); $140 billion is Defense Department full cost estimate through June 30, 1974; $155 billion is unofficial full cost estimate through June 30, 1974, as in Table 14–1.

[2] Product of column one times column two.

Sources: Column 3, Table 14–3; Column 4, Table 14–1.

percent (example II in Table 14–4). Applying this 278 percent to $110 billion, which is approximately the officially estimated incremental cost of the war, yields $311 billion as the probable value of Vietnam war veterans' benefits. In fact, Table 14–4 indicates that several alternative ways of interpreting the U.S. historical experience with veterans' benefits yield Vietnam veterans' benefit estimates in the neighborhood of $300 billion.

Thus, upon reflection, it seems Professor Clayton's original estimate of $220 billion for the ultimate value of Vietnam war veterans' benefits (see Table 8–1) might be somewhat low, although at first it appeared surprisingly high since at the time it was made it was twice the estimated full budgetary cost of the war. The $220 billion looks especially high to those who are not accustomed to thinking of the aggregate value of government outlays over a sweep of years. It may help to acclimatize oneself to this practice by looking backward instead of forward and by comparing the multiple-year veterans' benefit totals with the values of GNP in the original war years. This procedure also makes Professor Clayton's estimate appear low. As shown in Table 14–5 the present estimated value of veterans' benefits from World War I would amount to about twice the value of a year's GNP at the time it was fought, and World War II benefits would amount to about 1.4 times a year's GNP when it was being fought. Veterans' benefits from the Korean War (more comparable to the Vietnam war since it too was less than an all-out effort) are estimated at about 30 percent, and $220 billion of Vietnam veterans' benefits would be a low 27.5 percent of GNP during the peak Vietnam war years.

For several reasons the experience of the Veterans Administration in disbursing veterans' benefits after previous wars is not an ideal guide to estimating the value of benefits to veterans of the Vietnam war. For one thing, it does not take account of future veterans' benefits that may be extended by fifty state governments, which would have to be added to the cost of federal benefits. For another, future benefits to veterans of the Vietnam war will obviously depend in part upon the content of veterans' benefit laws that have not yet been written and which cannot be accurately foreseen. Historically, we can discern a trend toward granting more generous benefits to veterans, a trend which broadly parallels the increasing concern by governments about a variety of social and economic problems that have arisen in modern industrialized countries. In the United States a landmark in this trend was the enactment of the G.I. Bill of Rights for veterans at the end of World War II, with its generous provision of educational allowances, among other benefits. If the trend toward

TABLE 14-5

**VETERANS' BENEFITS AS PERCENTAGES OF AVERAGE
GNP'S DURING WAR YEARS**

	Percent
World War I	200
World War II	140
Korean War	30
Vietnam War ($220 B. estimate)	27.5

Source: Veterans' benefits from Table 8–1; GNP from *Survey of Current Business,* various issues.

more generous benefits should continue in the decades ahead, estimates of the value of the stream of benefits over the next one hundred years that might be appropriate to today's standards would fall far short of reality.

Another problem that interferes with efforts to extrapolate future veterans' benefits on the basis of experience with past wars is that for all earlier wars except the Korean War, there has been much less doubt about the original cost of the war itself than exists today about the original cost of the Vietnam war. The main reason for doubt about its original cost is that the Vietnam war marks the first time this country has fought a war when it was already fully armed and spending scores of billions of dollars on its military establishment before, during, and after the war itself. According to the official estimates of the full cost of the Vietnam war, at its peak the Pentagon was spending about twice as much on other military activities as it was spending to fight its war in Vietnam. Therefore, estimates of the original cost of the war have to be separated out of the department's total expenditures by statistical approximation, and the principal estimators themselves remain in sharp disagreement about how much it should be said to have cost. Moreover, since the U.S. government never *declared* war against North Vietnam, even the time period during which the war can be said to have been fought is in doubt. All cost estimates used in Table 14–4 are based on the official arbitrary start-up date of July 1, 1964, and a termination date of June 30, 1974. Thus, servicemen who served in Southeast Asia before July 1, 1964, and who may be required to serve there after June 30, 1974, and who may later receive veterans' benefits are excluded from the estimates. Thus, the original cost of the Vietnam war—which is the basis we have used thus far to estimate the cost of veterans' benefits —may itself be too low.

A Dissent by the Defense Department

Professor Clayton's estimate of the ultimate value of veterans' benefits looks modest when compared, as in Tables 14–4 and 14–5, with benefits veterans have actually received, or are expected still to receive, from earlier United States' wars. However, economic and financial analysts at the Defense Department expressed a directly contrary opinion in reviewing an earlier draft of this chapter, concluding, instead, that Clayton's estimate is unreasonably high. Their analysis of his work took the following form. First, they provisionally accepted $220 billion (his initial estimate) and, using the time pattern of Veterans' Administration outlays following previous wars, they phased out the $220 billion. They found that 90 percent of it would probably be spent by the year 2040, seventy-three years after the first VA payments to "Vietnam era veterans" in 1967. In comparable time-phasing exercises, it was found that 91.35 percent of total Spanish-American War veterans' benefits had been paid after seventy-three years and 97.4 percent of Civil War veterans' benefits had been paid. These comparisons looked essentially reasonable considering that Vietnam war veterans will probably live longer than Civil War veterans did.

While thus accepting the proposition that $220 billion could be spent on benefits to veterans of the Vietnam war, the Defense Department analysts hold that only the benefits dispensed by the VA because of service-connected disabilities should be counted as part of the cost of the war. To isolate these benefits, they advance the following breakdown of the three main categories of VA costs according to whether they are, or are not, service-connected.

According to the Defense Department, "There is no question that the costs of pensions or medical treatment for veterans injured in the service should be related to Defense. However, that covers only a portion of VA costs [and according to the above breakdown] roughly half of VA costs [are service-connected and therefore] . . . could be related directly to military service, and half could not." Basically, the Defense Department analysts oppose treating nonservice-connected veterans' benefits as defense-related and in this way counting them as part of the cost of the war. Such benefits, they hold, provide the equivalents of social welfare benefits that the government would distribute whether or not there had been a war in Vietnam, and one would not need to be a veteran to participate in them. As a department memorandum puts it, "If we abolish all veterans' legislation, public spending would not fall by the amount of the VA budget. Without the war, it is likely that additional amounts would have been spent [by the federal government] for education, training,

TABLE 14–6

VETERANS'ADMINISTRATION COSTS, FISCAL YEAR 1974
(Percentages)

	Total Costs	Distribution by Type	
		Service Connected	Non-Service Connected
Income Security	54	29	25
Education and Training	22	3	19
Health and Medical	24	18	6
Total	100	50	50

Source: Notes: Chapter 14, note 4.

health, and income security—the very purposes for which the VA spends its money.''

On the strength of this argument, defense analysts would cut 50 percent off Professor Clayton's $220 billion estimate of Vietnam war veterans' benefits, reducing it to $110 billion in order ''to recognize that about half of these costs would have been incurred anyway, under some heading other than veterans.'' The Defense Department would also prefer to state the value of future veterans' benefits in terms of the present value of the flow of future benefits discounted at 5 percent, and for this reason they would further reduce Clayton's estimate to a present value of only $23.1 billion.

But further, the department analysts believe that even this low figure of $23.1 billion—which is only 10.5 percent as large as Clayton's original $220 billion estimate—is about four times too high. Therefore, they propose substituting an entirely different method of estimating the probable cost of veterans' benefits.

Their alternative method begins by asking how many *additional* veterans there are because of the war, a question easier to ask than to answer because, like all incremental-type questions, the answer depends upon one's assumption of what *might have* happened if something else—in this case the war—had not happened. To approach the question of what military manpower *might have been* without the war, they suggest seven alternative estimating procedures. One set of procedures assumes that military manpower in 1965–74 would have remained at its 1964 level or at the 1955–64 average level, and another set assumes that base line manpower would have trended downward after 1969 as it actually did, even without the war. The unweighted average of incremental Vietnam war military manpower yielded by the seven methods used by the defense analysts was 1.02 million and the midpoint of the range of seven estimates was 1.05 million. Accordingly, they regarded 1 million men as "a reasonable figure." This figure, they write, "would involve the assumption that, without the war, military manpower would have fallen from the fiscal year 1964 level, but not by as much as the base line force has [actually fallen]."

To arrive at an estimate of veterans' benefits, they multiplied the million incremental veterans by $442, the average VA cost per veteran over the years 1957–73, measured in 1974 dollars. They then assumed the average veteran would draw benefits for fifty years and arrived at an estimated total cost of Vietnam war veterans' benefits of $22.1 billion. They converted this sum into estimated future current prices and discounted it at 5 percent back to 1974, arriving at a 1974 value of veterans' benefits of $17.3 billion. They accepted only half of this sum, or $8.6 billion as a charge against the Vietnam war, assuming the 50 percent service-connected disability ratio would hold, and deflated it back to the fiscal year 1969, (a peak war year) by a price index for federal purchases to arrive at their preferred figure of $5.8 billion as the value of benefits to be received by veterans of the Vietnam war.

The Issue Is Joined

With this second Defense Department estimate of the cost of Vietnam war veterans' benefits, we can clearly draw the issue between their method of estimating the benefits and Professor Clayton's method. Astonishing as it seems, their preferred method yields a figure ($5.8 billion) which is barely 2.6 percent of Professor Clayton's original $220 billion estimate.

How are we to explain such an unbelievably large difference? Neither method is ideal, or "correct," and they differ fundamentally. Clayton draws a historical parallel between veterans' benefits from earlier U.S. wars, while the Defense Department uses a "pure forecast" of benefits that a specified number of veterans can expect to receive, based upon half of VA costs per veteran over the past sixteen years. It is impossible to say in the abstract which method is "better"—a historical parallel or a pure forecast. Instead, we must examine the major differences between the two to decide which seems more reasonable.

Which Benefits Should Be Counted? / The Pentagon argues that only half of veterans' benefits should be counted as part of the cost of the war, on the ground that the other half would have been a charge on the public purse even if the war had not taken place. Its analysts believe that in the future nonservice-connected *veterans'* benefits will be no more generous than benefits available to ordinary citizens. In this sense they reject the applicability of historical parallels, because after earlier wars veterans *did* receive many more benefits than were available to the ordinary citizen.

The contrary argument is that the Veterans' Administration disburses public funds to veterans under legislation that Congress passes for the express purpose of rewarding veterans for the sacrifices they have made. Politically powerful veterans' groups regard these benefits as a right and therefore they had better remain a part of any measure of the cost of the war. As for the future, benefits available to Vietnam war veterans may be expanded, and if so, they will probably not be extended to other groups until much later; large-scale federal aid to education, for example, was not introduced until about twenty years after World War II's GI Bill of Rights. Possibly, also, a coalition of conservative politicians may succeed in accelerating the rate at which the Nixon-Ford administration is curtailing the government's social and economic programs, but if so, veterans' benefits would almost certainly be exempted so that once again, as during most of U.S. history, veterans would be receiving more generous treatment than other citizens.

Current Prices or Discounted Future Values?

The estimated ultimate values of Vietnam war veterans' benefits are shown in Table 14–4 in current prices, in line with the policy of using current prices for all estimates contained in this book. The same procedure is followed in reporting the costs of U.S. wars in Table 383 in the *Statistical Abstract* for 1972. As an alternative, the attempt could have been made to show future costs in terms of discounted present values and past costs in terms of the purchasing power of some selected year. In theory, at least, that would have made the estimates more easily comparable through time, but it would have produced a hodgepodge of price- and time-adjusted figures that could have been compared with one another and with readily available published figures only with great difficulty. The Defense Department itself, in discussing its own costs, always stresses current dollar figures. The most frequently used Defense Department estimates of the budgetary cost of the war, for example, ($140 billion total cost and $112 billion incremental cost) are current price estimates covering a span of years in which average prices paid by the federal government rose some 65 percent.

How Many Veterans? / Another reason the Defense Department's estimate of Vietnam war veterans' benefits is so extremely low is that it is based upon a very restricted view of the number of veterans that should be counted. In other U.S. wars, all personnel who served were counted as veterans, eligible for benefits, because they had served in this or that war. For the Vietnam war, however, the Defense Department did not even estimate with its seven methods the cost of *all* personnel who served in the war, but only the cost of *incremental* personnel.

The department's analysts point out in defense of their methods, that even in the absence of overt wars such as in Vietnam, "we create an immense number of veterans in normal peacetime operations, and would have created over 5 million of them without the war, had we simply kept on as we were after 1964." That is, because of its "enormous turnover in military personnel," the department argues that more than 5 million of the 6.6 million veterans it actually created in 1964–73 would have been created through the normal turnover of its military personnel. This high turnover is a key factor in its calculation of an incremental increase of only about 1 million military personnel because of the war.

All seven of the methods used to estimate the incremental number of veterans provided smaller totals than other methods might have done. For example, U.S. military strength in the fiscal year 1974 is more than 15 percent less than it was in fiscal 1964, and in arriving at an estimate of the cost of the 1965–73 phase of the war, one should at least consider that if the detente that began in 1963–64 had not been aborted by the war, the armed forces could have been reduced as early as 1965. This would sharply have increased the incremental number of veterans forced to serve because of the war. Also, the incremental number of veterans would have been higher if base line force requirements set forth by responsible independent agencies, such as the Brookings Institution and the Urban Coalition, had been introduced into the calculations along with those of the Defense Department itself.

How Large the Benefits?
The Defense Department's estimate of the cost of the Vietnam war veterans' benefits that is most directly comparable to Professor Clayton's estimate is $22.1 billion, stated in current (1974) dollars

TABLE 14–7

THE DEFENSE DEPARTMENT'S ESTIMATES OF VIETNAM WAR VETERANS' BENEFITS AS A PERCENT OF THE WAR'S ORIGINAL COST AND OF AVERAGE GNP DURING THE WAR YEARS

Veterans' Benefits (Defense Department Estimates)	As Percents of Four Estimates of the War's Original Cost				As Percents of Average GNP During the War Years
	$112 b	*$140 b*	*$155 b*	*Av of 3*	
$22.1 bil	19.7	15.8	14.3	16.6	2.8
$11.1 bil	9.9	7.9	7.2	8.3	1.4

Source: Table 14–4, Table 14–5, and text.

and including both service-connected and nonservice-connected benefits. It will be recalled that the Department believes only half of this sum, or $11.1 billion, should be counted as a cost of the war because the other half would probably represent payments for other than service-connected disabilities. One way to approach these estimates is to compare them with veterans' benefits from past wars as a percentage of the original costs of the wars and as a percentage of average GNP during the war years. These percentages applicable to the Vietnam war are shown in Table 14–7. It uses the same three alternative estimates of the original cost of the Vietnam war that are used in Table 14–4, and also an average of these three estimates.

Concerning the comparison with the war's original cost, benefits would be 16.6 percent and 8.3 percent of the average of the three alternative estimates of the cost of the war, depending on whether all benefits or only service-connected benefits are counted. Concerning the comparison with average GNP during the war years, the parallel percentages would be 2.8 and 1.4. These very low percentages are in sharp contrast to the historical record shown in Tables 14–3 and 14–5. History shows that for all past U.S. wars, veterans' benefits averaged 319 percent of the original cost of the war, and that for the four most recent wars the estimated percentage is 210 percent. Similar percentages of GNP during past war years average 123 percent for the three most recent U.S. wars. When "pure forecasts" of economic variables differ so extremely from all previous comparable historical experience, they must be rejected as unhelpful.

In estimating the cost of future veterans' benefits, the estimator's confidence is not enhanced by the knowledge that past conscientious efforts to forecast VA outlays have not been successful. In fact, two of the best-known ones have been very much too low. John M. Clark, in a memorable 1931 study of World War I costs,[14] estimated that less than $100 million a year would be paid to that war's veterans by 1975, but in 1970 they were already nineteen times that large, at $1.9 billion. Twenty-five years later, in 1956, the President's Commission on Veterans' Pensions (the Bradley Commission) predicted that VA expenditures would not reach $6 billion a year until 1985, but they did so in 1964—twenty-one years ahead of schedule.[15]

The most satisfactory estimate at present is believed to be the $233 billion estimate in Table 14–8. It bears the same proportion to the estimated $155 billion unofficial estimate of the full cost of the Vietnam war that estimates of veterans' benefits from the most recent two U.S. wars (World War II and the Korean War) bear to the original costs of those wars (141 percent). This proportion is very much smaller than similar proportions for four of the last five United States wars (see Table 14–3).

Extra-Budgetary Economic Costs

In estimating the cost of the war, the Defense Department was, of course, estimating only its budgetary cost, and even this only within

TABLE 14–8

FUTURE BUDGETARY COSTS OF THE VIETNAM WAR
($ billions)

1. Making up postponed investments in military facilities*	6.7
2. U.S. government's postwar costs in Southeast Asia (20 years)	40.0
3. Vietnam war veterans' benefits (ultimate cost)	233.0
4. Interest on Vietnam war debt**	25.1
Total	304.8

* One-half of $13.5 billion estimate by Defense Department in Joint Economic Committee Hearings, June 6, 1969, p. 318, and June 12, 1969, p. 691. See accompanying text for justification of taking one-half.

** Midpoint between $22 billion estimate by Professor Clayton (Table 8–1) and $28.2 billion estimate by Tom Riddell.

its own time and content constraints. The economic cost of the war over time will be vastly greater than its budgetary cost from fiscal 1965 to 1973. But even during those years, when the bulk of the fighting took place, the economic cost of the war was greater than its budgetary cost. Two major items are taken up under the heading of extra-budgetary economic cost. First, the extra economic cost associated with the drafting of servicemen and secondly, the foregone earnings of servicemen who were killed while fighting the war.

The men and women in the U.S. armed forces increased by 900,000 from 1965 to the wartime peak in 1968, but the U.S. government did not pay the market price for their services. Instead, many were remunerated at rates of pay far below even the minimum wage set for civilian labor. The true economic cost of the services of drafted servicemen and of reluctant volunteers was not the low pay they received but rather what they would have been earning and producing in jobs of their own choice if they had not been forcibly drafted. Estimates of the monetary value of these earnings that were sacrificed by men in the armed forces vary widely, depending upon which of many different plausible assumptions are used in making the estimate.

An impressive and often-quoted estimate of the added economic cost of the Vietnam war attributable to the drafting of servicemen is by Professor Robert Eisner of Northwestern University. Professor Eisner constructed a supply curve for voluntary recruits to the armed forces based on estimates by the President's Commission on an All-Volunteer Armed Force (the Gates Commission)[16] of the added budgetary cost of volunteer armed forces of different sizes. His purpose, he writes, is to "attempt to answer the question as to how much more [would have] had to be paid to maintain a volunteer armed force for the Vietnam war than would have had to be paid to maintain a presumably smaller force in peacetime."[17] His estimates of this cost for the Vietnam war years through 1970 are shown in Table 14–9.

Professor Eisner used the planned size of the armed forces for 1970 (3.456 million) whereas the actual size turned out to be 3.066 million. After making this and certain other adjustments to his calculations, Cornell University's Air War Study Group arrived at an estimate of $60 billion for the excess of the economic over the budgetary cost of the draft for the years 1966–71.[18]

Professor Eisner's estimate is a comprehensive one. Among other things it is intended to allow for "costs to the economy of actions to avoid the draft, such as prolongation of student status and uneco-

TABLE 14–9

ESTIMATES OF ADDED ECONOMIC COST OF CONSCRIPTION

Fiscal Year	Average Armed Forces (millions of men)	Added Cost of Conscription (billions of $ 1970)
1966	2.870	2.9
1967	3.344	13.9
1968	3.483	19.5
1969	3.534	21.8
1970	3.456 (est.)	18.3
1966–70		76.4

Source: Robert Eisner, "The War and the Economy" in Sam Brown and Len Ackland, eds., *Why Are We Still in Vietnam?* (New York: Random House, 1970), p. 119.

Servicemen who fought the Vietnam war were paid much less than the market value of their services. Therefore, the true economic cost of the war must include an estimate of the difference between their low military pay and what they would have been earning if they had been working in jobs of their own choosing.

Making use of this relationship, Professor Eisner has estimated how much more it would have cost to fight the Vietnam war with an all-volunteer force than we would have had to pay for a smaller armed force in the absence of the war. This table contains his estimates.

---

nomic occupational choice, as well as other, extra nonmilitary costs related to the draft." He adds that "estimates of added budgetary costs of a volunteer armed force are measures of the 'conscription tax,' or the serviceman's evaluation of that part of the value of his military service for which he is not paid when he is drafted."[19] Professor Eisner believes his estimates of the market-oriented cost concept that he sets out to measure are conservative.

It is possible to take a more narrow view of the extra economic cost of conscription. The estimate summarized in Table 14–10 seeks to measure only the direct cost to the men who participated in the war and compares their beginning military pay with the earnings of beginning civilian workers. It completely ignores, for example, "the fact that many draftees or 'reluctant volunteers' would have been quite unwilling to choose freely military service at the same wage as

TABLE 14–10

ESTIMATE OF SACRIFICED CIVILIAN EARNINGS BY MEN SERVING IN THE VIETNAM WAR

$5,400 Average between yearly wage of beginning un-skilled blue-collar worker and beginning civil-service worker (FS-3 or wage-board 5)[1]
−$1,655 Military base pay, grade E-2 (private)[2]
=$3,745 Difference between GI's pay and earnings from roughly equivalent civilian jobs

2,582,650 Man-years spent by U.S. servicemen in Vietnam (sum of year by year averages, 1965–72)
+1,291,325 Estimated man-years of Vietnam war backup troops[3]
=3,873,975 Estimated man-years spent by U.S. servicemen on Vietnam war

$3,745 × 3,873,975 = $14.6 billion aggregate difference be-tween pay of Vietnam war troops and earnings from roughly equivalent civil-ian jobs, 1965–72.

[1] Roughly equivalent civilian earnings cited by Roger T. Kelly, assistant secretary of defense, in Hearings before the U.S. House of Representatives Committee on Armed Services, February 1971.

[2] July 1967 rate adjusted to average 1970 rate to be made comparable to civilian earnings. Data from Department of Defense (Comptroller), *The Economics of Defense Spending,* July 1972, pp. 132, 134.

[3] Military personnel in line of communication and training at approximately half of military personnel in Vietnam. Charles Schultze and Associates, *Setting National Priorities, The 1971 Budget;* The Brookings Institution, Washington, D.C., 1970, p. 51.

This table contains a rock-bottom minimal estimate of the economic sacrifice exacted from U.S. servicemen who fought the war in Vietnam, due to the fact that military pay was lower than the civilian wages they might have been earning. It is based on the difference between beginning military pay during the war years and the beginning wages of civilian workers at that time.

It is a minimal estimate because (1) it applies only to men who fought in Vietnam rather than to all servicemen who were added because of the war and (2) it compares military pay to only the lowest-paid civilian jobs.

they might have earned as a civilian."[20] It also assumes that all draftees and reluctant volunteers would have been employed at relatively unremunerative rates of pay if they had retained their civilian status, in arriving at its estimate of $14.6 billion. Thus, it is probably a minimal estimate of how large the excess of the economic over the budgetary cost of the draft would be. The figure contained in Table 14–11 ($37 billion) is about midway between Professor Eisner's estimate (as amended to $60 billion) and this minimal estimate.

TABLE 14–11

EXTRA-BUDGETARY ECONOMIC COSTS OF THE WAR
($ billions)

1. Excess of economic over budgetary cost of the draft	$37.0
2. Foregone earnings of deceased U.S. servicemen*	33.7
Total	$70.7

*The product of 56,245 men times $15,000 times 40 years = $33.7 billion.

Indirect Costs and Burdens

To catalog the social and political indirect costs of the Vietnam war would be a grim undertaking indeed, and one could justify assigning dollar costs to some of them. An attempt might be made to quantify the investment in human capital that might have taken place except for the war's displacement of educational outlays at all levels; assumptions could have been made about how productive the billions of dollars poured into the war might have been if they had been invested in the country's physical capital stock instead; that part of the cost of the higher crime rate resulting from the intensified neglect of our inner cities and their unfortunate inhabitants because of the war could have been estimated; similarly, with the part of the drug problem that can be attributed, directly and indirectly, to the war.[21] The list could go on, but the tie-in to the war would become increasingly tenuous and difficult to fix objectively. A line must be drawn someplace between costs that are and costs that are not mainly attributable to the war. The costs described in this chapter represent one man's judgment of where to draw the line.

Some readers may be surprised to find the recession of 1970–72 and a measure of excess inflation in 1969–72 included among the indirect costs and burdens of the war. First, consider the recession. If we imagine the economy in 1965–72 as it might have been without the war, it also would not have had the strong inflationary thrust of 1966–68. Without that kind of inflation, a Friedmanesque administra-

TABLE 14–12

INDIRECT COSTS AND BURDENS OF THE WAR
($ billions)

Vietnam recession of 1970–72	$185
Net effect of excess inflation on the monetary value of GNP, 1969–72	140
Increased net foreign indebtedness resulting from deterioration of net exports, 1964–65 to 1972	45
Impoverishment resulting from worsened international terms of trade after February 1973 (annual rate)	8
Total	$378

tion (if it could have been elected absent the war) would not have been determined to cut back demand at a time when the underacknowledged war was also subtracting demand, thus precipitating the recession. Secondly, how about the inflation that has grown almost continuously more serious ever since the Vietnam war escalation started? It simply does not seem appropriate to leave it out in the counting up the cost of the war. To most economists it does not fit the description of an economic cost, although most would have to agree that it probably represents the single most painful effect of the war to the vast majority of Americans. The method used to assign a dollar value to inflation through the year 1972 as one of the social burdens of the war is explained below.

If You Add It All Up

When all four major categories of cost are brought together as in Table 14–13, they add up to the enormous sum of approximately $900 billion. This sum is so vast it defies comparison with anything except the gross national product itself. That is, in order of magnitude terms, the calculable dollar economic cost of the Vietnam war is roughly on a par with the $930 billion value of all goods and services produced in the United States in 1969, one of the peak years of war spending. We must add at once that not all of this sum had to be paid at one time, nor does all of it have to be taken away from us in the form of taxes. Moreover, we must recall that the most basic costs of wars cannot be measured in dollars at all but take their toll in the form of lost and broken lives, the degradation of public life and the brutalization of peoples' attitudes. It must also be admitted that the time periods covered by the estimates are, in the nature of the case, somewhat arbitrary. For the Pentagon, the war "began" on June 30, 1964, but the estimates in this book go back to the immediate post-World War II years when the United States began pouring funds into Vietnam. Most estimates end with calendar years 1972 or 1973, but since most Veterans Administration spending for the war is still to come, this component of its cost is projected into the future.

The figure of about $900 billion for the identifiable dollar cost of the war to the American economy seems certain to arouse controversy. One reason it will be controversial is because we economists usually look at relatively short-term marginal changes in our figures instead of trying to estimate the cost over a period of years of a single massive blunder in government policy. In arriving at an estimated dollar equivalent of the economic cost of the war, I do not for a moment claim that the Vietnam war was the *only* unfavorable economic factor operating on the economy in the 1960s and early 1970s. I claim only that it was by far the *major* one and that it, and it alone, provides the thread of continuity that gives unity and meaning to the wretched performance of the U.S. economy in the years after 1964.

TABLE 14–13

DOLLAR COST OF THE VIETNAM WAR— THE ESTIMATES COMBINED
($ billions)

Past budgetary costs (Table 14–1)	$128.4–171.5
Future budgetary costs (Table 14–7)	304.8
Extra-budgetary costs (Table 14–10)	70.7
Indirect costs and burdens (Table 14–11)	378.0
Total	$882–925

Table 8–6 brings together estimates of the economic cost of the war Defense Department comptroller that "there is no one correct basis for stating the cost of the war." This table groups the war's costs into four different categories: *past* budgetary costs to the U.S. government, *future* budgetary costs to the U.S. government, *extra*budgetary economic costs, and *indirect* costs and burdens.

Cost figures on such a gigantic scale are awkward to deal with and difficult to comprehend. The dollar figures cover a period of more than one hundred years and take no account of past or future inflations. If we yield to the temptation and add them up, they total about $900 billion, a figure so enormous that it defies comparison except with the size of the U.S. GNP itself, which was $930 billion in 1969.

It is not easy to comprehend a cost of such great magnitude—in part because of its sheer size and in part because it was built up from diverse sources and covers a span of more than one hundred years. Another reason it is hard to grasp is that a certain ambiguity attaches to the very word "cost" itself. This is a word that most people use unreflectively, perhaps as many as several times a day, but it is nevertheless a word that can have a number of different connotations. If we go back over the twenty individual components that make up the total in Table 14–13, we find that as many as *ten* different connotations of the word "cost" are used in one or more components. And yet most people think they know more-or-less exactly what they mean by "cost." These are the ten different connotations of the word we have been using.

1/ Cost in its traditional economic sense of forgoing alternatives—in this case the things we might have done in 1965–74 instead of fighting the Vietnam war. When Washington shifted the nation's priorities we gave less money and attention to domestic social concerns such as the war on poverty, model cities, education, and new residential housing and devoted more to one particularly ill-starred military project.

2/ Cost in its most basic economic sense of forgoing productive activity altogether. Many billions of dollars of goods and services will never come into existence that might have been produced by young men killed while fighting the war. Others, those who were wounded, will be paid veterans' pensions instead of making the full-bodied economic contributions they might have made. Also, the Vietnam recession of 1970–72 cost the nation billions of dollars' worth of nonproduced goods and services.

3/ Cost in the sense of spending vast sums of money to draft men into the military forces, to equip them with expensive weapons, and to send them to war. The Defense Department's estimate of the incremental cost of the war represents cost in this sense.

4/ Cost to these men in the sense of having to allocate their time to less remunerative and less desirable activities than they would have engaged in as civilians. Professor Eisner's market-oriented estimate of "the conscription tax" is designed to quantify this cost.

5/ Cost in the sense of re-equipping soldiers and paying them more because they have been assigned to more dangerous tasks. In part this cost is measured by the difference between the Defense Department's full and incremental war cost estimates.

6/ Cost in the sense of having to build facilities in the future that should have been built in the past. This kind of cost is typified by the extent to which the Defense Department will have to carry out construction projects and maintenance costs in the future that were postponed because of the war.

7/ Cost in the sense of taxes that we and our descendants will have to pay in the future because the Vietnam war was fought. Interest payments on the Vietnam war debt and benefits Vietnam veterans will receive fall into this category. Economists usually play down the significance of cost in this sense, calling it "a mere transfer payment" because the government levies taxes in order to pay interest and veterans' benefits. That may be how it looks to a statistician who is measuring the gross national product, but it is a solid *cost* to those taxpayers who are neither veterans nor holders of government debt.

8/ Costs in the sense of expensive military gifts given by the U.S. government in the name of the American people to Southeast Asian military regimes that cannot stay in power without them. These too are "merely transfer payments" to those who estimate gross national product, but they go outside the country and are a charge against the productive power of the U.S. economy.

9/ Cost in the sense of a general loss in value of United States gross national product compared to the gross products of many other countries. The effect of the war-induced inflation in causing a deterioration of the U.S. international terms of trade illustrates cost in this sense.

10/ Cost in the sense of increased debt owed by the American economy as a whole to the rest of the world because of the sharp increase in the U.S. balance of payments deficit arising from the war and the inflation it generated.

Besides lumping together dollar cost estimates comprising "costs" in all of these different senses of the word, the approximately $900 billion in Table 14–13 includes a large component that does not fit the usual definition of cost at all—a measure of the amount by which war-induced excess inflation raised the monetary value of the GNP without increasing its real value. Finally, because the estimates a span of more than one hundred years, they are harder to comprehend, however expressed. Most of the estimates are expressed in current, or "ordinary," dollars and have not been processed to take out price changes or to adjust for widely separated points in time.

Among the four main categories of war cost estimates in Table 14–

13, by far the largest two categories are the indirect costs and the future budgetary costs. Strange as it seems, these are the two aspects of its cost that are most often ignored in many accounts of the cost of the war. Many such accounts emphasize only its past budgetary cost to the U.S. government, but in Table 14–13 this accounted for only about one-fifth of all the items shown in the table.

APPENDIX A

INFLATION AND GOVERNMENT POLICY

In this appendix we discuss the general problem of inflation and how the responsible agencies of the U.S. government are supposed to deal with it. To some readers this will be a familiar story, but to those not already familiar with the economics of inflation, this digression provides a valuable background for understanding the main theme of the critical years 1965–68 when the government failed to keep its Vietnam war from injecting the virulent strain of inflation into the civilian economy that is still ravaging it.

In all modern economies it is now an accepted responsibility of governments to try to prevent both inflation and deflation from gaining a foothold, because both can be extremely disruptive—economically, socially, and politically.[1]

In the 1930s governments did not act either wisely or in time to prevent the Great Depression from erupting, spreading around the world, and paving the way for the rise of ruthless dictators and the outbreak of World War II. In the years since World War II governments have proven themselves able to avert another great depression, but they have been far less successful in controlling inflation.

Modern-day inflations are of two general types: demand-pull and cost-push. In a demand-pull inflation, demand exceeds supply and buyers compete against one another for limited supplies, thus "pulling" prices upward. In a cost-push inflation, upward pressure on prices comes from the cost side (that is, the supply side) rather than from the demand side and *sellers* are said to "push" prices upward as they pass their cost increases along to buyers. Sometimes, when a strong cost-price spiral gets under way, it is not easy to tell whether demand-pull or cost-push is dominant at any one time. At other times, however, it is not difficult to tell which of the two is dominant in causing prices to start upward. For many years economists stressed the dangers of demand-pull inflation to the exclusion of concern about the cost-push variety. They felt that competition could be relied upon to keep costs down and that, therefore, any increase in prices must be due to the effects of excess demand. Today, however, most economists have abandoned this view.

The initial impact of the Vietnam war on the U.S. economy was to activate a demand-pull inflation, because the government stepped up its demands on the economy when it was already fully employed. That is to say, in 1965–68 the sharp increase in government *demand* "pulled" prices up at a time when additional *supply* was very difficult to come by. The productive power of the economy is justly famous, however, and by 1969 supply had caught up and there was no longer any excess demand in the economy. By 1969, in other words, the inflation had transformed itself into one of the cost-push type in which labor, management, and moneylenders were all demanding higher rewards, in part because they expected inflation to continue. Since one man's rewards are another man's costs, cost-push inflation took over and "pushed" prices upward in 1969–71.

Historically, price rises resulting from cost-push inflations have been less serious than those resulting from demand-pull inflations, but once started, cost-push type inflations may be harder to bring under control. There are six main policies a government can introduce, either singly or in combination, to protect the economy from an inflation the government itself sets off by sharply increasing its spending. In the years since 1965 the government has resorted to all of them at one time or another, although haltingly, erratically, and ineffectively.

1/ *Increase taxation.* If the government decides to increase its spending sharply, as for the Vietnam war, a simple way to protect against inflation would be to increase taxes by a similiar amount so that the increase in government spending would be offset by a decline in private incomes. The 10 percent income-tax surcharge took effect in July 1968, but that was more than three years after the main decision had been made to escalate the war.

2/ Decrease other government spending. In theory, an alternative way to offset increased spending for the Vietnam war would have been to curtail other government spending by an amount equal to the increase in war expenditures. However, the increase in the cost of the Vietnam war was too rapid and too great for this technique to have been practicable if used alone. However, after the war inflation got under way the Defense Department did cut back on its non-Vietnam war spending and President Johnson forced cuts in the antipoverty program and elsewhere in the government.

3/ Reduce the money supply and/or tighten credit. This third policy instrument rests with the Federal Reserve System, a quasi-autonomous body, rather than with the President and Congress as the first two do. According to economic theory, any inflation can be ultimately choked off if it is denied an adequate money supply. But monetary policy works abitrarily and only after indeterminate lags, and there were severe practical obstacles to its use to offset the effects of the Vietnam war when it was tried in 1966 and 1969.

4/ Encourage imports and/or discourage exports. More imports, by adding to the supply of goods in a country, can help to keep its prices from rising so fast, while a decline in exports reduces the pressure of demand at home. Reducing import barriers and/or revaluing the currency (that is, increasing its international value) are familiar ways of trying to accomplish these purposes. In the case of the United States in the late 1960s, however, twenty-odd years of excess military spending abroad had so weakened the balance of payments that neither of these policies was feasible. Instead, a collapse of confidence in the dollar in 1971–73 forced a *devaluation* of the dollar which made inflation worse.

5/ Direct wage and price controls. These are very unpopular with most economists and with centers of economic power such as big business and big labor. When matters got out of hand by the summer of 1971, however, because other available measures had not been used properly, the Nixon administration reluctantly turned to direct controls. But like the other inflation preventives, direct controls, too, were used ineffectively. Besides being too late, they were not carefully coordinated with government policies in other fields and they were relaxed prematurely in early 1973, making possible the two-digit inflation of 1974 and 1975.

6/ *An incomes policy.* This term, more widely used in Europe than in the United States, refers to government efforts of various kinds to persuade business and labor to refrain from pushing their price- and wage-setting powers to the limit in a full employment economy. In other words, it denotes a government policy of trying to induce business and labor to limit their incomes voluntarily. The method of doing so differs from country to country. In the United States, the Council of Economic Advisers set voluntary wage-price guideposts in 1962 and asked labor and management not to exceed them. This is the weakest of all controls, sometimes referred to as "jawboning," because it does not have the sanction of law. The guideposts were helpful in 1962–65 when the economy itself was in a healthy state. They collapsed under the impact of inflation in 1966, but the administration plaintively invoked them for a long time after the chance of their being effective had expired.

Given these six types of overall policies to control inflation, how, one may ask, are they to be decided upon and carried out in practice in the gigantic, highly complex, American economy?

Under the American system of governmental checks and balances, overall economic stabilization policies are mainly the result of various actions and interactions among three different agencies of government. The executive branch—ultimately the President himself—proposes economic policies (except monetary policies), Congress disposes of his proposals according to its own preferences and antiquated system of rules, while the Federal Reserve System is responsible for setting monetary goals and policies.

Within the executive branch the President relies almost exclusively on three government agencies to advise him on matters of high-level economic policy.

1/ *Office of Management and Budget (until 1970, the Bureau of the Budget).* This is the key agency on expenditure policies. In preparing the President's budget message (submitted to Congress every Januury and covering the government's fiscal year commencing in the following July), it reviews the spending plans of all federal agencies and, in theory, at least, is concerned with how national priorities are set.[2]

2/ *The Treasury Department.* The Treasury is charged with financing government expenditures, either through collecting taxes or borrowing in the nation's capital markets. Treasury economists advise the President and Congress concerning new taxes and the adjustment of existing taxes in order to lromote economic stability. The Treasury also, rather than the State Department, is responsible for U.S. international monetary and financial policy.

3/ The Council of Economic Advisers. The CEA is headed by three economists appointed by the President. These men, with the aid of a relatively small staff, advise the President on all aspects of overall economic policy. It has no administrative responsibilities, spends little money, and has no constituency—except the President. It was set up by the Employment Act of 1946 (sometimes called the Full Employment Act) to assist the President in achieving the broad purposes of the act, the most significant of which was "to promote maximum employment, production, and purchasing power."

These three agencies are known collectively in Washington vernacular as "the troika" (a Russian vehicle drawn by three horses abreast). Their relationships to one another, to the President, and to Congress differ from one administration to another depending upon the personalities involved and, especially, upon the particular President's style of operation. G. L. Bach, a careful student of economic policy-making in Washington, describes their relationships during the Vietnam war buildup as follows:

> *[Under President Kennedy] the troika rapidly developed into a powerful forum for discussing overall government economic policy. The chairman (William McChesney Martin) was invited from the Federal Reserve, making a quadriad, when the issues being discussed involved monetary policy. The President himself usually attended meetings; he was intrigued by issues of economic policy and read avidly the memos sent to him. . . .*

> *President Johnson, unlike his predecessor, had little interest in detailed discussions of economic issues. The quadriad, which had thrived under President Kennedy, gradually atrophied, not by design, but because it did not well serve the Johnson administration's style.*[3]

As this passage suggests, the Federal Reserve's role in overall policy-making is less easy to categorize than the roles of the troika agencies. Its seven-member board of governors is the seat of ultimate power in the American banking system and is appointed by the President. Overall monetary policies are usually made by the Federal Open Market Committee, so named because it determines the Fed's purchases and sales of government securities "in the open market." These purchase and sales operations have become the major channel through which the Fed affects the size of reserves held by commercial banks. It is the size of these reserves, in turn, that affect the money supply, because they determine how much credit the banks can extend to the private sector of the economy. Federal Reserve authorities also can change the ratio of commercial banks' reserves to deposits (a power rarely used), and they can raise or lower the Federal Reserve discount rate, which is the interest rate member commercial banks must pay to borrow from the Federal Reserve Bank. Discount rate changes have come to have great psychological importance, because they are interpreted as a symbol of changes in the Fed's monetary policies.

Relations among the executive branch, Congress, and the Federal Reserve vary in cordiality from time to time, although the effectiveness of each is obviously dependent on the cooperation of the other two. The Fed is nominally free to set monetary policy independently of both Congress and the President, but the record shows that it has usually adjusted its philosophy and policy orientation to conform broadly with the dominant views of whatever presidential administration is in power. There is often more tension between Congress and the President and between Congress and the Fed, although under the heavy impact of the Vietnam war relations among all three became severely strained from time to time.

NOTES

CHAPTER 1
ECONOMIC CONSEQUENCES OF THE WAR IN VIETNAM:
HOW SIGNIFICANT WERE THEY?

1. The South Vietnamese embassy estimated 30 percent of the civilian casualties were children under the age of thirteen years. "Impact of the Vietnam War," Foreign Affairs Division, Congressional Research Service, Library of Congress, Washington, D.C., 1971.

2. Accepting the Defense Department's official estimate of the cost of the war ($140 billion), this means U.S. taxpayers paid more than $150,000 per corpse.

3. Library of Congress. "Impact of the Vietnam War," p. 11.

4. Peter R. Kann, "War and More War," Wall Street Journal, December 22, 1972.

5. In a widely noted study, Professor Wassily Leontief pointed out that if the cost of the Vietnam war in 1967 were to be distributed to all of the civilian sectors of the economy, say by a tax cut, the average increase in business and personal expenditures in that year would have been 3.9 percent. Wassily Leontief, "Economic Effect of Vietnam War Spending," U.S. Congress Joint Economic Committee Hearings, April 27, 1967.

6. Arthur M. Okun, The Political Economy of Prosperity (New York: W.W. Norton, The Brookings Institution, 1970), p. 62.

7. Withal, he received overoptimistic reports from both his military and economic advisers. His Council of Economic Advisers wrote in January 1966: "The Vietnam conflict finds us well prepared. The procurement and personnel increases are modest . . . by comparison with total supply capabilities." For national defense spending the council included in its projections for the fiscal year 1966–67 a $10.3 billion increase over the fiscal year 1964–65, a sum of money only 46 percent as large as the increase that actually occurred. See President's Council of Economic Advisers, Economic Report of the President, 1966 (Washington, D.C.: U.S. Government Printing Office), p. 59.

8. "In only seven other countries of the world is total output in a year as large as the increase in our output last year." Lyndon B. Johnson, Economic

Message to Congress, January 27, 1966. Reprinted in U.S. Council of Economic Advisers, *Economic Report of the President, 1966* (Washington, D.C.: U.S. Government Printing Office), p. 6.

9. Budget of the United States, fiscal year 1966, presented to Congress January 25, 1965, p. 68.

10. Lyndon Johnson's view of his Southeast Asian adversary is well known. He once expressed it colorfully to John McCone, director of the CIA, in upbraiding him because, Johnson complained, the CIA did not "even know anything about a raggedyass little fourth-rate country" like North Vietnam. David Halberstam, *The Best and the Brightest,* New York: Random House, 1972, p. 512.

11. U.S. Senate, Committees on Armed Services and Appropriations, "Supplemental Military Procurement and Construction Authorizations, Fiscal Year 1967," January 1967, pp. 96–97.

12. Figure 3–2 also records the Nixon administration's economic recession of 1970–71 when total output stagnated for about a year and a half. By the end of 1970 the gap between actual and potential GNP was proportionally larger than at any other time shown excepting only the years 1958 and 1960.

13. The Defense Materials System, in effect since the end of the Korean War to assure military priority over civilian orders in case of conflict, continued to be used in on-the-spot situations but was no substitute for an overall economic mobilization plan. (See President's Council of Economic Advisers' 1966 *Report,* p. 60.)

14. A former high State Department official writes, for example, that in Vietnam affairs "Defense Department officials seemed to run the show on both military and non-military matters . . . while the State Department seemed resigned to playing a reactive, even peripheral, role." Chester L. Cooper, *The Lost Crusade,* (New York: Dodd, Mead, 1970), p. 255. For a similar view by another former high State Department official, see Roger Hilsman, *To Move a Nation* (Garden City, N.Y.: Doubleday, 1967).

15. This irresponsible behavior by the American government toward the economy was unique to the Vietnam war. During both World War II and the Korean War Washington succeeded reasonably well in protecting the civilian economy from the direct inflationary effects of war. After World War II, when Congress was considering Marshall Plan aid to Europe, it conducted detailed studies to determine whether the domestic economy could withstand the inflationary effects of large foreign aid appropriations. Finally, in 1954 the Eisenhower administration carefully considered what it would have cost to go to war in Vietnam to help the French and then decided not to do so.

16. Murray L. Weidenbaum, "After Vietnam: Our Vietnamized Economy," *The Saturday Review,* May 24, 1969.

17. Ibid.

18. R.P. Oliver, "The Employment Effect of Defense Expenditures," *Monthly Labor Review,* September 1967.

19. Weidenbaum, "After Vietnam."

20. The full cost of the war, according to the present official definition, was used to calculate the percentages in Figure 1–9.

CHAPTER 2
THE VIETNAM WAR:
LANDMARKS ON THE WAY IN AND ON THE WAY OUT

1. In 1967 the United States maintained defense commitments to 46 countries; it had 302 major military bases overseas. U.S. House of Representatives, Subcommittee of the Committee on Appropriations, Department of Defense Appropriations for 1973, Hearings Part III, p. 167.

2. In other words, the U.S. government spent almost 2 1/2 times as much fighting for the status quo in one small underdeveloped country as it spent "promoting economic development" in *all* less developed countries in a quarter of a century.

3. Estimates of the aid North Vietnam received from the USSR and China vary, but the total probably did not exceed $4 or $5 billion over the *entire period of the war.* This is the equivalent of about *two months'* spending on the war by the U.S. government at its peak in 1968 and 1969. Neither of the two giants of the Communist world wished to get more involved than they felt necessary in a war in Southeast Asia. Hanoi sought to remain neutral in the struggle between them since it needed aid from both. They, in turn, quarreled about supplying the aid. China accused the USSR of not supplying enough modern weaponry and the USSR accused China of obstructing the flow of Soviet aid to the North Vietnamese.

A view of the war that many Americans eventually came to share was put forward early in 1967. "American aggression is . . . the cause of the war in Vietnam. . . . The U.S. government alleges that the vital interests of the Americans are jeopardized in Vietnam. But in this way it is possible to declare any part of the earth, any island or continent, to be a sphere of their interests. It is not difficult to imagine the chaos that would set in in international relations if other world powers were to start acting in a similar way. . . . There can be no toleration of claims of any state to a special position in the world, to its right to decide the fate of other peoples, to institute a quarantine for entire areas against social and political . . . [change]." Premier Aleksei N. Kosygin of the USSR, quoted in the *New York Times,* February 9, 1967.

4. Different people became disenchanted with the war at different times. The following memorable remarks by Sen. John Stennis of Mississippi, chairman of the Senate Armed Services Committee, were made on April 25, 1967. "I don't know just how much a westerner can teach an Asiatic in an Asiatic country about self-government, or how fast this can be done. They have their ideas about those things and we have ours. I am beginning to feel like there is

a missed connection there in some way." Testimony before the Joint Economic Committee, p. 94.

George F. Kennan, who originated the doctrine of "containing" communism when he was at the U.S. State Department, characterized Johnson's Vietnam policy as a "massive miscalculation and an error . . . for which it is hard to find any parallels in our history." Kennan portrayed Johnson and his advisers as behaving "like men in a dream, seemingly insensitive to outside opinion, seemingly unable to arrive at any realistic assessment of the effects of their own acts." *New York Times,* February 29, 1968.

About two months earlier, Gen. David M. Shoup, retired U.S. Marine Corps Commandant, said Johnson's contention that the Vietnam war was vital to United States interests was "pure, unadulterated poppycock." *New York Times,* December 19, 1967.

5. "Military spending . . . tends to have first claim [on the federal budget] with nondefense programs getting what is left over despite the urgency of their demands. . . . In both the Truman administration before the Korean War and in the Eisenhower administration after it, the tendency was to deduct the estimated cost of domestic programs from anticipated federal revenues . . . and then allocate the remainder to the military." Adam Yarmolinsky, *The Military Establishment* (New York: Harper & Row, for the Twentieth Century Fund, 1971), p. 240.

"Until 1969, the military services were not given budget targets but requested what they viewed as required to meet the threat. . . . Since then, the services have been given targets [called fiscal guidance], and the entire department in fact operates under such a specific target." U.S. Department of Defense (Comptroller). *The Economics of Defense* (Washington, D.C.: U.S. Government Printing Office, 1972), p. 168.

6. As Eric Goldman tells us, "President Johnson assumed that foreign policy was something you had, like measles, and got over with as quickly as possible. . . . At the farthest stretch of his modernity, he reached thinking that was basically of a Cold War type." Eric Goldman, *The Tragedy of Lyndon Johnson* (New York: Alfred A. Knopf, 1969), pp. 527–528. The point being made in the text, however, does not depend upon any particular President's having an inadequate background in foreign affairs.

7. United Nations Conference on Trade and Development, Geneva, Switzerland.

CHAPTER 3
"GETTING THE COUNTRY MOVING": 1961–64

1. Arthur M. Okun, *The Political Economy of Prosperity* (New York: W.W. Norton, for The Brookings Institution, 1970), pp. 33–41.

2. Walter Heller, *New Dimensions of Political Economy* (New York: W.W. Norton, 1967), p. 61.

3. Their diagnosis was the same as that of an economic policy task force headed by Professor Paul Samuelson of the Massachusetts Institute of Technology that had reported to Kennedy before his inauguration. The Task force had told him that the recession of 1960–61 had been "superimposed upon an economy which in the last few years has been sluggish and tired," a fact that was more significant than the fact of the recession's existence *per se.*

4. Herbert Stein, *Fiscal Revolution in America* (Chicago: University of Chicago Press, 1969), p. 3750.

5. Herbert Stein remarks that Eisenhower "spoke so often and so earnestly about balancing the budget that he was thought to be making a fetish of it." Ibid., p. 347. G.L. Bach concludes a study of economic policies of the Eisenhower administration by noting that the administration's policies "appear to have been overrestrictive . . . especially in 1959–60." *Making Monetary and Fiscal Policy* (Washington D.C.: The Brookings Institution, 1971), p. 109. Some observers attribute Kennedy's win over Nixon in 1960 to the recession of 1960–61.

6. Kennedy had taken only one economics course at Harvard.

7. As Walter Heller was to put it later, "In 1961 . . . the problem of the economic adviser was not what to say (the activist-oriented gap analysis made that clear) but how to get people to listen." Heller, *New Dimensions of Political Economy,* p. 27.

8. Ibid., p. 29.

9. Stein, *Fiscal Revolution in America,* p. 395.

10. For example, Rep. Wilbur Mills, a key member of Congress on matters of taxation.

11. Stein, *Fiscal Revolution in America,* p. 385.

CHAPTER 4
TAKING THE NEXT STEP: THE ANTIPOVERTY PROGRAM, 1964–65

1. In social science jargon these people were structurally unemployed rather than cyclically unemployed. That is, they were not temporarily out of work because the country was in a recession phase of the business cycle but more or less permanently out of work because of a structural mismatch between the jobs available and the low level of their skills, aspirations, and ability to work. It follows that such people are not helped very much when the country's growth rate increases.

2. Michael Harrington, *The Other America* (New York: Macmillan, 1969), pp. 169, 186.

3. James L. Sundquist, "Jobs, Training and Welfare for the Underclass," in Kermit Gordon, ed., *Agenda for the Nation* (Washington, D.C.: The Brookings Institution, 1968), p. 49.

4. Statistically, households are defined as poor if their income falls below what is necessary to maintain a minimal consumption level. The line is unavoidably arbitrary; in 1964 it was $3,000 for a family of four (about $60 a week). The social and psychological problems of poverty certainly persist when incomes rise above the bare minimum necessary for subsistence. To add some flexibility to the concept, the Social Security Administration has developed what it calls a "near poor" category with incomes ranging up to one-third higher than the poverty standard.

5. James Tobin catches a common attitude of mainstream Americans toward poverty in their midst by citing the following incident. "The nationwide attitude toward Negro poverty was similar to that of the ingenuously puzzled and indignant white residents of a northern Wisconsin county on learning that the federal government considered it to be one of severe poverty; it did not occur to them that the dismally low incomes of the many Chippewa Indian residents would count in this assessment." "Raising the Incomes of the Poor," in Gordon, *Agenda for the Nation,* p. 79.

6. Heller, *New Dimensions of Political Economy,* p. 20.

7. Herbert Stein writes, "The [Kennedy] administration had a list of domestic programs for which it wanted to increase spending. These included federal aid to education, urban renewal, regional, economic development, manpower training, and the provision of medical care for the aged." *Fiscal Revolution in America,* pp. 387–388.

8. President's Council of Economic Advisers, *Economic Report of the President, 1965,* p. 166.

CHAPTER 5
TWO WARS IN CONFRONTATION–ONE AGAINST POVERTY AND ONE AGAINST NORTH VIETNAM

1. President Johnson presented the Tonkin Gulf resolution to Congress, later interpreted as authorizing the prosecution of the war in Vietnam, in August 1964, just three months after he had proclaimed the Great Society in an address at the University of Michigan.

2. In late 1966, when the direction of change in priorities had become clear, Sargent Shriver protested feelingly but futilely, "The poor will feel they have been shortchanged. They will feel they have been double-crossed. The

poor will feel that democracy is only for the rich." *New York Times,* November 23, 1966.

3. President's Council of Economic Advisers, *Economic Report of the President, 1966,* pp. 4 and 11. At this time he had preliminary GNP estimates that were much too low—$9 billion too low for 1965 and $25 billion too low for 1966, and thus the danger of inflation at the time was seriously underestimated.

4. *New York Times,* April 20, 1966.

5. Unemployment fell below 4 percent at the end of 1965.

6. The Bureau of the Budget's requirement that government agencies make five-year cost projections was only beginning to get under way in 1965.

7. President's Council of Economic Advisers, *Economic Report of the President, 1966* (Washington D.C.: U.S. Government Printing Office, 1966), p. 31.

8. Ibid., p. 11. It would be hard to exaggerate the extent to which the administration shifted its priorities from the domestic antipoverty program to the war in Vietnam between January 1965 and January 1966. Compare, for example, the guns-ahead-of-butter statement in the text with the following statement written one year earlier: "Although several million people will be assisted [by Great Society programs in 1965] *this is only the beginning* of the nation's long-range war on poverty. Continuing effort, carried out with skill and imagination, will be required. . . ." President's Council of Economic Advisers, *Economic Report of the President, 1965* (Washington, D.C.: U.S. Government Printing Office, 1965), p. 167.

9. While the poverty program was hit hard by budget-cutting, many of the customary pork-barrel items were shielded in the 1966–67 budget. "For example, it was recommended that the Department of Agriculture start construction of 35 watershed projects and 1600 miles of forest roads; that the Bureau of Reclamation start work on three new projects with a total cost initially estimated at $1 billion, that the Corps of Engineers start building 25 new river and harbor projects and begin designing 23 more. . . . The January 1966 budget did not contemplate the firm policy of no new starts on public works that was maintained during the Korean War." Murray L. Weidenbaum, *Economic Impact of the Vietnam War* (Washington, D.C.: The Center for Strategic Studies, Georgetown University, 1967), p. 25.

Two unflattering interpretations of this record are possible. Either Johnson's commitment to the antipoverty program was only rhetorical or the meat ax was applied to the budget of January 1966 so crudely—and perhaps in such haste—that programs were dropped out on the altogether irrational ground of last in, first out. The antipoverty program was, after all, a rank newcomer compared to the ones described above.

10. John C. Donovan, *The Politics of Poverty* (New York: Pegasus, 1967), p. 64. Donovan writes perceptively of the antipoverty program's fall from grace and I have leaned on his treatment in the text.

11. The antipoverty program's $1.6 billion 1966–67 budget was 8 percent of the supplemental appropriations for the Vietnam war of $19.3 billion between August 1965 and March 1966.

12. *New York Times,* November 30, 1966. The low priority items Johnson cut out of the budget at this time, as reported in approximate amounts, were (in billions of dollars):

Highway Construction	0.5
Housing and Urban Development	0.5
Health, Education and Welfare	0.3
Corps of Engineers	0.1
Agriculture	0.4
Interior	0.1
Agency for International Development	(0.4)*
Office of Economic Opportunity	0.1
Department of Defense	0.6
Elementary and Secondary School Aid	0.4
Miscellaneous	0.1
TOTAL	3.1

*Cut made earlier in the year

Of these cuts, 42 percent were in Housing and Urban Development, Health, Education, and Welfare, Office of Economic Opportunity, and Elementary and Secondary School Aid.

13. Ibid.

14. Donovan, *Politics of Poverty,* p. 91. The cutback was from an already low level in terms of national priorities. In 1967 just the retired pay of military personnel was $300 million greater than the OEO's spending for the war on poverty.

15. *New York Times,* March 15, 1967. At about the same time, Budget Director Charles L. Schultze told the House Ways and Means Committee, "Our military effort in Vietnam has not suffered in any way from a shortage of funds. We have provided every plane, every gun, and every cartridge needed to support operations in Vietnam." Hearings on "Temporary Increase in Debt Ceiling," January 1967, p. 10.

16. Donovan, *Politics of Poverty,* p. 92.

17. President's Council of Economic Advisers, *Economic Report of the President, 1969,* pp. 202, 204. "The recently adopted programs related to the antipoverty program that were operating below authorized levels were (in billions of dollars):

Elementary & Secondary Education	2.0
Higher Education	1.3
Housing & Community Development	0.6
Area Re-development	0.5

Health Training & Research	0.4
Total, per year	4.8"

18. Ibid. The *new* efforts in civilian programs related to the antipoverty program were (in billions per year):

Education	7.0
Preschool	1.0
Elementary & Secondary	2.5
Higher	3.0
Vocational	0.5
Health	3.8
Kiddie Care	0.5
Medicare for Disabled	1.8
Comprehensive Health Centers	1.0
Hospital Construction & Modernization	0.5
Nutrition	1.0
Community Service Programs	0.8
Jobs and Manpower	2.5
Public Jobs	1.8
Manpower Development Training Act	0.5
Employment Service	0.2
Social Security and Income Support	7.5
Public Assistance	4.0
Social Security Improvements	3.5
Economic Area & Special Development	2.2
Entrepreneurial Aid	0.5
Area Redevelopment	0.5
Rural Development	1.0
Indian Assistance	0.2
Urban Development	5.5
New Cities	0.5
Land Acquisition & Planning	0.5
Urban Mass Transportation	0.5
Model Cities	2.0
Other Urban	2.0
Rapid Interurban Ground Transit	0.1
Total per year	30.4

In addition to these *new* programs, the council listed others totaling $9.3 billion that were not, however, as directly related to fighting poverty as the ones above. The council also listed $1.2 billion more of underfinanced existing programs that were not directly related to fighting poverty. Details were supplied by the council for each of the listed new programs.

19. For a similar calculation for the years 1965–67, see President's Council of Economic Advisers, *Economic Report of the President, 1968,* p. 69.

20. According to the Council of Economic Advisers, 1969, this operation would have cost $9.7 billion in 1967. *Economic Report, 1969,* p. 153. For further discussion of this matter see Arthur M. Okun, *The Political Economy of Prosperity* (New York: W. W. Norton, for The Brookings Institution, 1970), p. 125, and Kermit Gordon, ed., *Agenda for the Nation* (Washington, D.C.: The Brookings Institution, 1968), p. 105.

21. Okun, *Political Economy of Prosperity,* p. 125.

22. Lest anyone doubt that the United States escalated the war in Vietnam with "zest," let him recall that there were only two votes cast in Congress against the Gulf of Tonkin resolution in August 1964. Let him also reread the 1966 rhetoric of Sen. Robert F. Kennedy and let him recall the public anxiety in 1966–67 over whether the U.S. military establishment was being hindered from carrying on its work in Southeast Asia by a "bomb shortage."

23. *New York Times,* April 20, 1966: As shown in footnote 17, federal aid to the schools was substantially underfunded in 1969, and was, in fact, one of the first programs to be cut back.

24. Chester L. Cooper, *The Lost Crusade, America in Vietnam* (New York: Dodd, Mead, 1970), p. 263.

25. Martin Luther King, Jr., *The Trumpet of Conscience* (New York: Harper & Row, 1967), pp. 22–23.

CHAPTER 6
ESCALATING THE WAR IN VIETNAM: HOW NOT TO FINANCE A WAR

1. Typical of the attitude of economic overconfidence at the time was the conclusion of an article in *Fortune* that "the United States could fight several Korean wars with just its annual increase in output; the Vietnam buildup, at its present pace, probably will not push the [U.S.] economy to capability." Gilbert Burcke, "The Guns, Butter and Then-Some Economy," *Fortune,* October 1965.

2. Chester L. Cooper, *The Lost Crusade, America in Vietnam* (New York: Dodd, Mead, 1970).

3. *Business Week,* February 5, 1966, p. 125.

4. "By 1964 and early 1965 . . . there was reason to think that, with a long period of price stability behind us, the country might gradually attain high employment and stay close to it without reviving inflation." Committee for Economic Development, *"The National Economy and the Vietnam War,"* New York, April 1968.

5. President's Council of Economic Advisers, *Economic Report of the President, 1965*, p. 68.

6. *New York Times*, July 16, 1965. Inside the government in the spring of 1965 economists were looking ahead to the budget they would send to Congress in January 1966 "and shaping a program *to promote a continuing advance*" in the GNP. Arthur M. Okun, *The Political Economy of Prosperity* (New York: W.W. Norton, for The Brookings Institution, 1970), pp. 50–51 (Italics added).

7. Before an economy reached full employment the main risk was thought to be that it would not be adequately stimulated. Once at full employment there were risks in both directions—*of inadequate and of excessive stimulation*. "It is easy to prescribe expansionary policies in a period of slack. Managing high-level prosperity is a vastly more difficult business." Gardner Ackley, "The Contribution of Economists to Policy Formation," *Journal of Finance*, Vol. 21 (May 1966), p. 176.

8. See graph of actual and potential GNP on page 44.

9. Testimony of the Hon. Robert C. Moot, Assistant Secretary of Defense (Comptroller) at Hearings of the Subcommittee on Economy in Government of the U.S. Congress's Joint Economic Committee, June 6, 1969, pp. 374–375.

10. Charles E. Metcalf, "Fiscal Policy and the Poor," *Public Policy*, Vol. 18 (Winter 1970), pp. 197–198.

11. David Halberstam, *The Best and the Brightest* (New York: Random House, 1972), pp. 596–597.

12. White House Presidential news conference, July 29, 1965; President's report to the American people on radio and television following the military incident in the Gulf of Tonkin, August 4, 1964.

13. Halberstam, *Best and Brightest*, pp. 399, 604 (italics in original).

14. Ibid., p. 595.

15. Personal conversation with the author.

16. Okun, *Political Economy of Prosperity*, p. 68.

17. As brought out in subsequent congressional investigations, the relevant information on prime contract awards, defense industry new orders, backlogs and inventories, manpower data, etc., was not customarily made available in one place, even within the Department of Defense.

In February 1966, Defense Secretary Robert McNamara, who many observers think knew better, asserted "defense expenditures will . . . be no more of an inflationary element in fiscal years 1966 and 1967 . . . than they were in . . . 1960–64, and therefore by themselves are not sufficient cause for predicting inflation." U.S. House of Representatives, Committee on Appropriations, "Department of Defense Appropriations 1967," Part I, 1966, pp. 4–5.

18. The Defense Department estimates the lead time (i.e., the time that elapses between placing the order and paying for the product) in procuring aircraft for the Vietnam war was eighteen months and that for ammunition it

was six months. U.S. Senate Armed Forces and Appropriations Committees, "Supplemental Military Procurement and Construction Authorizations, Fiscal Year 1967," January 1967, p. 163.

19. Other, more complex problems were also created by the sudden impact on the economy of Vietnam war spending. Sen. John Stennis, chairman of the Senate Armed Services Committee, describes an acute situation that developed as the government placed the procurement of clothing and tentage suitable for the Vietnam climate "on a crash basis." This diverted large supplies from the domestic market, resulting in a vast increase of textile imports to satisfy U.S. civilian demand. These imports dismayed the U.S. textile industry and provided part of the animus for the subsequent pressure it brought to bear successfully on President Nixon to restrict U.S. textile imports. U.S. Congress, Joint Economic Committee, Hearings on *The Economic Effects of Vietnam Spending,* April 1967, p. 73.

20. Murray L. Weidenbaum, *Economic Impact of the Vietnam War* (Washington, D.C.: The Center for Strategic Studies, Georgetown University, 1967), pp. 11–20. He points out that the same failure to distinguish between the effects of new orders and higher government expenditures bedeviled public policy in the early phase of the Korean War.

21. Newspapers headlined an "Administration-Federal Reserve Showdown": Professor Seymour Harris, chairman of the Department of Economics at the University of California, San Diego, accused the Fed of "using a monetary sledgehammer . . . depriving the people of $40 billion" (of GNP); Professor James Tobin of Yale, a former member of the Council of Economic Advisers, speaking of "new defense expenditures of unannounced but apparently modest size" deplored the Fed's "unilateral decision" when "the signs of inflation are remarkably few." Letters to the *Los Angeles Times* and *New York Times,* respectively,

22. G.L. Bach, *Making Monetary and Fiscal Policy* (Washington, D.C.: The Brookings Institution, 1971), p. 122.

23. "According to one White House aide, the President saw the increase in interest rates as almost a personal, vindictive act on the part of Chairman Martin (of the Federal Reserve)." Ibid., p. 125.

24. Ibid., p. 123.

CHAPTER 7
THE BREACH OF 1965 BECOMES THE DEADLOCK OF 1966–68

1. Edwin L. Dale, "The Inflation Goof," *New Republic,* January 4, 1969.

2. David Halberstam, *The Best and the Brightest* (New York: Random House, 1972), p. 607.

3. In order to avoid having a tax increase bog down in congressional debate over reforming the structure of taxation, an across-the-board equal percentage increase on all income taxes was proposed. At first 6 percent,

then 8 percent, and finally 10 percent was selected, as the magnitude of the inflationary impact of the war became clearer.

4. Ackley, who was closely associated with President Truman during the Korean War and with President Johnson during the Vietnam war, believes Johnson understood the economics of war better than Truman did, but under the circumstances Congress would not grant him a tax increase. Johnson, according to Ackley, "was probably the best informed President we ever had on economic matters. He used to carry our [CEA] memos around in his pockets" (Personal conversation with the author).

5. Halberstam, *Best and the Brightest,* p. 608.

6. Dale, "Inflation Goof."

7. Ibid.

8. Ibid.

9. In mid-1967 Congress scolded both the administration and the Pentagon for misleading it so long about the cost of the war. It is "obvious . . . that the lack of accurate expenditure data during calendar 1966 handicapped the Congress seriously in reaching appropriate tax, spending, and other economic policy decisions. . . . [Vietnam costs] outran the original estimates by $14 billion in fiscal 1966 and $12 billion in fiscal 1967. The size of these increments and their promulgation after the fact, as it were, had a disruptive effect on the conduct of fiscal and monetary policy. For example, had it been known early in the spring of 1966 that $12 billion over and above the fiscal 1967 budgetary estimates would be appropriated for the Vietnam war, Congress certainly would have given more serious consideration to a tax increase or spending cut and quite probably would have enacted one or the other or both. Such action would have . . . avoided the havoc caused by the excessive reliance on restrictive monetary policy in 1966." Joint Economic Committee, *Report on Economic Effect of Vietnam Spending,* July 7, 1967, pp. 3, 5–6.

10. The January 1966 budget contained small and clearly inadequate mini-tax changes that slightly increased federal revenue. Excise tax cuts on telephone service and automobiles were rescinded, corporate tax payments were speeded up, and graduated withholding of individual income taxes was introduced.

11. Support for the tax increase by outside economists was sporadic and belated, in part because many who might have spoken out were opposed to the administration's war in Vietnam and in part because the enormity of its cost was not made clear by the government itself. It was late in the game— September 11, 1967—when an open letter signed by 260 economists favored the tax increase. Some prominent economists appended a clause to that

letter insisting that "support for a tax increase does not imply support of all federal policies, foreign and domestic." *New York Times,* September 11, 1967. *The Times* printed an editorial *opposing* the tax increase as late as December 3, 1967 (Section E, p. 10).

12. The assumption of the Johnson administration that limitless resources were available to the U.S. economy was indicated by a statement by Secretary of Labor Willard L. Wirtz in protesting the raising of the Federal Reserve discount rate in December 1965. "There can be no tolerance for the suggestion that expansion of the economy must be slowed down . . . while there is still so much to be done." *Washington Post,* December 12, 1965.

13. Hyman Minsky, "The Crunch of 1966—Model For New Financial Crises?" *Trans-action,* March 1968, pp. 44–51.

14. By midsummer the growth in the money stock had fallen to zero.

15. Minsky, *"Crunch of 1966,"* p. 212.

16. The Federal Reserve was severely attacked in Congress, where high interest rates are always unpopular, for its performance in the spring and summer of 1966. In September Congress passed a law empowering federal supervisory agencies to set ceilings on the interest rates banks and other savings institutions would be allowed to pay.

17. Housing starts fell more than 40 percent in nine months. "[In 1966] tight money worked like a fiscal action pinpointed to finance defense through a substantial excise tax on the purchase of new homes. That type of tax program would have been hooted off Capital Hill for its obvious inequity and illogic." Arthur M. Okun, *The Political Economy of Prosperity* (New York: W.W. Norton for The Brookings Institution, 1970), pp. 80–81.

State and local governments had learned by 1969–70, when severely tight money again discriminated against them, that high levels of military spending were exacerbating their difficulties. Five mayors of major cities testified in opposition to the Nixon administration's proposed defense budget, calling for unspecified budget reductions. Yarmolinsky chapter in *The Annals of the American Academy,* 1973, p. 7.

18. A 1967 Commerce Department survey of business investors' behavior in 1966 remarked upon "the small and significantly delayed" effect of monetary policy on business investment, in sharp contrast to its "shock effect . . . on housing." Jean Crockett, Irwin Friend, and Henry Shavell, "The Impact of Monetary Stringency on Business Investment," *Survey of Current Business,* August 1967.

Professor Daniel Suits of the University of California put the relationship between the Vietnam war and the business investment boom of 1966 into technical language in testimony before a congressional committee. Professor Suits said the multiplier for war outlays is 1.85 (i.e., $1 spent on war adds $1.85 to the GNP) but that if one adds "the second and third order effects" of war expenditures that arise because they exert pressure on business to add to its investments in fixed assets and inventories, "then this multiplier could be three." U.S. Congress, Joint Economic Committee, *Hearings on the Economic Effects of Vietnam Spending,* April 26, 1967.

19. Fiscal policy was called into play by the administration in the fall of 1966 to try to curb the investment boom. The investment tax credit was suspended in October, only to be reintroduced again in the spring of 1967. This was one of the several "backings and fillings" of governmental economic policies that added to the public's sense of confusion and consternation during the Vietnam war period.

20. See, for example, Notes: Chapter 6, note 19.

21. In other words, if wage increases are greater than labor's increasing productivity they cut into profit margins. Then managements pass along such increases in the form of higher prices in order to recover their previous profit margins. This is, of course, an example of cost-push inflation at work (see Appendix A).

22. See John Sheehan, *The Wage-Price Guideposts* (Washington, D.C.: The Brookings Institution, 1967).

23. *New York Times,* August 21, 1966.

24. Okun, *Political Economy of Prosperity,* p. 77.

25. President's Council of Economic Advisers, *Economic Report of the President, 1967,* p. 5.

26. Murray L. Weidenbaum, a close and perceptive observer of how the Vietnam war inflation got started, resorts to a paleozoological analogy to characterize the events described in this chapter. "A major error occurred in domestic policy in the U.S. during 1966," he writes. "In this era of sophisticated information system, it still seems that a parallel can be drawn with the prehistoric brontosaurus whose internal communication system was so primitive that when another animal started chewing on the end of its tail, it lost its entire tail before the news reached the brain." *Economic Impact of the Vietnam War* (Washington, D.C.: The Center for Strategic Studies, Georgetown University, 1967), p. 41.

CHAPTER 8
THE BUDGETARY COST OF THE WAR

1. Excepting the Spanish-American War which, as wars go, was very short and inexpensive at the time.

2. Another source estimates total (i.e., military and economic) U.S. aid to South Vietnam, Cambodia, and Laos at over $1.1 billion "in the five years before the expansion of the war in 1965." "Impact of the Vietnam War," Congressional Research Service, Foreign Affairs Division, Library of Congress, Washington, D.C., 1971, p. 3.

3. James L. Clayton, testimony before U.S. Congress, Joint Economic Committee, *The Military Budget and National Economic Priorities,* Hearings, June 4, 1969, p. 146.

4. Judging from the table, the estimate of Vietnam war veterans' benefits looks conservative compared to those of the next four wars listed in the table. It is odd that his estimate for World War II veterans' benefits is so relatively small, given both the increase in benefits that he mentions and the rising price level. His estimate of the interest cost of the Vietnam war also seems modest, especially considering the general expectation that interest rates will continue to be high in the future.

5. Casualties through July 8, 1972, were: 45,810 U.S. deaths from hostile action; 10,234 from other causes, for a total of 56,044 deaths. The total wounded was 303,208, of which 153,103 required hospitalization and 150,105 did not. Total dead and wounded through July 8, 1972, was 359,252. Information supplied by the Office of the Assistant Secretary of Defense, Public Affairs, by letter July 20, 1972.

6. Clayton, testimony, p. 148.

7. Ibid.

8. U.S. Congress, Joint Economic Committee, *Economic Effect of Vietnam Spending,* Hearings, April 24, 1967, p. 1.

9. Ibid.

10. Ibid., July 7, 1967, p. 5.

11. U.S. Senate Committee on Appropriations, Hearings on H.R. 7224, Mutual Security Appropriations for 1965, 84th Congress, First session, p. 140.

12. Raymond E. Manning, "Cost of U.S. Wars," Library of Congress, Legislative Reference Service, October 1956, p. 31.

13. U.S. Congress, House of Representatives, Subcommittee of the Committee on Appropriations, Department of Defense Appropriations for 1971, Part I, p. 487.

14. The account in the text is based upon extensive discussions and correspondence with present Defense Department officials and on some discussion and correspondence with Robert N. Anthony, Assistant Secretary of Defense (Comptroller) from 1965 to 1968. Anthony does not accept all of the opinions expressed in the accompanying text.

15. According to the Defense Department full costs "cover all the forces engaged plus their support . . . all costs of aircraft operations in the theatre, fuel, parts, maintenance and base operations. . . . All ammunition consumed

in the theatre is reflected under [*sic*] full costs. Since the base line units involved would consume some ammunition in peacetime training, only the difference is included in the incremental cost." Department of Defense press release, July 18, 1972.

16. December 9, 1967, p. 1053.

17. Personal correspondence with the author dated July 20, 1973, and August 20, 1973.

18. Raphael Littauer and Normal Uphoff, eds., *The Air War in Indochina* (rev. ed.) (Boston: Beacon Press, 1972), p. 100. According to Defense Department definitions, however, the *use* of military equipment is not counted as a war cost, only the *purchase* of identical equipment to replace war losses.

19. In a personal letter to the author dated October 5, 1972.

20. Personal correspondence with the author dated April 6, 1973.

CHAPTER 9
THE DOLLAR: A CASUALTY OF THE VIETNAM WAR

1. For a detailed account of the role of government spending in the U.S. balance of payments, see Robert Warren Stevens, *The Dollar in the World Economy* (New York: Random House, 1972), chapters 12–14; "The Dollar and Bretton Woods, A Post-Mortem," *Bankers' Magazine* (Boston), Spring 1973; and "The Public Sector of the Balance of Payments," presented at the Midwest Economics Association meetings, 1974 and reprinted in *Economics and Business Review*, University of Nebraska, Fall 1974.

2. Within overall goals set by the defense-foreign-policy establishment some efforts were made to reduce the Pentagon's direct spending abroad. For example, the "Buy American" regulations were tightened requiring the Pentagon to substitute U.S.-made goods for foreign-made goods. Thus, although U.S. troops were stationed in many countries because those countries could not afford to maintain as large military establishments as the Pentagon thought desirable, American servicemen were restricted in their local spending, "being required to eat ham sandwiches flown in from Washington," as one soldier with an ironic turn of mind put it.

3. The pinch on domestic supplies was especially acute in 1966–69 because the very rapid buildup of military procurement was concentrated on purchases of vehicles, ammunition, communication equipment, and basic army supplies to fight a mainly conventional type war. Most of these items are directly competitive with both U.S. exports and U.S. civilian demand.

4. Leonard Dudley and Peter Passell, "The War in Vietnam and the U.S. Balance of Payments," *Review of Economics and Statistics*, November 1968, pp. 437–442. An estimate that the additional indirect cost was $2.4 billion was subsequently revised to $2.0 billion.

5. Bernard Udis and Associates, *Adjustments of the U.S. Economy to Reductions in Military Spending,* prepared for the U.S. Arms Control and Disarmament Agency, ACDA document E-156 (Washington, D.C., 1970), pp. 381–395.

6. This sum falls considerably short of the $53 billion deterioration in the net liquidity position of the U.S. economy *vis-à-vis* the rest of the world from 1965 to 1972, a deterioration that will have to be made good in some way acceptable to the other countries of the world in the years to come.

7. U.S. net capital exports in 1971 and 1972 were $9 billion and $8 billion, respectively.

8. Morgan Guarantee Trust Co. of New York, *World Financial Markets,* February 23, 1973, p. 4. Exchange rates between the dollar and other currencies varied widely after the world currency realignments. The Japanese yen appreciated 37 percent against the dollar, the German mark 30 percent, the French franc 23 percent, and the Canadian dollar 5 percent. Against the currencies of the group of ten leading members of the IMF, the dollar depreciated by 17 percent.

CHAPTER 10
"MOMENTS OF TRUTH" FOR THE DOLLAR AND FOR U.S. INTERNATIONAL ECONOMIC POLICY

1. U.S. imports shot up 60 percent between their 1964–65 average and 1968, and the balance on current account collapsed from $5 billion surplus to a $0.5 billion deficit.

2. The Johnson administration had been forced to impose the first-ever mandatory controls on the outflow of U.S. private capital on January 1, 1968, when it also asked Congress to impose a penalty tax on foreign travel by Americans. At the time, the 1968 crisis was called a loss of confidence in the gold value of all currencies, but since all were tied to gold via the gold convertibility of the dollar, it was fundamentally a dollar crisis.

3. Peter G. Peterson, *A Foreign Economic Perspective* (Washington, D.C.: U.S. Government Printing Office, 1971). As subsequently released to the public in December 1971 the two-volume report is a model government publication, including splendid color graphs prepared by the CIA.

4. The United States has also contributed to the undermining of GATT rules. It maintains quota limitations on a number of imports, of which oil was the most prominent until it was removed in May 1973; in recent years the United States has forced a number of its weaker trading partners into accepting voluntary export restrictions on shipments to it in flagrant violation of the rules, purposes, and spirit of GATT. There are now seventy such agreements covering many products, (including steel, beef, mushrooms, and cotton, woolen and synthetic textiles. (See, e.g., Richard N. Cooper, "Trade Policy Is Foreign Policy," *Foreign Policy,* Winter 1972–73, pp. 18–36.)

5. In an address to the American Club of Paris, February 22, 1971.

6. The facts of the case hardly support the unions' claims, however. Unemployment rose by 2.2 million workers from 1968 to 1971 and the merchandise trade balance worsened by $2.4 billion. Each $1 billion of exports is estimated to provide some 70,000 jobs and thus there was a loss of some 170,000 jobs in the foreign sector. This accounted for about 7.5 percent of the increase in unemployment.

7. At the time of writing, officials from twenty countries are at work trying to design new international monetary institutions to replace those destroyed by the United States in August 1971.

8. Peterson, *Foreign Economic Perspective,* p. 4. It is symptomatic of the long sleep by those responsible for foreign economic policy that Peterson refers to "Marshall Plan strategy." The Marshall Plan came to an end in 1952, nineteen years before the Peterson report was written.

9. U.S. Congress Joint Economic Committee, Subcommittee on economy in Government, Hearings, June 3–24, 1969, p. 645.

CHAPTER 11
"WINDING DOWN THE WAR": NEW MEN AND NEW IDEAS TO CENTER STAGE

1. In a television interview with representatives of three major networks on July 1, 1970. Distributed in printed form as "A Conversation with the President" by the U.S. State Department, Department of State Publication 8545, Washington, D.C., 1970, p. 26. Defense Secretary Melvin Laird said of the Nixon Doctrine: "Our objective for the future is that the United States will not need to rely on its own manpower to achieve the objective of self-determination for our friends and allies in Asia and to thwart Communist aggression in that part of the world. Under the Nixon Doctrine we have, we will maintain, and we will use as necessary sea and air resources to supplement the efforts and the armed forces of our friends and allies who are determined to resist aggression." U.S. House of Representatives Appropriations Committee, Defense Department Hearings for 1972, Part I, p. 36. A *Wall Street Journal* writer put it more succinctly: it meant "the transfer of the fighting and dying to the South Vietnamese forces." Richard J. Levine, "The Pentagon as Laird Leaves," *Wall Street Journal,* January 3, 1973.

2. Bernard Udis, ed., *Adjustments of the U.S. Economy to Reductions in Military Spending,* U.S. Arms Control and Disarmament Agency, Document E-156, December 1970.

3. Ibid., p. 6. In one section of this report Lawrence R. Klein and Kei Mori were able to project econometrically "combinations of policies that could bring about a smooth transition." Their various budget projections entailed a level of unemployment "beneath 6 percent under all but the worst of circumstances." By late 1970, however, they felt constrained to add that their unemployment estimates might be low by, say, between 0.2 and 0.5 points. Ibid., p. 119.

4. President's Council of Economic Advisers, *Economic Report of the President, 1969* (Washington, D.C.: U.S. Government Printing Office), pp. 181–211.

5. Ibid., pp. 189, 191.

6. See Chapter 7 for a discussion of the policy deadlock of 1966–68.

7. It was the first time since the 1920s that conservative Republicans had been in power. Eisenhower, in 1952–60, was essentially an "Eastern establishment" type of Republican. "The 1968–69 Nixon creed, with heavy support from libertarians and conservatives, looked back to the days before the New Deal. At the beginning of his administration in 1969, Mr. Nixon was prepared to make a serious effort to reverse the trend begun by Franklin D. Roosevelt in 1932 and to shrink the role of the federal government in the national economy." Leonard Silk, *Nixonomics* (New York: Praeger, 1972), p. 197.

8. *Time,* February 1, 1971, p. 72.

9. Silk, *Nixonomics,* pp. 28–29.

10. Source of monetary data: Federal Reserve Bank of St. Louis, Mo.

11. For a discussion of the quadriad in 1961–63, see Appendix A. In 1971 the quadriad was Paul McCracken at the Council of Economic Advisers, George Shulz at the Office of Management and Budget, John Connally at the Treasury, and Arthur Burns at the Federal Reserve.

12. In a speech at Pepperdine College, Los Angeles, December 1, 1970. The vital importance to the country of keeping the Federal Reserve relatively free from political pressures is shown by the fact that the Federal Reserve foresaw, before the Johnson and Nixon administrations did, both the need to restrain the economy when Vietnam war spending started upward in late 1965 and the need to abandon the unworkable policy of Game Plan II at the beginning of 1971.

CHAPTER 12
"WINDING DOWN THE WAR": GAME PLAN III—INFLATION AND RECESSION

1. January 27, 1969. Weekly Compilation of Presidential Documents.

2. Leonard Silk, *Nixonomics* (New York: Praeger, 1972), p. 8.

3. Robert V. Roosa, in an address to the annual combined luncheon of the American Finance Association and the American Economic Association at the New York Hilton Hotel, December 29, 1969.

4. In U.S. Congress, Joint Economic Committee Hearings, "Midyear Review of the Economy, 1971," p. 73.

5. The letter is partially reprinted in Roger Miller and Raburn Williams, *The New Economics of Richard Nixon: Freezes, Floats, and Fiscal Policy* (Scranton, Pa.: Harpers Magazine Press, 1972), pp. 17–20.

6. See Appendix A for a discussion of the full employment budget.

7. Federal Reserve Bank of St. Louis, Mo.

8. In current dollars, spending was about the same in 1968 and 1969, but in real terms it was down about 5 percent in 1969.

9. President's Council of Economic Advisers, *Economic Report of the President, 1969* (Washington, D.C.: U.S. Government Printing Office), p. 193. (Italics added)

10. "We all know why we have an unemployment problem. Two million workers have been released from the Armed Forces and defense plants because of our success in winding down the war in Vietnam." Richard M. Nixon in a television address to the nation, August 15, 1971.

CHAPTER 13
AFTER THE WAR—THE PEACE DIVIDEND AND NEW WAR COSTS

1. The committee used a figure of $22 billion, but the preliminary estimate of the incremental cost of the war with which it was working was subsequently revised upward by $2.5 billion.

2. The $3 billion was the amount by which the committee estimated federal revenues (less the 10 percent surtax) would exceed built-in govermental costs (including defense).

3. U.S. Department of Defense (Comptroller), *The Economics of Defense Spending,* July 1972, p. 148.

4. Ibid., p. 150.

5. See Charles L. Schultze and Associates, *Setting National Priorities. The 1973 Budget* (Washington, D.C.: The Brookings Institution, 1972), pp. 61–63, for a fuller treatment of these points.

6. Edward R. Fried and Associates, *Setting National Priorities. The 1974 Budget* (Washington D.C.: The Brookings Institution, 1973), p. 293.

7. The National Urban Coalition, *Counterbudget,* (New York: Praeger, 1971), p. 267.

8. Edward R. Fried and Associates, *Setting National Priorities,* p. 297.

9. Statement by Don R. Brazier, Acting Assistant Secretary of Defense (Comptroller), before the subcommittee on Defense Department appropriations of the House Committee on Appropriations, supporting fiscal 1974 budget estimates, Table 14.

10. Edward R. Fried and Associates, *Setting National Priorities,* pp. 292, 334.

11. Ibid., p. 406.

12. The Urban Coalition, *Counterbudget,* p. 273.

13. *The Center Magazine,* January-February 1974, p. 54. A publication of the Center for the Study of Democratic Institutions, Santa Barbara, California.

14. Note, for example, this observation from among many that could be chosen. "About 130 new systems, estimated to involve a total procurement cost of at least $140 billion, are under development or in procurement and new systems, once started, have proved notoriously difficult to cancel." Charles L. Schultze and Associates, *Setting National Priorities: The 1971 Budget* (Washington, D.C.: The Brookings Institution, 1970), p. 35.

15. The Commerce Department makes these estimates in inflation-free dollars of 1958 purchasing power in order to eliminate the effects of inflation from the calculations. In Table 13–5 the estimates are converted back into dollars of the current year's purchasing power in order to make these estimates of the GNP gap comparable with other estimates of the cost of the Vietnam war contained in this book.

16. The frequent failure of dollar measures to convey an adequate sense of social cost is illustrated by Table 13–5, showing that the country *gained* $21 billion by exceeding its potential GNP in 1966 and 1968. In reality, however, the country paid an enormously high social cost for those extra bits of production because in squeezing them out, the seeds of a virulent inflation were sown, an inflation that is still ravaging the economy as these lines are being written in the spring of 1973.

17. Inflation is often measured by the percentage decline in the purchasing power of the dollar that accompanies it. Measured in this way, the Vietnam war inflation caused the consumers' dollar to lose more than one quarter of its purchasing power between 1964 and the beginning of 1973.

CHAPTER 14
THE ECONOMIC COST OF THE WAR

1. Robert Leckachman, "The Cost in National Treasure: $400 Billion Plus," *The Saturday Review* (December 1972), pp. 44–49.

2. Tom Riddell, "The $676 Billion Quagmire," *The Progressive* (October 1963), pp. 33–37.

3. Murray L. Weidenbaum, *Economic Impact of the Vietnam War* (Washington, D.C.: The Center for Strategic Studies, Georgetown University, 1967), p. 21.

4. Defense Department comments on an earlier draft of this chapter. Other references to Defense Department views in this chapter also refer to these unpublished comments.

5. Edward R. Fried and Associates, *Setting National Priorities: The 1974 Budget,* (Washington, D.C.: The Brookings Institution, 1973), p. 333.

6. Ibid., p. 331.

7. Ibid., p. 333.

8. Ibid.

9. David Halberstam, *The Best and the Brightest* (New York: Random House, 1972), p. 597.

10. Tom Riddell, "The $676 Billion Quagmire," p. 35.

11. According to the Veterans Administration, it expects to have disbursed $10.2 billion to "Vietnam era veterans" between 1967 and 1974, which would leave $223 billion to be paid in the future.

12. Professor Clayton originally took 200 percent as a medium level multiple of the original cost of the Vietnam war, as falling between a high of 300 percent and a low of 100 percent. At the time of his estimate, the full cost of the war was estimated at $110 billion. Subsequently, he revised this procedure and used 183 percent (derived from the Korean War ratio in Table 14–3) instead of 200 percent. See his article, "The Fiscal Costs of United States Wars," *Western Political Quarterly* (September 1972).

13. Defense Department comments on an early draft of this chapter.

14. John M. Clark, *The Costs of the World War to the American People* (New York: Yale University Press, 1931), p. 203.

15. *Veteran's Benefits in the United States* (Washington, D.C.: U.S. Government Printing Office, April 1956), p. 106.

16. Discussed in Appendix C of *The Report of the President's Commission on an* All-Volunteer Armed Force (Washington, D.C.: U.S. Government Printing Office, February 1970). (Known as The Gates Commission Report.)

17. Quoted from a letter to the author dated May 14, 1973.

18. Cornell University Air War Study Group, *Air War in Indochina*, p. 240. The size of the armed forces fell below 2.5 million men to 2.392 million in 1972 and the unemployment rate was 5.6 percent. Since the excess draft cost estimates are very sensitive to these variables and since military pay rates were then much higher, I assume no added cost for 1972.

19. Robert Eisner, "The War and the Economy" in Sam Brown and Len Ackland, eds., *Why Are We Still in Vietnam?* (New York: Random House, 1970).

20. See note 19 above.

21. Tom Riddell estimates a cost of $27 billion as a result of drug addiction by Vietnam veterans and computes the loss of the productive work of draft evaders and deserters at $16.3 billion. "The $676 Billion Quagmire," p. 36.

APPENDIX A
INFLATION AND GOVERNMENT POLICY

1. We need not dwell here on the tendency for most economists to worry more about the problems of deflation, while many bankers and business people worry more about the problems of inflation. Both inflation and deflation are unacceptable beyond fairly narrow margins.

2. Among American institutions whose inadequacies were uncovered by the Vietnam war, an important one has been the nonmethod by which national priorities were set in cold-war-minded Washington. The following two excerpts from congressional hearings in 1969 illustrate the problem:

(1) Chairman Proxmire: Mr. [Stuart L.] Udall, you served in the cabinets of Presidents Kennedy and Johnson. Can you tell us whether you had a chance to argue the civilian case within the administration, for example at cabinet meetings?

Mr. Udall: No, neither of the Presidents that I served under had any systematic institutional way whereby there was a forum where you could argue domestic priorities against military priorities. It just was not a subject that was discussed.

(2) Mr. Charles L. Schultze, U.S. Budget Director from 1965 to 1967: "We need to get ourselves into a position where political leaders can view the expert recommendations of the military with the same independent judgment, decent respect, and healthy skepticism that they view the budgetary recommendations of such other experts as the Commissioner of Education, Surgeon General, and the Federal Manpower Administration.

"[Consider] . . . the procedures used by the Budget Bureau to review the budget of the Defense Department. In all other cases agency budget requests are submitted to the Bureau, which reviews the budgets and then makes its own recommendations to the President, subject to appeal by the agency head to the President. In the case of the Defense budget, however, the staff of the Budget Bureau and the staff of the Secretary of Defense jointly review the budget requests of the individual armed services. The staffs make recommendations to their respective superiors. The Secretary of Defense and the Budget Director then meet to iron out differences of view. The Secretary of Defense then submits his budget request to the President and the Budget Director has the right of carrying to the President any remaining areas of disagreement he thinks warrant Presidential review."

Representative Moorhead: "Secretary McNamara . . . was asked if his recommendation had ever been reversed when he had a difference with the Bureau of Budget. And he said, in four years, no. He said, 'Maybe there was one time, but I can't recall it.' "

U.S. Congress, Joint Economic Committee, Subcommittee on Economy in Government, Hearings, June 3–24, 1969, pp. 261, 54, 336.

3. G.L. Bach, *Making Monetary and Fiscal Policy* (Washington, D.C.: The Brookings Institution, 1971), pp. 117, 121.

INDEX

Page numbers in italics indicate an illustration of the subject mentioned.

Abel, I. W., quoted, 118
Acheson, Dean, 35; quoted, 120
Ackley, Gardner, 75–76; quoted, 69
    See also Ackley-Okun Report
    (1969)
Ackley-Okun Report (1969), 123–24,
    141–42, 144–45, 150, 152–53
AFL/CIO, 118. *See also* Unions
Agricultural products, and balance
    of payments, 116
Airline mechanics' strike (1966), 80
Air War Study Group (Cornell University), 100–101, 164, 167, 182
American Revolution: cost of, *83;*
    and veterans' benefits, *171*
American Statistical Association,
    Ackley's speech to (1969), 69
Anthony, Robert N., 87–88; vs. Moot,
    97–98, 165; quoted, 101
Antipoverty program. *See* War on
    poverty
Arms race, *12*
Australia, and Vietnam war, *166*

Bach, G. L., quoted, 73, 195

Balance of payments crises, 13, 16,
    20, 63, 78, 103–11 *passim,* 193; and
    cost of war, *186,* 189; phases of
    (1966–72), 112–20. *See also* Exports; Imports
Banking industry: Federal Reserve
    Board and, 77–78; and gold, 112,
    132. *See also* Commercial banks;
    Discount rate; Interest rates
Bao Dai, Emperor (Vietnam), *166*
Bell and Howell Company, 114
Benoit, Emile, 108
Bombings, 4, 30, 33, 54, 67, 114; cessation of (1968), 31, 122 (*see also*
    De-escalation); and cost of war,
    94, 100–101, 165
Bommarito, Peter, quoted, 118
Bradley Commission, 181
Bretton Woods Agreement (1944),
    103–104, 110–11, 115; end of, 113,
    119–20
Brookings Institution, 147, 151, 152,
    154, 168, 169, 179
Bundy, McGeorge, 69
Bureau of the Budget, 67, 194

Burke-Hartke bill (1971), 118
Burns, Arthur, 125; and Recession of 1970–71, 129–31, 133
Business cycle, "new economics" and, 41–43
Business Week, 66

Cabinet Co-ordinating Committee on Economic Planning for the End of Vietnam Hostilities. *See* Ackley-Okun Report (1969)
Cambodia: casualties, 3; U.S. aid to, *166,* 170; U.S. invasion of (1970), 31–32
Cambridge University (England), 41
Camp David conferences (1973), 132–33
Canada: dollar of, 110; and peace talks, 31
Casualties, 2, *3;* cost of, 85, 182, 188; first, 121
Cease-fire (1973), 168, 169. *See also* Peace talks (Paris)
China: Truman and, 29; and Vietnam, 34
Civilian industries, and military production, 14–16
Civil War: cost of, *83,* 84; and veterans' benefits, *171, 172,* 175
Clark, John M., 181
Clayton, James L., 82–85, 89, 164; and veterans' benefits, 170–81 *passim*
Clifford, Clark, 154
Cold War: and balance of payments deficits, 104–105, 119–20, 130; Vietnam and, 32, 34–35, 163; weapons of, 14, *15*
Commerce Department, Bureau of Economic Analysis, 157–159
Commercial banks, 78, 196
Common Market (European), 115, 116
Community Action Programs, 49
Connally, John, 131, 133
"Conscription tax," 183, 188. *See also* Draft

Consumer Price Index, 72, 79, *126, 127, 161*
Consumers: meat boycott (1973), 160; purchases (1966–68), 20, 23, 80
Cooper, Chester L., quoted, 66
Cornell University, Air War Study Group, 100–101, 164, 167, 182
Cost allocation problem, 163
Cost-benefit analysis, 37–38
Cost of war, 4, 14, 23, *25,* 26, 33, 57, 82–102, 163–90; categories, 164; *full* vs. *incremental (see* Full costs; Incremental costs); and GNP, 165, 186–88, 189; and peace dividend, 145–162; "residual," 168–70; ten different connotations of, 188–89. *See also* Defense spending; De-escalation—cost of; Draft—cost of; Escalation—cost of
Cost-push inflation, 7, 8, 113, 134, 135, 137, *138,* 191, 192. *See also* Inflation
Council of Economic Advisers (CEA), 195; Johnson's, 5, 56, 58, 69, 70, 73, 75, 123–24 (*see also* Ackley, Gardner; Okun, Arthur M.); Kennedy's, 41, 43, 45, 48, 79, 194 *(see also* Heller, Walter); Nixon's, 125, 127 (*see also* McCracken, Paul)
Council on International Economic Policy (Nixon's), 114
Credibility gap, 88, 119. *See also* Secrecy on war
"Credit crunch of 1966," 77–78, 80
Crime rate, 185
Cuba, U.S. trade arrangements with, 117

Dale, Edwin L., quoted, 76
De-escalation (1968 on), 8, 31–32, 62, 66, 121–43; and balance of payments deficits, *107,* 113, 114; and casualties, *3;* cost of, 95, 100, 141–43, 146, 149, 155, *156, 158,* 161–62. *See also* Game Plans (Nixon's)

Defense industries, workers in, *22*

Defense spending, 35–36, *71;* and de-escalation (*see* De-escalation —cost of); and escalation, 73, 74–77, 86–88, *90, 140* (*see also* Cost of war; Escalation—cost of); and foreign countries (*see* Foreign aid—military); and GNP, *64,* 98–100, 150; 1963–65, 29, 67; and peace dividend, 98, 144–55; postponed investments, 165, 167–68, 169. *See also* Cost of war; Escalation

Deficit spending (1966–68), 17, 20, 76, 77, *139. See also* Balance of payments deficits; Escalation—financing of

Demand-pull inflation, 7, 112, 113, 134, 135, 137, *138,* 191–92. *See also* Inflation

Democratic Republic of Vietnam. *See* North Vietnam

Detente. *See* Soviet Union—detente with U.S.

Devaluations (currency), 105, 110, 112–13, 193. *See also* U.S. dollar crises

Diem, Ngo Dinh, 28–29, 53–54

Dien Bien Phu, battle of (1954), 28

Discount rate, 72–73, 75, 196. *See also* Federal Reserve System; Interest rates

Donovan, John C., quoted, 57

Draft (military), *12;* cost of, 164, 182–85, 188; end of, 67 (*see also* Volunteer Army); and escalation, 54, 68. *See also* Defense spending; U.S. Armed Forces

Drug problem, 185

Dudley, Leonard, 108, *109*

Dulles, John Foster, 35

Economic Opportunity Act (1964), 49; Title II, 55. *See also* Office of Economic Opportunity; War on poverty

Economic Report of the President (Johnson's, 1969). *See* Ackley-

Okun Report (1969)

Economic Report of the President, The (1970), 128

Education, federal aid to, 178, 185, 188

Eisenhower, Dwight D., 36, 125; economic policy of, 40–41, 44–45; and interstate highway program, 26; and Vietnam, 28

Eisner, Robert, 164, 182–85, 188

Elderly, and peace dividend, 159–60

Election of 1960, 40

Election of 1964, 29–30, 49, 53

Election of 1968, 31–32, 37, 122, 123, 186

Election of 1970 (congressional), 129

Election of 1972, 32, 130, 135

Employment (full): and full employment budget, 137–40; and inflation, 6, 11, 14, 17, 63–65, 67, 86, 112, 123, 155, *156;* and tax cut (1964), 46, 54; and wage-price guideposts (1962–65), 194. *See also* Unemployment

Employment Act of 1946, 13, 195

Environmental considerations, 167

Escalation (1965–68), 1–2, 30–31; balance of payments deficits and, 104–107, 112–13, 115–16; cost of, 88, *90,* 91, 95, 102, *140,* 146, 155, *156* (*see also* Cost of war; Defense spending—and escalation); financing of, 18–24, 62–73 (*see also* Deficit spending [1966–68]); and GNP (*see* GNP—in escalation period); and inflation, 6–7, 10–11, 52–53, 54, 57, 63–73 *passim,* 74–81, *126,* 155, 157, 186, 191, 192; vs. War on poverty, 52–61 (*see also* War on poverty—defeat of). *See also* Bombings; Federal Reserve System—and escalation; Gulf of Tonkin Resolution (1964)

European Common Market, 115, 116

European Free Trade Area, 116

Exports: decrease in, 16, 20, 78, 104, 107, 110, 116; and trade policy,

Exports *(continued)*
193. *See also* Balance of payments crises; Imports

Federal Open Market Committee, 195–96
Federal Reserve System, 194, 195–96; and "credit crunch" of 1966, 77–78, 80; easy money policy (1967–68), 124, 125–27; and escalation, 16, 63, 72–73, 74, 75, 77–78, 193; and recession of 1970–71, 113, 129–31
First National City Bank of New York, 118
Ford, Gerald R., 178
Foreign Affairs magazine, 29
Foreign aid: "economic," *166,* 168–70; military, 103–105, *106, 166,* 168–70
Foreign trade. *See* Balance of payments crises; Exports; Imports
"Four-Point Do-Nothing Plan" (Game Plan II), 128–31, 140
Fowler, Henry, 31
France: and peace talks, 31; and Vietnam, 27–28, 30, *166*
Friedman, Milton, 125–29, 185–86
Full costs, 92–102 *passim, 166,* 173, 179, 188. *See also* Cost of war; Incremental costs
Full Employment Act (Employment Act of 1946), 195
Full employment budget, 137–40. *See also* Employment (full)

Galbraith, J. K., 136–37
Game Plans (Nixon's): I, 127–29, 140; II, 127–31, 140; III, 132–43
Gates Commission, 182
GATT, 116
Geneva Conference (1954), 28
G.I. Bill of Rights, 173–74, 178. *See also* Veterans' Benefits
Gilpatrick, Roswell L., quoted, 29
GNP. *See* Gross National Product

Gold (and U.S. dollar), 104, 105, 110, 112–13; Nixon and, 118–19, 130, 132, 133
Goldwater, Barry, 29, 49
"Gradualism" policy (Nixon's), 127, 130, 131. *See also* Game Plans—I and II
Great Britain: and Common Market, 115; and currency stability, 111, 112; and detente, 67; 19th-century diplomacy of, 33–34; and peace talks, 31
Great Depression (1930s), 191. *See also* New Deal
Great Society programs, 24, 26, 29, 38, 48–49, *50–51,* 68, 75–76; cutbacks in, 16, 22, 52; cost of, *25;* and peace dividend, 144, 145. *See also* War on poverty
Gross National Product (GNP), *10;* Actual and Potential *(performance gap),* 43–45, 139, 157–59; and cost of war, 165, 186–88, 189; decline in, 24 *(see also* Recession of 1970–71); and defense spending, *64,* 98–100, 150; in escalation period, 11, 16, *18–19,* 20, 23, 60, 63, 67, 69, 70, 72, 74; and "excess" inflation, 160; Friedman and, 125; North Vietnam compared to U.S., 8, 33; and veterans' benefits, 173, 180; and World War II, 89
Ground troops, commitment of (1965), 67–68. *See also* Escalation
Gruening, Ernest, 35
Gulf of Tonkin resolution (1964), 30, 35, 38, 54, 133; repeal of, 32

Harrington, Michael, 47–48, *50,* 60
Heller, Walter, 41, 43, 45; quoted, 48
Hoover, Herbert, 129
Housing industry, collapse of (1966), 13, 20, 78, 80, 188
Humphrey, Hubert, 31, 36

Imports, 7, 78, 105, 110, 120, 193;

Nixon surcharge on, 133; protectionism and, 115, 118–19. *See also Balance of payments crises; Exports*

Incomes policy, 194. *See also* Wage-price guideposts (1962–65)

Income tax. *See* Tax cuts; Tax increases

Income tax surcharge (1968), 16, 66, 77, 113, 124, 193. *See also* Tax increases—Johnson and

Incremental costs, 86–87, 92–102 *passim,* 145, 164–65, *166,* 168, 188; and veterans' benefits, 172–73, 179. *See also* Cost of war

Inflation, 2, 6–7, 23–24, 191–96; and balance of payments deficits, 105–107, 111, 112–13, 115, 119; and cost of war, 85, 185–90 *passim; cost-push* vs. *demand-pull,* 7, 8, 113, 134, 135, 137, *138,* 191, 192; and de-escalation, 122–43 *passim;* and deficit spending (*see* Deficit spending [1966–68]; Employment [full]); and escalation (*see* Escalation—and inflation); "goof" of 1966, 74–80 *passim;* and "new economics," 41; Nixon's Game Plans vs., 127–29, 132–43 *passim;* and peace dividend, 146, *148,* 149, 155–62. *See also* Recession of 1970–71

Interest rates: decrease in (1970–71), 113; and housing industry, 20, 78; increase in, 13, 16, 17, 77–78. *See also* Discount rate; Federal Reserve System

International Monetary Fund, 110

International monetary system, 103–20. *See also* Bretton Woods Agreement (1944); U.S. dollar crises

Interstate highway program, *25,* 26

Japan: economy of, 115; and Vietnam (surrender of, 1945), 27

"Jawboning," 194. *See also* Wage-price guideposts (1962–65)

Job Corps, 60. *See also* War on poverty

Johnson, Lyndon B.: budget messages, 8–9, 56, 124; and credibility gap, 88 (*see also* Secrecy on war); economic failures of, 10–11, 13–14, 17, 23–24, 63, 72–73, 119, 134, 195 (*see also* Inflation); Economic Report of the President (1969) (*see* Ackley-Okun Report [1969]); vs. Federal Reserve System, 72–73; Nixon compared to, 121–22; and secrecy (*see* Secrecy on war); and taxes (*see* Tax cuts—Kennedy-Johnson [1964]; Tax increases—Johnson and); and Vietnam war, 29–39 *passim* (*see also* De-escalation; Election of 1968; Escalation; Gulf of Tonkin resolution [1964]). *See also* Great Society programs; War on poverty

Joint Chiefs of Staff, 24, 68

Kennedy, John F., 124–25; economic policy of, 11, 40–46, 74, 79, *139,* 195 (*see also* Employment [full]; Wage-price guideposts [1962–65]); and space program, *25,* 26; and tax cut (*see* Tax cuts—Kennedy-Johnson [1964]); and Vietnam war, 28–29; and War on poverty, 47–48, 49, 56

Kennedy, Robert F., quoted, 54, 60

Keynes, John Maynard, 41

King, Martin Luther, Jr., quoted, 60–61

Kissinger, Henry, 32

Korean war, *12,* 27; cost of, *83,* 84, 89, *140;* and military production, 14, 15, 75; and unemployment, 11; U.S. aid following, 169–70; and veterans' benefits, *171, 172,* 173, 174, 181; Vietnam war compared to, 4, 5, 63, 65, 68

Laird, Melvin, 86, *87;* quoted, 94

Landowners, and peace dividend, 159

Laos: casualties, 3; U.S. aid to, *166, 169*

Latin American Free Trade Area, 116

Lekachman, Robert, 164

Library of Congress, 89

Liquidity crises (1966 and 1969–70), 13, 77–78

London *Economist,* 96

Long Binh, Vietnam, U.S. air base at, 33

McCarthyism, 27

McCracken, Paul, 125, 137

McNamara, Robert, 33, 38, 69; and cost of war, 86–88, 150; and inflation "goof" of 1966, 75, 76; quoted, 10–11

McNeil, Wilfred, quoted, 89

Manpower development and retraining programs (JFK), 48

Manufacturing, earnings in, 20–21

Marshall Plan, 23, 114, 120

Martin, William McChesney, 195

Meat boycott (1973), 160

Medicare and Medicaid, 85, 145

Mexican war: cost of, *83;* and veterans' benefits, *171*

Military Assistance Advisory Group (MAAG), 28

Military budgets. *See* Defense spending

Military production, shift in, 14–16. *See also* Defense spending; U.S. Armed Forces

Minh, Ho Chi, 28

Minority groups, and peace dividend, 159–60

Missile buildup (early 1960s), 67

Model cities progam, 188. *See also* War on poverty

Monetary policy. *See* Federal Reserve System

Moot, Robert C.: vs. Anthony, 97–98, 165; quoted, 91

Morse, Chandler, quoted, 100

Morse, Wayne, 35

Municipal bonds, 78

National Liberation Front (Vietcong), 28, 32; casualties, 3; Tet offensive, 31, 113. *See also* North Vietnam

National Security Council, 114

Neighborhood Youth Corps, 60

New Deal, 36, 48, 49

"New economics," 41–46 *passim;* and escalation, 62, 66

"New Federalism" (Nixon), 24

"New orthodoxy" (Stein), 43

New York Times, 30, 75

New Zealand, and Vietnam war, *166*

Nixon, Richard M.: and balance of payments crises, 113–20 *passim,* 133 (*see also* Gold; U.S. dollar crises); vs. Burns, 130–31, 133; and Cambodian invasion, 31–32; and cost of war, 94, 178; and de-escalation, 124–43 (*see also* De-escalation; Game Plans [Nixon's]); economic failures of, 6–7, 8, 14, 24, 63, 119–20, 134–35 (*see also* Inflation; Recession of 1970–71; Unemployment—Nixon and; Wage-price controls); Johnson compared to, 121–22; and tax cuts, 131, 133, 153, 155. *See also* Bombings; Election of 1968; Election of 1972; Peace dividend; Watergate

"Nixon Doctrine," 122–23

North Vietnam: bombings of (*see* Bombings; Escalation); casualties, 3; and peace talks, 32 (*see also* Peace talks); U.S. economy compared to, 8–10, 33. *See also* National Liberation Front (Vietcong)

Office of Economic Opportunity (OEO), 49; and escalation, 54–57. *See also* War on poverty

Office of Management and the Budget, 194

Okun, Arthur M., quoted, 5, 58–59, 60, 71, 80. *See also* Ackley-Okun Report (1969)
"Old orthodoxy" (Stein), 43–44
Oligopolistic industries, and peace dividend, 159

"Pacification" campaign (1966–67), 31. *See also* Escalation
Paris negotiations. *See* Peace talks
Passell, Peter, 108, *109*
Paul, Pope, 31
Peace and growth dividend. *See* Ackley-Okun Report (1969)
Peace dividend, 98, 144–62. *See also* Ackley-Okun Report (1969)
Peace talks (Paris), 168; cease-fire (1973), 168, 169; Johnson and, 31; Nixon and, 32; and truces, 141
Percy, Charles H., 114
Performance gap (of GNP), 43–45, 139, 157–59
Peterson, Peter G., 114–18 *passim,* 120
Philippines: U.S. trade arrangements with, 117; and Vietnam war, *166*
Planning Programming Budgeting (PPB), 37–38
Poor, and peace dividend, 159–60
Postwar period. *See* Peace dividend; Recession of 1973–75
Poverty, Harrington on, 47–48, *50,* 60
"Poverty gap," 59–60
Poverty programs. *See* War on poverty
Preferential trade agreements, 116–17
President's Commission on All-Volunteer Armed Force (Gates), 182
President's Commission on Veterans' Pensions (Bradley), 181
President's Council of Economic Advisers. *See* Council of Economic Advisers (CEA)
Protectionism, 115, 118–19
Proxmire, William, 86

Puerto Rico, U.S. trade arrangements with, 117

Recession of 1948–60, 41
Recession of 1970–71, 7, 8, 13, 23, 24, 63, *71,* 113, 118, 122, 123; and cost of war, 161–62, 185–90 *passim;* Nixon's Game Plans vs., 126–43 *passim;* and peace dividend, 158–62
Recession of 1973–75, 155, 156, 162
Re-escalation (1972–73), 32
Refugees, 3
"Residual costs," 168–70
Reston, James, quoted, 30, 57
Riddell, Tom, 164, 165, 170
Rivers, Mendel, 69
Roosa, Robert, quoted, 136
Roosevelt, Franklin D., 36; and New Deal, 48, 49; and Vietnam, 27
Rusk, Dean, 35

Savings and loan associations, 77
Savings banks, 77
Schulze, Charles L., 76
Secrecy on war, 8, 12–13, 17–19, 23–24, 34, 102, 110; Johnson and, 7, 23–24, 65–69 *passim,* 74–76
Selective Service Act of 1971, 147
Shriver, Sargent, 48
Silk, Leonard, quoted, 128
Small businesses, and peace dividend, 159–60
Social security system, 26
South Korea, *166. See also* Korean War
South Vietnam: casualties, 3; "pacification" campaign (1966–67), 30–31; property damage, 4; U.S. aid to, *166,* 168–70. *See also* Diem, Ngo Dinh; Thieu regime
Soviet Union: detente with U.S., 29, 67, 179; and North Vietnam, 34; and peace talks, 31
Space program, *25,* 26

Spanish-American War: cost of, *83*, 84; and veterans' benefits, *171*, 175

State and local government services, cutbacks in, 16, 22, 78, 159–60

State Department, 195

Statistical Abstract, 82, 164, 178

Stein, Herbert, quoted, 43, 45

Stennis, John, 69

Stock prices, declines in, 13

Student unrest, 17, 23

Symington, Stuart, 86, *87*

Tax cuts: Kennedy-Johnson (1964), 45–46, 66–67, *139;* Nixon and, 131, 133, 153, 155; and peace dividend, 144; and war on poverty, 48, 54

Tax increases: Johnson and, 16, 17, 66, 68, 75–76, 77, 80–81, 113, 124, 193; "new economics" and, 41; Truman and, 65

Tay Ninh Province (Vietnam), 4

Tet offensive (1968), 31, 113

Thailand: U.S. aid to, 105, *166;* U.S. troops in, 84

Thieu regime: Johnson and, 31, 121–22; Nixon and, 32, 121–22

"Third Country" troops, cost of supporting, *166*

Timber industry (Vietnam), 4

Time magazine, 125

"Transfer payments," 189

Treasury Department, 194

"Troika, the" (U.S.), 195

Truces, 141. *See also* Peace talks

Truman, Harry S.: and China, 29; and Korean war, 65

Truman Doctrine, 122–23

Unemployment: under Eisenhower, 40–41; 1965–68, 74, 79; Nixon and, 7, 8, 24, 118, 124–25, 128, 130, 132, 135, *138,* 142–43 (*see also* Recession of 1970–71); and peace dividend, 155–62 *passim;* tax cut (1964) and, 46; World War II and Korean war and, 11, 63

Unions: and *cost-push* inflation, *7,* 136, 137, *138;* and international trade policy, 7, 118; and peace dividend, 159–60; and wage-price guideposts (1966), 79–80

United Nations: conference on international trade and development (1964), 38–39; and peace talks, 31; strengthening of (need for), 155; U.S. support for, 154

United Rubber Workers, 118

U.S. Armed Forces, *6, 12,* 31, 182; pay increases for, 146–50 *passim;* reductions in (since 1964), 148–49. *See also* Bombings; Casualties; Defense spending; Draft; Veterans' benefits; Volunteer army

U.S. Congress: Burke-Hartke bill (1971), 118: Joint Economic Committee, 73, 82–85, 86, 88. *See also* U.S. House of Representatives; U.S. Senate

U.S. dollar crises, 31, 78, 103–20, 193; Nixon and, 113–20, 130, 132, 133–34, 135. *See also* Devaluations; Gold

U.S. House of Representatives: Armed Services Committee, 69; Ways and Means Committee, 76. *See also* U.S. Congress

U.S. Senate: Armed Services Committee, 69, 86; Foreign Relations Committee, 28, 32–33. *See also* U.S. Congress

University of Chicago, 125

University of Michigan, Johnson's "Great Society" speech at, 48–49

Unorganized workers, and peace dividend, 159–60

Urban Coalition, 150, 154, 179

Veterans Administration (VA), 173–81 *passim,* 187

Veterans' benefits, *83,* 84, 85, 147, 170–81, 188, 189

Vietcong. *See* National Liberation Front

Vietnam war, history of, 27–39, 165, 187. *See also* Bombings; Cost of war; De-escalation; Escalation; Peace talks; Re-escalation

Volunteer army, 145, 147; cost of, 182–83

Wage-price controls: absence of, 5, 11, 17, 24; Burns and, 130–31, 133; imposition of (1971), 17, 63, 66, 113–14, *126*–27, 133, 134, 135; Nixon vs., 125, 127–28, 130–31, 136–37, 193

Wage-price guideposts (1962–65), 63, 194; end of (1966), 79–80

Wages (1966–68), 20–21, *22*

War of 1812: cost of, 84, *83;* and veterans' benefits, *171*

War on poverty, 47–51; agencies and programs, *50–51;* defeat of, 13, 23, 52–61, 155, 160, 162, 188, 193; legislation, *50–51;* proclaimed, 26, 38, 48. *See also* Great Society programs

Washington Post, 137

Watergate, 17, 19, 34, 76, 102

Weidenbaum, Murray L., 164, 165; quoted, 14–15

West Germany: and dollar crisis, 117; France and, 27

Westmoreland, General, 113

Wheeler, Gen. Earle G., 170; quoted, 24, 68

Wholesale price index, 128. *See also* Consumer Price Index

World War I: cost of, *83,* 84; and veterans' benefits, *171, 172,* 173, 181

World War II, 191; cost of, 82–84, *83,* 89; U.S. dollar and, 103–104 (*see also* Bretton Woods Agreement); U.S. production during, 10; and unemployment, 11, 63; and veterans' benefits, *171, 172,* 173, 181; Vietnam and, 27; Vietnam war compared to, 4, 5, 63

Wriston, Walter B., quoted, 117–18

Yale University, JFK's commencement address (1962), 45